Mega-Schools, Technology and Teachers

Education for All (EFA) has been a top priority for governments and intergovernmental development agencies for the last 20 years. So far the global EFA movement has placed its principal focus on providing quality universal primary education (UPE) for all children by 2015.

The latest addition to **The Open and Flexible Learning series**, *Mega-Schools, Technology and Teachers* addresses the new challenges created by both the successes and the failures of the UPE campaign. This book advocates new approaches for providing access to secondary education for today's rapidly growing population of children and young adults and examines:

- the creation and expansion of Mega-Schools, which combine distance learning and community support and have a proven track record of increasing access at scale.
- how to prepare the 10 million new teachers that are required to achieve Education for All by 2015 by focusing on classroom-based in-service training.
- strategies for using technology to scale up distance education cost-effectively.
- the creation of a 21st century educational ecosystem that integrates open schooling and teacher education with communities and their school systems.
- successful examples of open schools and teacher education programmes operating at scale around the world.

Readers will be delighted to find that Sir John Daniel, best-selling Routledge author of *Mega Universities and Knowledge Media*, delivers another insightful and practical book on educational technology. *Mega-Schools, Technology and Teachers* will be of interest to all who are concerned by the central educational challenge of our times: providing secondary education to tens of millions of young people around the world.

John S. Daniel has been president and CEO of the Commonwealth of Learning since 2004 after previous appointments as assistant director-general of UNESCO, vice-chancellor of the UK Open University and president of Canada's Laurentian University.

Open and Flexible Learning Series

Series Editors: Fred Lockwood, A.W. (Tony) Bates and Som Naidu

Activities in Self-Instructional Texts
Fred Lockwood

Assessing Open and Distance Learners
Chris Morgan and Meg O'Reilly

Changing University Teaching
Terry Evans and Daryl Nation

Contemporary Perspectives in E-Learning Research: Themes, Methods and Impact on Practice
Gráinne Conole and Martin Oliver

The Costs and Economics of Open and Distance Learning
Greville Rumble

Delivering Digitally
Alistair Inglis, Peter Ling and Vera Joosten

Delivering Learning on the Net: The Why, What and How of Online Education
Martin Weller

The Design and Production of Self-Instructional Materials
Fred Lockwood

Designing Video and Multimedia for Open and Flexible Learning
Jack Koumi

Developing Innovation in Online Learning: An Action Research Framework
Maggie McPherson and Miguel Baptista Nunes

Distance and Blended Learning in Asia
Colin Latchem and Insung Jung

Exploring Open and Distance Learning
Derek Rowntree

Flexible Learning in a Digital World
Bettery Collis and Jef Moonen

Improving Your Students' Learning
Alistair Morgan

Innovation in Open and Distance Learning
Fred Lockwood and Ann Gooley

Integrated E-Learning: Implications for Pedagogy, Technology and Organization
Win Jochems, Jeroen van Merriënboer and Rob Koper

Interactions in Online Education: Implications for Theory and Practice
Charles Juwah

Key Terms and Issues in Open and Distance Learning
Barbara Hodgson

The Knowledge Web: Learning and Collaborating on the Net
Marc Eisenstadt and Tom Vincent

Leadership for 21st Century Learning: Global Perspectives from International Experts
Donald Hanna and Colin Latchem

Learning and Teaching with Technology: Principles and Practices
Som Naidu

Learning and Teaching in Distance Education
Edited by Som Naidu

Learning with Digital Games: A Practical Guide to Engaging Students in Higher Education
Nicola Whitton

Making Material-Based Learning Word
Derek Rowntree

Managing Open Systems
Richard Freeman

Mega-Schools, Technology and Teachers
Achieving Education for All

John S. Daniel

Routledge
Taylor & Francis Group

NEW YORK AND LONDON

First published 2010
by Routledge
270 Madison Avenue, New York, NY 10016

Simultaneously published in the UK
by Routledge
2 Park Square, Milton Park, Abingdon, Oxon OX14 4RN

Routledge is an imprint of the Taylor & Francis Group, an informa business

© 2010 Taylor & Francis

Typeset in Minion by EvS Communication Networx, Inc.
Printed and bound in the United States of America on acid-free paper by Sheridan Books, Inc.

Library of Congress Cataloging in Publication Data
Daniel, John S., 1942–
Mega-schools, technology, and teachers : achieving education for all / John S. Daniel.
p. cm. — (Open and flexible learning series)
Includes bibliographical references and index.
1. Education, Elementary—Developing countries. 2. Educational equalization—Developing countries. 3. Distance education—Computer-assisted instruction—Developing countries.
I. Title.
LB1556.7.D48D36 2010
372.9172'4—dc22
2009033155

ISBN 10: 0-415-87204-9 (hbk)
ISBN 10: 0-415-87205-7 (pbk)
ISBN 10: 0-203-85832-8 (ebk)

ISBN 13: 978-0-415-87204-1 (hbk)
ISBN 13: 978-0-415-87205-8 (pbk)
ISBN 13: 978-0-203-85832-5 (ebk)

To:
Kristin
Julian, Anne-Marie and Catherine

Contents

List of Figures and Tables

Figures

Tables

Series Editor's Foreword

The numbers that are presented in this book *Mega-Schools, Technology and Teachers* by Sir John Daniel, and the challenges he identifies, are staggering. Even with the success of the Education For All (EFA) campaign it is estimated that by 2015 there will be 30 million children who will be unable to receive a primary school education. Furthermore, it is also estimated that the world will need a further 10 million teachers by this date and that there will be over 400 million children aged 12–17 years who will be unable to benefit from a secondary school education. Any naïve belief that we can simply scale-up conventional teaching methods, including the provision of teachers, to meet the demands for primary and secondary school education is laid bare.

For those of us working in the field of education this book makes uncomfortable reading—especially as it challenges many of our long held assumptions about quality provision. Assumptions associated with the primacy of pre-service teacher education compared to in-service training practice, of the superiority of public rather than private educational provision, of the exclusivity of small group teaching rather than mass education…and, of course, the role that Communication and Information Technology can contribute.

This book offers us a new concept—that of Mega Schools and a synthesis of ideas that demonstrate that it is possible that Open Schools can have a positive role to play alongside conventional schools, that Distance Learning practices and Communication and Information Technology can be combined for the benefit of both learners and teachers. The book also offers us compelling evidence from around the world, combined with a range of case studies, that illustrate that with imagination and innovation, coupled with entrepreneurship and commitment we can raise to the challenge facing us.

In the opening pages of this book Sir John admits that in writing it he experienced 'a growing sense of shame' that whilst a senior member of UNESCO he uncritically accepted the conventional wisdom of experts about how best to achieve Education for All (EFA). I'm sure that after reading this book you will agree that he has more than corrected any lapse. The challenge Sir John outlines for us is formidable. If we are not to experience a similar feeling of shame we need to think and act differently. The vision Sir John offers is one that is achievable and one that millions of future adults will thanks us for.

Fred Lockwood

Acknowledgements

Our work at the Commonwealth of Learning (COL), which aims to scale up the opportunities for learning on which the future of humankind depends, inspired me to write this book. I have chosen to focus on just two of our activities, open schooling and teacher education, because they contribute decisively to the core task of global development: the achievement of Education for All. Let me thank first the colleagues leading this work, Frances Ferreira (open schooling) and Abdurrahman Umar (teacher education), who have advised me patiently and kindly shared their draft publications.

My warm appreciation goes to all my COL colleagues for creating such an intellectually stimulating environment. Kodhandaraman Balasubramanian, Willie Clarke-Okah, Angela Kwan, John Lesperance, Wayne Mackintosh, Joshua Mallet, Tanyss Munro and Ian Pringle have all given me ideas. I am especially grateful to our Board Chair, the Honourable Burchell Whiteman, for his encouragement and to our Vice-President, Asha Kanwar, who has willingly increased her workload to give me more time to write. It is also a pleasure to acknowledge Dave Wilson's wise counsel, Amy Monaghan's ingenious help in tracking down documents, Annette Bacchus' useful tutorial in formatting documents and Alex Hennig's impressive design skills. Royalties from this book will be shared with COL.

A career in higher education and distance learning spanning four decades has brought me into contact with many institutions. One of the pleasures of this research has been getting in touch again with some wonderful colleagues. All have been most generous in sharing their recollections of events and pointing me to new sources of information. My particular thanks go to two special friends who, after reviewing the whole manuscript, challenged and encouraged me with their perceptive comments: Desmond Bermingham and Stamenka Uvalić-Trumbić.

Other colleagues have been good enough to check passages about their institutions or programmes. The text has been enriched by the inputs and suggestions of Jophus Amanuah-Mensah, Mahmood Butt, Charlie Reed, Bernard Cornu, Anne-Marie Laliberté Denis, Glen Farrell, Alice Flores, Crystal Gips, Anwarul Islam, Maxim Jean-Louis, Jean-Michel Lacroix, Rehana Masrur, Sugata and Sushmita Mitra, Bob Moon, Widad Othman, Alejandro Pisanty, Sheldon Shaeffer, Abhimanyu Singh, Daniel Tau, James Tooley, Michel Umbriaco, Jesus Vazquez-Abad, and Paul West. I thank them for their help and take responsibility for errors of fact or interpretation that remain.

Many other researchers, writers and educational leaders have inspired me by their arguments, findings and insights. I express particular appreciation to Dominique Abrioux, Tony Bates, Bob Bernard, Svava Bjarnason, Nick Burnett,

Hubert Charles, Chris Colclough, Susan D'Antoni, Gajaraj Dhanarajan, Judith Eaton, Ann Floyd, Brenda Gourley, Janet Jenkins, Ruth Kagia, Badri Koul, Diana Laurillard, Keith Lewin, John Naughton, Steve Packer, Frits Pannekoek, Hilary Perraton, Geoff Peters, Caroline Pontefract, Colin Power, Bob Prouty, Greville Rumble, Jamil Salmi, Amartya Sen, Kamalesh Sharma, Ram Takwale, Qian Tang and Peter Williams.

This is the second book that I have contributed to this series. I congratulate Fred Lockwood for his longevity in the role of Series Editor. It is a pleasure to thank him for nursing me through the process once again and for sharing documents that he had collected on open schooling.

In the year that I began primary school my father was appointed principal of one the emergency teacher training colleges that Britain created after World War II in order to supply the additional teachers required by a reformed education system. I honour his memory and like to think that he would have enjoyed reading my reflections about similar challenges in a new century.

Glossary of Acronyms

ACU	Association of Commonwealth Universities
AIOU	Allama Iqbal Open University, Pakistan
AVU	African Virtual University
BGCSE	Botswana General Certificate of Secondary Education
BOCODOL	Botswana College of Distance and Open Learning
BRAC	Bangladesh Rural Advancement Committee
CAPES	Certificat d'aptitude au professorat de l'enseignement du second degré
CAPET	Certificat d'aptitude au professorat de l'enseignement technique
CERI	Centre for Educational Research and Innovation (OECD)
CNED	Centre National d'Enseignement à Distance
COL	Commonwealth of Learning
CPD	Continuing Professional Development
CSET	California Subject Examinations for Teachers
CSU	California State University
CTCS	Certificate in Tertiary and Community Studies (UPNG)
DEEP	Digital Education Enhancement Project
DFID	Department for International Development (UK)
eAC	eAfrica Commission
EFA	Education for All
FTI	Fast-Track Initiative
GER	Gross Enrolment Ratio
GMR	Global Monitoring Report
GNP	Gross National Product
HITW	Hole in the Wall
IB	International Baccalaureate
IDLN	Indonesia Distance Learning Network
IRFOL	International Research Foundation for Open Learning
IRI	Interactive Radio Instruction
IT	Information Technologies
ICT	Information and Communications Technologies
IUFM	Institut Universitaire de Formation de Maîtres (France)
LH	Learning Hub
LIVES	Learning through Interactive Voice Educational System
MCDE	Malawi College of Distance Education
MDG	Millennium Development Goal

MIE	Minimally Invasive Education
MIT	Massachusetts Institute of Technology
NCE	Nigerian Certificate in Education
NCES	National Council for Educational Statistics
NEPAD	New Partnership for African Development
NER	Net Enrolment Ratio
NGO	Non-Governmental Organisation
NIIT	National Institute for Information Technology
NIOS	National Institute of Open Schooling (India)
NOLNET	Namibia Open Learning Network
NTI	National Teachers' Institute (Nigeria)
NUT	National Union of Teachers (Nigeria)
ODL	Open and Distance Learning
OECD	Organisation for Economic Cooperation and Development
OER	Open Educational Resource
OFSTED	Office for Standards in Education (UK)
OFTP	Ontario Federation of Teaching Parents
OLPC	One Laptop Per Child
OUM	Open University Malaysia
PC	Personal Computer
PERMAMA	Perfectionnement des Maîtres en Mathématiques (Québec)
PGCE	Post-graduate Certificate of Education
PISA	Programme for International Student Assessment
PNG	Papua New Guinea
PTR	Pupil Teacher Ratio
QA	Quality Assurance
SLTP	Sekolah Lanjutan Tingkat Pertama (Junior Secondary School, Indonesia)
TEI	Teacher Education Institution
TESSA	Teacher Education in Sub-Saharan Africa
TFA	Teach For America
UE	University of Education (Pakistan)
UKOU	United Kingdom Open University
UN	United Nations
UNDP	United Nations Development Programme
UNESCO	United Nations Educational, Scientific and Cultural Organisation
UPE	Universal Primary Education
UPNG	University of Papua New Guinea

Introduction

Education for All (EFA) is a longstanding human aspiration that still eludes many countries. This book starts from four beliefs in proposing ways to attain this lofty goal.

First, EFA is a vital ambition because education nourishes the human spirit, improves the quality of lives and holds the key to the future of humankind on planet Earth. It may also promote higher material living standards, but its fundamental value is to give people greater freedom to choose their futures.

Second, government action is essential to give all citizens access to learning opportunities. This does not mean that the state has to be the principal provider of education. As nations evolve into knowledge societies their people will require better initial education and regular training throughout their lives. Public funds are insufficient to support all the learning opportunities needed. Governments' main role is to establish—and to enforce without corruption—legislation that maximises the accessibility, appropriateness and effectiveness of education and training. Countries must embrace all cost-effective methods of schooling and foster innovative ways of providing it.

Third, harnessing technology, which has already increased the availability and quality of products and services everywhere while reducing their cost, is crucial to the achievement of EFA. Technology is the application of scientific and other organized knowledge to practical tasks by organizations consisting of people and machines, so it draws on non-scientific knowledge as well as applied science. Technology is about practical tasks rather than theory and always involves people and their social systems. Achieving EFA is a practical task focussed on people.

Fourth, education in the 21st century requires more emphasis on learning and less on teaching. Indeed, our ideal is the adoption of a culture of self-directed learning by individuals and communities. Technology can encourage this transition.

Chapter 1 starts from first principles to defend the assertion that educating everyone is important. In historical terms this is a relatively new ambition. What is the justification for it? What progress has been made in the global campaign for EFA that has been gathering pace for two decades? For some years I had the privilege of being thoroughly immersed in this great project as Assistant Director-General of UNESCO. I am proud that it has brought universal primary education within reach for many countries but regret that the quality is often so poor. What are the consequences of this blend of success and failure?

The most urgent consequence of success is that tens of millions of children are completing primary school and seeking secondary education. Countries that have had to struggle to create a network of primary schools and provide the teachers for them do not have the resources to expand provision at secondary level using the same formulae. Alternative approaches must be used.

Moreover, the success of the EFA campaign is still only partial—in three ways. First, there will still be nearly 30 million children not going to primary school in 2015. A key requirement for giving them that opportunity, and for expanding secondary education, is to recruit and train more teachers; yet projections indicate a worldwide shortage of at least 10 million teachers over the next five years. Conventional methods of teacher education simply cannot meet the challenge so alternative approaches are also required there.

Second, success in achieving EFA has been incomplete because completion rates are low and pupil performance is often below par. This is partly a matter of resources but mainly the result of poor management and lack of accountability.

Third, only part of the EFA agenda has yet been seriously addressed. Strictly speaking, the term *EFA* covers the six goals for Education for All that were agreed at the World Forum in Dakar in 2000. These covered a broad spectrum of educational needs. After Dakar, however, to focus effort and make progress, the international community and many developing country governments concentrated mainly on the task of achieving universal primary education.

Now that universal primary education is within reach it is time to turn our efforts to some of the other goals, notably eradicating illiteracy, equipping youth and adults with the skills to earn livelihoods, and raising the quality of education everywhere. Alternative approaches to providing education will be particularly valuable if they can also tackle these challenges, as they already do at the tertiary level.

The huge task of achieving EFA demands a multiplicity of responses and we review three of them in chapter 2. First, we look at what can be done to expand and improve public secondary education in conventional settings. The reforms necessary to make this approach cost effective are so politically challenging that most developing countries will find it impossible to implement them in the foreseeable future, especially in the poorest communities. Although governments and development agencies are not blind to the weaknesses of state-run school systems, most are still in denial when it comes to acting on their own observations.

In trying to implement Article 26 of the Universal Declaration of Human Rights, the international community has focused too much on the aspiration that 'education shall be free' and not enough on the right of parents to 'choose the kind of education that shall be given to their children'. There is now incontrovertible evidence that large numbers of the poorest parents choose to pay for the education of their children in private schools. A second section of chapter 2 examines the extensive phenomenon of inexpensive private schooling in some of the most disadvantaged urban and rural communities of the developing world and asks how the private sector can help to cope with the secondary surge.

Third, through three high-profile projects we review claims that information and communications technologies (ICT) offer a cost-effective way of expanding access to quality education in the developing world. The One Laptop Per Child initiative was launched in 2005 with the aim of putting tens of millions of specially designed computers in the hands of children in poor countries. The Hole in the Wall project began in 1999 in India when children in a Delhi slum were given unsupervised access to computers in the street. Their surprising achievements inspired the radical concept of 'minimally invasive education'—a euphemism for saying that children can learn from computers without teachers. We also summarize evidence from the NEPAD eSchools Demonstration Project that was launched in schools in 16 African countries in 2005.

While each of these approaches may contribute to expanding secondary education, something more is needed to create truly effective systems. Public schools, especially in poor areas, need to be made more accountable to parents, and private schools must be able to operate in a transparent way instead of being the prey of corrupt officials. All schools need access to more and better learning resources. Computer-based projects should be integrated into wider systems so that they can achieve economies of scale and effect some substitution of capital for labour.

Open schools could both widen access and also integrate other responses to the challenge of expanding secondary education. Such schools, which already exist in some countries, can pursue diverse objectives through a variety of institutional structures and technologies. Chapter 3 examines the principles that underpin technology and its potential role in creating new approaches to secondary schooling and teacher education. We recall Adam Smith's analysis of technology at the dawn of the industrial revolution to argue that the genius of technology is to operate at scale, creating products and services of consistent quality at low cost.

Ever since the revelation of observing at first hand the revolution in higher education that the UK Open University launched in the early 1970s, I have had the immense privilege of being closely involved in the development of open and distance learning (ODL) worldwide. This is the most successful application of technology in education to date and has a crucial role to play in the expansion of secondary schooling and teacher education that is now required.

Open universities were the 20th century's most significant innovation in higher education. In an earlier book I coined the term *mega-university* for distance-teaching enrolling over 100,000 students. Open schools could be the most important development in secondary education in the 21st century, and here I use the term *mega-schools* to designate those with more than 10,000 pupils.

To demonstrate the potential—and the diversity—of open schooling we have brought together, in appendix 1, short descriptions of a number of the world's mega-schools and open schools. Chapter 4 distils the experience of these institutions into proposals for expanding open schooling to make it an integrative force that improves the capacity and performance of all elements of school systems, including public schools, private schools and applications of ICT.

Similarly, appendix 2 profiles a variety of applications of open and distance learning in teacher education and describes an attempt make international teacher migration more predictable. Chapter 5 examines the challenges of teacher recruitment and retention and recommends that all teacher education institutions now adopt open and distance learning as a means to re-focus their work on school-based professional development instead of pre-service training.

In chapter 6 we explore strategies for introducing and integrating these alternative approaches to secondary schooling and teacher education. Education has traditionally operated as a cottage industry. Scaling up provision requires a different mindset. We argue for a new educational ecosystem for the 21st century of which mega-schools and school-based teacher education programmes would be essential components.

Funding better education has historically been less attractive to governments, donors and foundations than investing in improvements in health. This is partly because health offers scalable technological opportunities for impact, such as immunisation, whereas support for education sinks readily into a bottomless pit of ongoing operating costs. A major advantage of deploying ODL in mega-schools and school-based teacher education is that once the systems are established they then have lower operating costs per student than conventional approaches. User fees—even at low levels—can cover much of those ongoing costs. The key objective for governments or funding bodies should be to establish versatile distance learning systems rather than focus on any currently fashionable technology. Technology changes but systems endure.

In the mid-1990s, in *Mega-universities and Knowledge Media: Technology Strategies for Higher Education,* I documented the emergence of the large distance teaching universities and suggested how they might take advantage of evolving technologies to ease the crisis of access in higher education. Since then mega-universities and open universities have continued to multiply and expand briskly—several of them now enrol over a million students. Even more importantly open, distance and technology-mediated learning has entered the bloodstream of all tertiary institutions so fully that it is no longer even possible to make a global estimate of how many people are studying through these methods. This has given a great boost to the adoption of a culture of self-directed learning by individuals and groups.

Secondary education is now due for a similar revolution. My fondest hope is that my recommendations will help to make that revolution a life-enhancing experience for millions of the world's children.

Researching this book has been an enriching voyage of discovery—accompanied by a growing sense of shame. I now realise that during my service at UNESCO, from 2000 to 2004, I accepted too uncritically the conventional wisdom that the best route to EFA is the expansion of free public education in conventional classrooms. It is little consolation that the development experts whom I respect held the same view. Yet the evidence that we were all wrong was accumulating even as the Dakar Framework and the Millennium Development Goals were being approved. This book is an attempt to make amends by showing that the 21st century has brought us better ways of improving the future for millions by achieving the vital goals of EFA.

1
Education for All
Unfinished Business

Everyone has the right to education. Education shall be free, at least in the elementary and fundamental stages. Elementary education shall be compulsory. Technical and professional education shall be made generally available and higher education shall be equally accessible to all on the basis of merit.

Education shall be directed to the full development of the human personality and to the strengthening of respect for human rights and fundamental freedoms. It shall promote understanding, tolerance and friendship among all nations, racial or religious groups, and shall further the activities of the United Nations for the maintenance of peace.

Parents have a prior right to choose the kind of education that shall be given to their children.

Universal Declaration of Human Rights, Article 26, 1948

There can be no contentment for any of us when there are children, millions of children, who do not receive an education that provides them with dignity and honour and allows them to live their lives to the full.

Nelson Mandela, 2007

Success and Failure

This chapter assesses progress towards the global goal of Education for All (EFA), argues that reaching the goal is vital for the future of humankind, and asserts that we shall not attain it without adopting new approaches.

The EFA campaign has scored notable successes. That these have been achieved by concentrating on Universal Primary Education (UPE), rather than tackling the whole learning agenda agreed at Dakar in 2000, does not detract from the impressive performance of many developing countries. In expanding primary schooling for their children they have achieved in a decade what took richer countries close to a century (Clemens, 2004). The challenge now—and the subject of this book—is to complete and extend this work. A number of countries, including some with large populations such as Nigeria, are still a long way

1

from universal primary education. Many more will have difficulty in extending universal schooling to the secondary level.

Yet pursuing the goal of universal primary and secondary education with vigour is vital for several reasons. First, as Cohen (1996, 2007, 2008) has argued, educating girls to secondary level is the most promising way of reducing population growth and limiting climate change. Since the industrial revolution the world's population has grown by a factor of 7, and each person's impact on the environment is now, on average, seven times greater. This means that the impact of the human population on the planet has grown by a factor of 50. Curbing population growth is the fastest way to reduce it.

Cohen, Bloom, Malin, and Curry (2007) estimate that giving children, especially girls, 10 to 12 years of quality education could well reduce fertility rates sufficiently to make a population scenario of 7.8 billion people by 2050 more likely than the 12 billion projected from current rates of growth. Women with secondary education have, on average, 1.5 fewer children than those with only primary schooling. A one-child difference per woman represents 3 billion more or fewer people on the planet by the middle of the century.

Second, education beyond primary level is essential for creating the pool of people with the cognitive skills to become the teachers, nurses and health workers on which society depends. Third, parents realise that primary schooling is only a foundation and that the real benefits to their children accrue from continuing their education at secondary level and beyond. There could even be a 'knock-back' effect if secondary education does not become available. Without the possibility of progression to that level, parents might be less keen to send their children to primary school, putting at risk the gains already made.

Completing the push to universal primary education and extending schooling at the secondary level should now be the principal priorities of the EFA campaign. Both will require the recruitment, training and retention of millions of new teachers. Over and above this requirement for teachers, extending education through secondary level will be an impossibly expensive process if traditional approaches are used.

Costing the extension of schooling is difficult but, without new methods, the next phase of EFA is likely to be more expensive than the last for three reasons. First, the children still not served by primary schools are more costly to reach because many are disadvantaged and live in remote areas. Second, parents may not be satisfied with the quality of current offerings and want something better. Third, education at secondary level is inherently more expensive both to governments and to families. Two decades ago UNESCO (1991) found that on average each secondary pupil cost 3.5 times more than each primary pupil in the least developed countries, with factors as high as 8 in Mali and 20 in Uganda (UNESCO, 1994). The higher direct costs of secondary schooling compared to primary, and the higher opportunity costs of sending older children to school instead of to work are major obstacles to expansion on the conventional model.

In an important study Lewin (2008, p. 66) showed that a country will find it practically impossible to achieve universal secondary schooling if the unit cost of secondary education is more than twice that of primary education. In most of sub-Saharan Africa the disparity remains much larger than this, with ratios of secondary to primary costs commonly between 3:1 and 6:1. Lewin outlines the policy options for getting this ratio down in conventional schools. Since they include paying teachers less and having them work a fuller timetable, it is an understatement to say that implementing such policies will present a challenge to governments.

Binder (2006) reported that nearly 400 million children in developing counties between the ages of 12 and 17 do not attend secondary school. Making various assumptions about cost structures, speed of implementation and repetition rates, she estimated that the annual cost of achieving universal secondary education for those children would fall between $22 billion and $45 billion annually. To put these figures in perspective, we note that despite heroic efforts the multi-donor Fast-Track Initiative for universal primary education, described on p. 13, has raised only a few billion dollars since its inception.

The implications of these costs for low-income countries could be a doubling of education budgets to bring them to nearly half of total government spending. This is not a realistic scenario. Binder concludes: 'these calculations reveal a seemingly rich potential in the workings of low-cost, high-performing education systems...' (2006, p. 482). We shall show that secondary education can be scaled up in innovative ways that not only make better use of scarce financial and human resources than traditional classroom teaching in state schools, but also have the potential to improve the quality and performance of conventional schooling, both public and private.

To set the scene we ask why extending education is such an important goal and then examine the progress of the EFA campaign so far.

Education for All—Why?

Why is there such broad agreement on the importance of education for all?

Education for Peace, Order and Good Government

Two centuries ago, in *The Wealth of Nations,* Adam Smith (1776a) argued for universal education on the grounds of public order and the preservation of freedom:

> The more (ordinary people) are instructed the less liable they are to the delusions of enthusiasm and superstition, which, among ignorant nations, frequently occasion the most dreadful disorders. An instructed and intelligent people, besides, are always more decent and orderly than an ignorant and stupid one... They are more disposed to examine, and more capable

of seeing through, the interested complaints of faction and sedition, and they are, upon that account, less apt to be misled into any wanton or unnecessary opposition to the measures of government. In free countries, where the safety of government depends very much upon the favourable judgment which the people may form of its conduct, it must surely be of the highest importance that they should not be disposed to judge rashly or capriciously concerning it.

Education as a Human Right

By the mid-20th century access to education had come to be seen as a human right and was incorporated into international law through the Universal Declaration of Human Rights (Article 26; United Nations General Assembly, 1948):

(1)   Everyone has the right to education. Education shall be free, at least in the elementary and fundamental stages. Elementary education shall be compulsory. Technical and professional education shall be made generally available and higher education shall be equally accessible to all on the basis of merit.
(2)   Education shall be directed to the full development of the human personality and to the strengthening of respect for human rights and fundamental freedoms. It shall promote understanding, tolerance and friendship among all nations, racial or religious groups, and shall further the activities of the United Nations for the maintenance of peace.
(3)   Parents have a prior right to choose the kind of education that shall be given to their children.

We draw attention to two features of this statement to which we shall return. First, we shall ask in chapter 2 whether the aspiration that 'education shall be free at least in the elementary and fundamental stages' is not, in reality, hindering the achievement of EFA in the poorest communities. This is related to the right of parents to choose what kind of education is given to their children. In the light of mounting evidence that the poorest people are often choosing private education, even in unrecognised schools, because they find it provides better quality than the public schools, it is time to question orthodox views about educational development.

Education for Economic Growth

In the late 20th century, as bodies like the World Bank began to take an interest in what they called 'human capital development', the focus of arguments justifying universal education acquired an economic spin. By 1990, when the World Conference on Education for All convened in Jomtien, Thailand, the notion that education contributed to economic growth had become a truism.

Easterly (2001, p. 84) performed a service by reviewing the relationships between economic development and a number of measures of educational expansion. Having found little correlation between economic growth and the expansion of primary education, he reviewed Mankiw's (1995) claim for a stronger correlation with the expansion of secondary enrolment but showed that this did not hold up either. Pscharapoulos (2008) presented a 50-year recap of research on the relative importance of various levels of education to economic growth in which he suggested that early childhood education was now the key factor. Given the confusion, Easterly concluded that 'education is another magic formula that has failed us on the quest for growth'. Hanushek and Wössmann (2007) are less dismissive but conclude that what counts is not a particular level of schooling but the quality of education on offer and the learning outcomes achieved.

Amartya Sen (1999) has urged a more holistic perspective on the role of education in development. For him the search for a single magic bullet to destroy poverty and create steady economic growth is an illusion. He argued that: 'The case for taking a broad and many-sided approach to development has become clearer in recent years, partly as a result of the difficulties faced as well as successes achieved by different countries over the recent decades. These issues relate closely to the need for balancing the role of the government—and of other political and social institutions—with the functioning of markets' (p. 126).

Even the World Bank, in which the search for single all-purpose drivers of development had a strong hold on professional thinking for several decades, has come around to the need for an integrated and multifaceted approach (Stiglitz, 1998).

Development as Freedom

Sen's integrated approach is based on the concept of development as freedom. For him development is a process of expanding the real freedoms that people enjoy. This broad process embraces all narrower views of development such as growth of individual incomes, facilities for education and health care, civil rights, technological progress and social modernisation. Viewing development as the expansion of freedoms puts the focus on the purposes that make development important rather than on some of the means of achieving it.

Freedom is central to the process of development for two distinct but complementary reasons. The first reason is evaluative: the primary assessment of the progress of development is whether the freedoms that people have are enhanced. The second reason is effectiveness, because the 'achievement of development is thoroughly dependent on the free agency of people' (Sen, 1999, p. 4).

Such a broad approach to development gives a vital role to education even if the expansion of schooling in a particular jurisdiction does not give an immediate economic pay-off. The history of Japan and other East Asian countries shows that universal education should be seen as a basis for economic development rather than its cause. Those economies greatly expanded education (and health care) before they broke out of poverty. But once other factors were favourable for economic growth the good levels of education and literacy allowed these countries to develop rapidly. Sen himself (1999, p. 42) argues that once it adopted a form of market economics China grew more rapidly than India because it already had higher levels of education and health care.

Today the examples of jurisdictions as diverse as Cuba and the Indian state of Kerala show that high levels of literacy and health care do not of themselves create economic growth. However, experience suggests that if such jurisdictions were to adopt economic policies that favoured growth they would develop more strongly than others starting without such a base. Political and economic freedoms promote economic growth (Bhalla, 1995).

Education as a Constituent of Development

Considering development as freedom makes education a constituent component of development as well as a means for promoting it. Education fosters some freedoms directly and, since freedoms strengthen each other, it has a knock-on effect that promotes development generally. The notion of agency also helps to change the concept of development from a process that is imposed on people by governments and development organizations to something that they do for themselves. This goes further than Easterly's (2006) contention that development occurs when people respond to incentives and not as the result of any grand plan imposed from above. Free human beings have their own aspirations.

Sen (1999, pp. 199, 220) illustrates this rather nicely by pointing out that because of its strong emphasis on women's education the birth rate in the Indian state of Kerala has fallen faster than in China with its coercive one-child policy. Educating women is a good example of education being a constituent of development since its effect in reducing both fertility and infant mortality has been widely demonstrated. Earlier we noted Cohen's (2007, 2008) argument that girls' education is the surest route to sustaining a liveable planet.

We conclude that educating people is a vital component of development. It should not be seen primarily as the creation of human capital for the purpose of economic production, but as the nurturing of human capability that gives people the freedoms to lead worthwhile lives. This suggests that education for the 21st century should develop their capacity to become self-directed learners, which is a major change from the focus on teaching and rote learning that still passes for education in some developing countries.

Education is not a luxury to be postponed until a society is prosperous. Along with elementary health care it is a public good that efficient societies at all levels of wealth should foster. Adam Smith believed that its importance justified public expenditure: 'For a very small expense the public can facilitate, can encourage and can even impose upon almost the whole body of the people, the necessity of acquiring those most essential parts of education' (Smith, 1776b).

The Long Saga of Striving for EFA

Some National Experiences

Nations came to aspire to education for all at different times and in different ways (Pollard, 1956). In Japan, for example, modernisation started when the country opened its door to the West in 1867 in the Meiji Restoration. In Meiji Japan, the national goal was to build a rich country and a strong army. Education was regarded as an important means to achieve these national goals and an Education Act was issued in 1872. Its main objective was to provide education to everybody, regardless of status and gender, so that the whole population would be able to enjoy happiness and prosperity equally. The Act stated that 'learning is the key to success in life, and no man can afford to neglect it…everyone should subordinate all other matters to the education of his children…. Henceforth, through out the land, without distinction of class and sex, in no village shall there be a house without learning, in no house an ignorant person.' In the light of current enthusiasm for technical and vocational education it is interesting that the single-minded emphasis on vocational education in the preamble to the Act alarmed some traditionalists (Pyle, 1969, p. 33).

Japan had useful foundations to build on. Even before the Meiji Restoration, feudal Tokugawa Japan had a comparatively high rate of literacy for a pre-modern society. Nearly 50% of boys and some 15% of girls were getting some kind of formal schooling outside their homes. In the 1860s literacy was probably approaching 30%. At the time of the Restoration, there were between 7,500 and 11,000 *terakoya,* or temple schools, and perhaps another thousand diverse educational institutions.

Across the Pacific in the United States, the first compulsory school attendance act was passed by Massachusetts in 1852. This state had already legislated on education 200 years earlier, although the Massachusetts Act of 1642 had nothing to do with school. It placed on parents, and on the masters of children who had been apprenticed to them, the responsibility for their basic education and literacy. Government officials were there to see that all children and servants could demonstrate competency in reading and writing. All this reflected the view that in a heterogeneous society the masses had to be educated in order to understand the written codes of the governing laws and documents of the new country.

Most educational historians reporting on the expansion of primary education take the enactment of legislation and the establishment of state schooling systems as their starting point. Compulsory education was enacted in Britain in 1880. In 1881, under the short presidency of Jules Ferry, France introduced universal primary schooling that was 'secular, free and compulsory' and open to both boys and girls. In 1882 further legislation made schooling compulsory for children aged 7 to 13 (CNED, 2008a, p. 7).

However, this historical approach ignores the extensive private schooling that existed, as in the case of Japan, before the state got involved. In *Education and the State* E.G. West (1994) suggested that in Britain and some other Western countries universal primary education was achieved predominantly though private schools. In the *Edinburgh Review* in 1813 James Mill, the father of John Stuart Mill, wrote of 'the rapid progress which the love of education is making among the lower orders in England. Even around London…which is far from the most instructed and virtuous part of the kingdom, there is hardly a village that has not something of a school, and not many children of either sex who are not taught more or less, reading and writing' (Tooley, 2009, p. 237).

This example is quoted by Tooley in his important work *The Beautiful Tree*. He shows that a similar situation existed in India before the British introduced government schools and that the peer-teaching methods used in these indigenous Indian private schools were being copied in schools in England early in the 19th century and influenced Pestalozzi (2000, p. 230).

The title of Tooley's book is a quote from Mahatma Gandhi. Speaking at Chatham House, London in 1931 he said: 'I say without fear of my figures being challenged successfully, that today India is more illiterate than it was fifty or a hundred years ago, and so is Burma, because the British administrators, when they came to India, instead of taking hold of things as they were, began to root them out. They scratched the soil and began to look at the root, and left the root like that, and the *beautiful tree* perished' (2009, p. 212).

I confess that learning of Gandhi's account of the development of education in India was personally embarrassing. For most of my time at UNESCO, India's Minister of Human Resource Development was Dr Murli Manohar Joshi of the Hindu nationalist Bharatiya Janata Party. We sat next each other at a number of international meetings and became well acquainted. On these occasions Joshi always began his speech by asserting, although without mention of Gandhi, that the British had destroyed a good pre-existing education system in India. At the time I assumed that he made this point to tease me. Now I realise that he was right.

Whatever the merits of the indigenous private education systems—and they were considerable—the colonial powers introduced systems of government schools in most developing countries. At independence these systems were taken over and developed further by the new governments. They naturally became the focus of attention for the intergovernmental bodies, particularly UNESCO and the World Bank, which tried to help governments expand and improve educa-tion. Indeed, until very recently UNESCO and many of its member governments automatically assumed that if education is a public good it must be provided free by the state as a public service. This was the prevailing ethos when the in-ternational community began to take steps to fulfil the aspiration of education for all that figures in both the UNESCO constitution of 1945 and the Universal Declaration of Human Rights.

The Jomtien Conference

We shall take up the story next in 1990 when four agencies of the UN system (UNESCO [United Nations Educational, Scientific and Cultural Organization], UNICEF [United Nations Children's Fund], UNDP [United Nations Development Programme] and the World Bank) convened the World Conference on Education for All in Jomtien, Thailand.

The conference was convened because in 1985 some 105 million children aged between six and eleven were not in school, the majority of them girls. Moreover, economic recessions and financial crises in various developing countries were eroding the increases in school enrolments and literacy rates achieved in the 1970s. Forecasts suggested that the number of out-of-school children might double to 200 million by 2000. 'Given the centrality of education to countries' economic and social growth this did not bode well for world development', noted the World Bank (2000, p. 3).

The purpose of the Jomtien conference was to stimulate international commitment to a new and broader vision of basic education: to 'meet the basic learning needs of all, to equip people with the knowledge, skills, values and attitudes they need to live in dignity, to continue learning and to contribute to the development of their communities and nations' (World Bank, 2000, p. 3).

The outcome of Jomtien was a set of six targets, adopted by 155 governments, 33 intergovernmental bodies and 125 non-governmental organizations, that were to be reached by the year 2000. The targets addressed, in summary:

- The expansion of early childhood care.
- Universal completion of primary education.
- Improvement in learning achievement (with targets).
- Reduction of adult illiteracy.
- Expanded training in essential skills for youth and adults.
- General education for sustainable development.

At Jomtien an International Consultative Forum on Education for All was established to monitor and promote progress towards these targets. It organized various events, including a 1993 summit of the nine highest population developing countries (the E9), a mid-decade meeting to assess progress, and regional/country meetings to report on the country assessments that had been commissioned.

Despite these efforts the targets were not achieved. Indeed, in absolute terms the world went backwards. In 1990 100 million children aged 6 to 11 were not in school and by 2000 this number had grown to 125 million.

Did this mean that the Jomtien conference was an embarrassing failure and that its participants were, in Easterly's words, 'as ineffectual as they were well meaning'? His own explanation was that this kind of global planning simply doesn't work:

The failure of government-sponsored educational growth is once again due to our motto: people respond to incentives. If the incentives to invest in the future are not there, expanding education is worth little. Having the government force you to go to school does not change your incentives to invest in the future. Creating people with high skills in countries where the only profitable activity is lobbying the government for favours is not a formula for success. Creating skills where there exists no technology to use them is not going to foster economic growth. (Easterly, 2001, p. 73)

But this is to take too simplistic a view of the role of international conferences and targets. Planning the achievement of EFA in dozens of countries and cultures across the world is not the same as planning to land a spacecraft on Mars. Chabbott (2003) stresses the role of international conferences like Jomtien in building a consensus between counties and organizations on appropriate goals. Jones (1988), in his account of UNESCO's early work in promoting literacy, describes the difficulty of bringing even the two European perspectives of Britain and France together in a common cause—a form of culture clash that I experienced directly when I headed UNESCO's Education Sector many years later.

Those who had set the Jomtien targets took a somewhat different view of the failure to achieve them, putting much of the blame on six major changes that had impacted on education during the 1990s. First, population growth—notably a 25% increase in the number of 6- to 14-year-olds in Africa and a 15% increase in South Asia, East Asia and the Pacific—had moved the goalposts out of reach. Second, many countries were afflicted by conflict and natural disasters. Third, HIV/AIDS began to reverse the development gains of previous decades and had particularly dire effects on education systems as children became AIDS orphans and teachers died. Fourth, because of the break-up of the Soviet Union and Yugoslavia, there were 20% more countries in the world by 2000 and education systems that had previously provided relatively complete coverage had been broken up. Fifth, there were major economic crises in many countries in Africa, Asia and Eastern Europe (which may have been exacerbated by the development policies of the West). Finally, the exponential rise of communication technologies created a 'digital divide' that further increased the disparities between developed and developing countries.

The World Bank concluded: 'The six developments of the 1990s impacted strongly on education and have forced a fundamental rethinking of EFA, its role, goals and means as part of the end of decade review. Clearly EFA can no longer be attained through business as usual, with the usual players. Even if all the firm commitments made in 1990 had been met, efforts during the 1990s would have proved inadequate' (World Bank, 2000, p. 9).

The Dakar Forum

Despite this statement it appeared that the international community did try to achieve EFA through business as usual by convening another World Forum on

Education for All in Dakar, Senegal in 2000. Was this simply an attempt to hit the nail harder because the first blows had not driven it home?

Certainly the Dakar Forum looked very much like a re-run of Jomtien. It was convened by the same intergovernmental organizations and attracted over 1,000 participants from 164 countries. Once again a set of six targets were agreed upon, with 2015 as the most common deadline (UNESCO, 2001a, p. 10).

We quote them in full:

- Expanding and improving comprehensive early childhood care and education, especially for the most vulnerable and disadvantaged children.
- Ensuring that by 2015 all children, particularly girls, children in difficult circumstances and those belonging to ethnic minorities, have access to, and complete, free and compulsory primary education of good quality.
- Ensuring that the learning needs of all young people and adults are met through equitable access to appropriate learning and life-skills programmes.
- Achieving a 50% improvement in levels of adult literacy by 2015, especially for women, and equitable access to basic and continuing education for all adults.
- Eliminating gender disparities in primary and secondary education by 2005, and achieving gender equality in education by 2015, with a focus on ensuring girls' full and equal access to and achievement in basic education of good quality.
- Improving all aspects of the quality of education and ensuring excellence of all so that recognised and measurable learning outcomes are achieved by all, especially in literacy, numeracy and essential life skills.

Writing in 2009 it seems likely that many countries will still fail to achieve some or all of these goals. Does this mean that nothing was learned from the Jomtien experience about how to ensure that EFA is actually achieved? Does it mean that setting targets is a waste of time? The World Bank (2000, p. 15) claimed that it had 'distilled at least eight core lessons from the past decade, which can help renew the final push towards EFA'. These were:

- Strong political commitment at the country level is the cornerstone of success.
- Quality is as important as quantity.
- Governments cannot deliver on EFA alone—partnerships with families and civil society are essential.
- Countries make better progress when they have developed sector policy frameworks that treat all levels and forms of education comprehensively.
- Inefficient use of education resources constrains progress, notably the failure to allocate funds for learning materials and in-service teacher training, both of which have a major influence on quality.

- Education must adapt quickly to new economic, technological and social challenges, such as the increased role of markets and information technology.
- Education must be cushioned during crises.
- Education expansion needs to be supported by a growing economy.

While most of these lessons may seem rather obvious, they did help to make the post-2000 EFA campaign more focused than the efforts of the 1990s. The beneficial influence of learning materials and in-service teacher education on quality is an important theme running through our study of open schooling and teacher education.

Internationally set targets do have a role to play—and many national governments now set targets for domestic policies. Although one could argue that the Universal Declaration of Human Rights said it all half a century ago by proclaiming that 'everyone has a right to education' and 'elementary education shall be compulsory', politics works in shorter cycles. Agreed targets with deadlines give ministers of education some leverage within their governments, they facilitate the mobilisation of international support, and they give non-governmental organizations a stick with which to beat governments and intergovernmental organizations that fall down on their promises.

The Millennium Declaration

The World Bank's submission to the Dakar Forum implied that it expected to be given the responsibility for leading the post-Dakar campaign for EFA. In the event the Dakar Framework for Action called on UNESCO to co-ordinate global efforts. Later in 2000, however, the world's heads of government met at the United Nations and approved the Millennium Declaration. This included a list of eight Millennium Development Goals (MDGs) that took up, in summary form, two of the Dakar EFA goals:

- Achieve universal primary education:
  Ensure that, by 2015, children everywhere, boys and girls alike, will be able to complete a full course of primary schooling.
- Promote gender equality and empower women:
  Eliminate gender disparity in primary and secondary education preferably by 2005, and at all levels by 2015.

We recall here our commentary on p. 4 about Article 26 of the Universal Declaration of Human Rights where we noted the aspiration that 'education shall be free at least in the elementary and fundamental stages'. The qualification 'free' was applied to primary education in the Dakar goals but omitted in translating the Dakar goal on primary education into an MDG. Why was this? Part of the reason was simply the desire to make the MDGs as concise and clear as possible.

But another likely factor was that during the 1990s the World Bank and the United States had begun to question whether insisting that primary education be provided free might not be an obstacle to achieving it.

The international development community rallied round the principle of free primary education for most of the first decade of the 21st century (Packer, personal communication, 2009). Even by the end of the decade, when the evidence that poor parents often elect to pay for the education of their children could not be denied, the establishment view still prevailed (UNESCO, 2008b, p. 144).

It is now time to revisit this principle in the light of the evidence we summarize in chapter 2, which shows that the principle of free provision can be an obstacle to extending primary education to the poorest communities as well as an excuse for hypocrisy.

The World Bank was given a key role in the wider campaign to achieve all the MDGs and subsequently focused most of its educational work in on the two goals cited above. It prefers quantifiable goals and was doubtless glad not to be responsible for progress towards the only other quantifiable EFA goal: adult literacy. Indeed, at Dakar leaders from the south had advised the Forum against getting involved in the 'quicksands of literacy' since the numbers (800 million adult illiterates in 2000) were daunting (Singh, personal communication, 2009).

Notwithstanding this tighter focus, the World Bank continued to play a constructive part in UNESCO's coordination meetings on the wider EFA agenda, although in its own discourse it began to use the term EFA to refer only to Universal Primary Education (UPE). For a fuller description of the EFA architecture see Packer (2008).

The Fast-Track Initiative

After some false starts, the World Bank began to bring the international donors together to support the UPE campaign under what was called the Fast-Track Initiative (FTI). This was launched at the Development Committee of the World Bank in 2002 with the aim of providing concentrated support to complete the task of achieving the quantifiable EFA goals in countries where conditions were judged to be propitious. A first group of 18 low-income and low-enrolment countries were selected as recipients for early external assistance. The three goals of the FTI were: (a) deeper commitment to education policy reform and the efficient use of resources in developing countries; (b) increased and better coordinated aid from industrialized countries, to be provided within the framework of Poverty Reduction Strategy Papers; (c) and improved assessment based on better data (UNESCO, 2002a).

The FTI injected a sense of urgency into the support for the UPE campaign, although some potential recipient countries felt that the bar of domestic policy reform and efficiency required was set too high. The 2002 EFA Global Monitoring Report (UNESCO, 2002b) identified 28 countries at risk of not achieving the three quantifiable EFA goals, yet only six were on the FTI list. There were further worries that the FTI fell short of the Global Initiative that countries had committed themselves to establish at Dakar.

By 2004 these concerns had abated somewhat and the FTI was gaining traction. Its focus had narrowed to the achievement of UPE and over thirty multilateral and bilateral agencies and regional development banks were contributing to it—although most of the funds came from only a few donors. To respond to fears that donors would be on the hook for the long-term operational support of education systems, the major part of the FTI was called an EFA-FTI Catalytic Fund. This attracted $236 million from four donors in that year, although this was insufficient even for the immediate needs of the first countries invited to join the FTI. There were also concerns about whether the World Bank, which had strict benchmarks for support in its Indicative Framework on Universal Primary Completion, would accept the judgments of in-country donor groups that an education sector plan was good enough to justify FTI funding (UNESCO, 2004a). A mid-term evaluation of the FTI has been conducted (FTI, 2009).

The 2009 EFA Global Monitoring Report (UNESCO, 2008a) judged that the FTI was still not meeting expectations, although the FTI Catalytic Fund had become an important source of finance for several low-income countries. Seventeen donors had pledged $1.3 billion for the period 2004–2011—most of it from the Netherlands, the UK, the European Commission and Spain. There was a similar concentration in recipient countries; with large grants to only five countries and thirteen others receiving less than $10 million. The report concludes:

> At the current rate the projected needs will simply not be met. Taking into account the eight countries that will have joined the current 35 covered by the FTI, there is a potential funding gap of $1 billion for countries that have had plans endorsed. By 2010, with another 13 countries having joined the FTI, that figure could have climbed to $2.2 billion. Working on the assumption that the Catalytic Fund would cover 40% to 50% of the financing gap, there is a shortfall of around $1 billion looming. If these deficits materialise, some countries currently receiving support will see aid flows interrupted and others may get no support at all. (UNESCO, 2008a, p. 36)

Our purpose in summarizing the history of the FTI is to show that despite the good intentions expressed at the EFA conferences, securing the adequate donor support—and even collecting on pledges made—is not straightforward. The campaign to achieve Universal Primary Education has been a long and difficult struggle and despite all the efforts and international arm-twisting many countries may still not make it by 2015.

EFA Coordination and Monitoring

Inevitably the increasing focus of donor interest on UPE, rather than the wider six-goal EFA agenda, also led UNESCO, which was thoroughly involved in the development and implementation of the Fast-Track Initiative, to give particular prominence to the UPE and gender goals in its own work. Two factors, however, ensured that UNESCO pursued its role of coordinating the wider campaign to achieve all six Dakar goals.

First, UNESCO convenes annually a High-Level Group on EFA, with representation from around the world that changes each year. This Group reviews the progress of the Dakar agenda in a general way and focuses each year on one of the goals in particular.

Second, every year since 2001 UNESCO has published an EFA Global Monitoring Report (GMR), a substantial research report that charts progress towards each of the EFA goals and offers a detailed analysis of one of them (UNESCO, 2001a; 2002a, b; 2003a, b; 2004a, b; 2005a, b; 2006a, b; 2007a, b; 2008a, b). The 2008 Report, marking the half way point between 2000 and 2015, reviews all six goals in detail. It provides an invaluable guide to the progress of the EFA campaign although some caveats are in order.

UNESCO, like other intergovernmental bodies, is a creation of national governments and must rely largely on them to supply the data that it collects in order to monitor progress towards EFA. A first problem is that data collection and analysis take time. Short of by-passing national governments and conducting its own household surveys around the world, it is not possible for UNESCO to publish data that is less than two years old. A wider problem is the reliability of the data. Statistical services are in their infancy in most developing countries and may not be equipped to verify the data they receive from schools. Given the pressure to achieve EFA, both school heads and politicians have an incentive to err on the side of optimism in presenting figures for school enrolment.

Another challenge in gathering data is that in the poorest areas of some countries there is extensive private schooling. Some of this is recognised by governments and may be recorded in the figures, but much is unrecognised and goes unrecorded. Tooley (2005) found tens of thousands of children attending unrecognised private schools in the poorest areas of China, Ghana, India, Nigeria and Kenya. They accounted for between 15% of primary enrolments in a poor neighbourhood surrounding Accra, Ghana and 23% in one of the slums of Hyderabad, India. This suggests that the official data on progress towards EFA may be a significant underestimate—unless enrolments in the unrecognised private sector are balanced by over-reporting from the state sector. However, we shall take the UNESCO data at face value and return in chapter 2 to the phenomenon of private schooling for the poor.

EFA: The Challenges Ahead

The UPE target has been a special focus of both planning and funding, so it is not surprising that most progress has been made towards this goal (UNESCO, 2008a). As the 2015 deadline for several of the MDGs approaches, governments and international bodies will no doubt be chastised for their failure fully to meet them. But the evidence does show that the drive towards UPE gained much greater momentum after Dakar—and who can say that getting 'only' 40 million additional children into primary school is anything but a remarkable success?

Numbers in primary school have increased much faster since 2000 than in the decade between Jomtien and Dakar. The average net enrolment rate rose from 54% to 70% between 1999 and 2006 in sub-Saharan Africa and from 75% to 86% in South and West Asia. In these regions, along with the Arab States, there were 40 million more children in school in 2006 than in 1999. The bad news, however, was that in 2006 75 million children, 55% of them girls, were still not in primary school. Furthermore, on present trends there will still be some 29 million children not in school by 2015. While these numbers are small as a proportion of the world's school-age children, they represent a failure of development in the countries in which they are concentrated. What can be done to bring schooling to these youngsters? Recruiting and training more teachers is an important part of the answer—to which we shall return.

But the impressive success in getting millions more children into and through primary school also generates a pressing challenge. What must be done to enable these children to continue learning after their primary education? Three areas require attention: expanding secondary schooling; encouraging lifelong learning; and battling the persistent inequalities in education systems.

Expanding Secondary Schooling

Primary schooling is often referred to as basic education and in many countries the definition of basic education includes schooling at the junior secondary level. Overall, enrolment in secondary education is rising, having increased by 76 million, to 513 million, between 1999 and 2006. The world average Net Enrolment Rate (NER) is now 58%, although that figure masks great disparities between regions and within countries. Developed and transition countries are approaching universal enrolment whereas the secondary NER in 2006 was only 25% in sub-Saharan Africa and 45% in South and West Asia. Furthermore, many of the children covered by these figures never make it beyond junior secondary. As the 2009 EFA GMR notes:

> The transition from lower to upper secondary is a dropout point in many education systems, especially in East Asia, Latin America and the Caribbean, the Arab States and sub-Saharan Africa. At the global level the average Gross Enrolment Ratio (GER) in 2006 was much higher in lower secondary education (78%) than in upper (53%). (UNESCO, 2008a, p.17)

Although the EFA GMRs track enrolments in secondary education there is, curiously, no EFA goal that relates directly to the secondary level. Goal 3 addresses it indirectly as 'ensuring that the learning needs of all young people and adults are met through equitable access to appropriate learning and life-skills programmes'. This is closely related to goal 4: 'achieving a 50% improvement in levels of adult literacy by 2015, especially for women, and equitable access to basic and continuing education for all adults'.

The 2009 report found that governments were not giving priority to the learning needs of youths and adults in their education policies, noting that meeting these needs will 'require more clearly defined concepts and better data' (UNESCO, 2008a, p. 5).

Figueredo and Anzalone (2003, p. 3) suggested that 'secondary education in developing countries has suffered from a sort of identity crisis, belonging to a nebulous zone where students are at once expected to broaden the academic skills learned in primary school and to prepare for the world of work or higher education'. According to UNESCO (2001d, p. 3), 'this double function adds a level of complexity to the expansion of secondary schooling that many countries have been disinclined to tackle'.

Nevertheless, even at the turn of the century, before it was clear that primary enrolments would accelerate rapidly after the World Education Forum in Dakar, there was a strong emerging consensus about the priority of expanding secondary education: 'without a sustained improvement in the coverage and quality of secondary education, developing countries will fall further behind relative to developed countries' (Watkins, 2000, p. 132).

Encouraging Lifelong Learning

The concept of lifelong learning, which is central to education and training in the 21st century, did not feature in the Dakar Goals. Those goals tried to marry the conceptual frameworks for education systems developed over many years in the industrialized world with the complex patterns of learning in countries where the education system is still a work in progress. It is an uneasy marriage.

For example, the distinction between formal and non-formal education is unhelpful in charting paths for post-primary education. Use of the term *formal education* has led to an unduly sharp focus on children of conventional age studying academic curricula in regimented classroom settings. This ignores the realities and needs of the 21st century, an era in which people must acquire knowledge and skills throughout life, often by engaging in self-directed learning.

Lifelong learning enables people to prepare for—and respond to—the different roles, situations, and environments that they will encounter during their lives. It must be supported by a variety of education, training and learning systems through which they can both learn and receive guidance and encouragement. For both individuals and communities lifelong learning is an important tool for improving livelihoods and the health and quality of society generally. This implies that the most appropriate learning systems are those that blur the distinction between formal and non-formal education and enable people to continue to build the four pillars of their education: learning to know; learning to do; learning to live together and learning to be (UNESCO, 1996).

The data from the UNESCO EFA GMRs indicate that there is a massive challenge of providing opportunities for learning on all these dimensions at the post-basic level, both formal secondary schooling and 'appropriate learning and life skills programmes'. The numbers are considerable. To achieve a global secondary NER of even 80% would require places to be found for some 200 million more youngsters. The number of inadequately educated young adults who need to pursue further learning is even larger. Binder (2006) estimated that there were 400 million children aged between 12 and 17 not attending secondary school. Greater still is the number of adult illiterates. The report noted little progress in this area, projecting that on current trends there will be over 700 million adults lacking literacy skills in 2015 (UNESCO, 2008a, p. 5).

Hubert Charles, the distinguished educator from Dominica then serving as UNESCO representative in Nigeria, summarized the situation in that country as follows: '...there is a high and growing demand for participation by mature students anxious to ensure their continued relevance in an ever-changing labour market. Other categories of learners are demanding (or have the right to expect) involvement in the learning process. The marginalised, the poor, the rural dwellers, and even those who have been incarcerated, should be embraced within the learning world. The challenge, therefore, lies in putting in place an effective and varied delivery system with state and non-state players catering to the initial preparation, as well as to remedial and renewal needs' (2008, p. 166).

Battling Inequality

New approaches are also needed to address another issue. The 2009 edition of the EFA GMR is entitled *Overcoming Inequality: Why Governance Matters* (UNESCO, 2008a, 2008b). Its headline message is: 'Progress towards the EFA goals is being undermined by a failure of governments to tackle persistent inequalities based on income, gender, location, ethnicity, language, disability and other markers for disadvantage. Unless governments act to reduce disparities through effective policy reforms, the EFA promise will be broken' (UNESCO, 2008a, p. 4).

The EFA movement appears to have realised, as never before, that inequalities of educational provision within countries are now as much of a problem as inequalities between countries. Indeed, on one measure countries are already equal: 'children from the wealthiest 20% of households have already achieved universal primary school attendance in most countries; those from the poorest 20% have a long way to go' (UNESCO, 2008a, p. 4).

Any serious attempt to scale up secondary schooling must address inequalities of provision that the 2009 EFA GMR related to various factors. In Senegal urban children were twice as likely to be in school as rural children. Within the cities, slum dwellers fared badly: their attendance rates in Nigeria were 20% lower than those of other urban children, whereas in Bangladesh and Guatemala they were lower than for rural children. Here again, however, we must enter a caveat: the 'discovery' that large numbers of poor children are attending unrecognised private schools casts doubt on the accuracy of these figures. In the slum of Makoko in Lagos, for example, a study estimated that 70% of the children attended unrecognised private schools (Tooley, 2009, p. 47).

There are large disparities in attendance and completion among different linguistic communities. These differences are related to other inequalities. 60 million children suffer from iodine deficiency, which hampers cognitive development, and 200 million from anaemia, which limits concentration. There were around 166 million child labourers in 2004. Many of them never see the inside of a school; others attend sporadically (UNESCO, 2008a).

Sugata Mitra and his colleagues (Mitra, Dangwal, & Thadani, 2008) have documented disparities in educational opportunity in a most revealing way. With the help of Google Earth, they worked out a route from New Delhi into the heart of rural north-eastern India that avoided all the major metropolitan and urban areas as far as possible. They then drove this route and, whenever they came to a primary school, administered a set of tests in English, Mathematics and Science to the children and conducted brief interviews with the teachers.

Plotting the test results for each school against distance from New Delhi showed an unmistakable downward trend that was traced to the attitude and quality of the teachers in remote areas. Mitra and colleagues comment: 'there are, and always will be, places in the world where good teachers will not want to go. How will learners in such areas get equal opportunity?' (2008, p. 4). Moreover, where the only real line of accountability for teachers is to a distant government office, their high rates of absenteeism and low commitment are well documented.

The correlation is not only a matter of geographic distance in developing countries. A study in the UK (Mitra, 2008) plotted performance of schools against the density of subsidised housing in their locations and found a similar trend. The variation in performance is again attributed, in large part, to the reluctance of good teachers to go to areas with a high concentration of subsidised housing.

These are telling examples of quality variations within countries that are analyzed more generally in the 2005 and 2009 EFA GMRs (UNESCO, 2004a, b; 2008a, b). There are now many studies that compare cognitive achievement in different countries. Some are global, like the OECD's Programme for International Student Assessment (PISA) that operates in 59 industrialized and middle income countries (OECD, 2009). Others, like the Southern and Eastern African Consortium for Monitoring Educational Quality, focus on particular regions.

Results indicate that in industrialized countries family background and peer groups tend to influence student outcomes relatively more than in developing countries, where school resources play a greater role. In the latter countries reducing class size and various school inputs such as meals, uniforms, learning materials and remedial teaching all improved achievement in particular circumstances (UNESCO, 2004a, p. 14).

Scaling up Secondary Schooling

The next chapter begins to explore new approaches that can help countries rise to the challenges posed by the successes and failures of the drive to achieve EFA. Most developing country governments do not have the resources to address these challenges in the traditional manner by expanding the public school system, even if it were effective. Already low-income countries spend less than others on education, even as a proportion of their GNP, and the share of national income devoted to education actually decreased in 40 of the 105 countries providing data between 1999 and 2006. Global comparisons are telling: 'In 2004, North America and Western Europe alone accounted for 55% of the world's spending on education but only 10% of the population aged 5 to 25. Sub-Saharan Africa accounts for 15% of this age cohort but only two per cent of global spending. South and West Asia, over one-quarter of this group, accounts for seven per cent of spending' (UNESCO, 2008a, p. 6).

These figures indicate that most developing countries simply will not have the resources to offer secondary schooling and lifelong learning opportunities to youth and adults by using traditional classroom models and relying on provision by the state. The numbers of children and young adults seeking education and training are so large that incremental additions to conventional systems will not address the challenge.

Furthermore, even were UPE to be largely achieved by 2015, the international development and donor community would be extremely unlikely, especially in a time of economic difficulty, to sign up for a follow-up campaign for Universal Secondary Education. In expanding secondary education countries are likely to be largely left to their own devices, which will be an expensive proposition if they rely on traditional approaches (Binder, 2006; Cohen, 2007). Many countries will find the task well nigh impossible unless the cost of quality secondary education can be drastically reduced by using alternative methods or making entire education systems work more effectively.

All this is summed up firmly by Figueredo and Anzalone (2003, p. 27): 'The cost of expanding conventional secondary education is prohibitive for many developing countries, and relying on lower-cost alternative systems will not only be attractive but also inevitable'.

In the rest of this book we shall explore alternative and synergistic approaches to completing the drive to EFA. There may be no silver bullet. Extending access to education and training on the scale required will require a multiplicity of initiatives.

The first requirement is for a change of perspective by governments. Instead of thinking of themselves primarily as providers of education, they should see their role as creating facilitative and incorrupt legislative and regulatory frameworks within which a multiplicity of providers can work towards EFA goals. Focusing on the state as the sole or main provider of education obscures its key function of monitoring the performance of the overall system.

In proposing a holistic approach to development, Amartya Sen stated that it required 'a balancing role of the government—and of other political and social institutions—within the functioning of markets' (Sen, 1999, p. 126). Back in 2000, as already noted, the World Bank argued that 'EFA could no longer be attained through business as usual, with the usual players' and that 'Governments cannot deliver on EFA alone—partnerships with families and civil society are essential' (World Bank, 2000).

As well as working to reform and improve their public education systems, governments must broaden their concept of education provision to embrace and encourage three other approaches in particular: private schools for the poor; initiatives based on information and communications technologies (ICT), and large scale open schools. Chapter 2 will assess the roles of public systems, private schools and ICT. Chapter 4 will examine open schooling in more detail, drawing on a general analysis in chapter 3 of the principles that underpin the use of technology in education and the descriptions of selected open schools given in appendix 1.

Scaling up Teacher Education

Schooling, whether conventional or open, requires teachers. The most recent projections are stark: 'Governments will have to recruit and train teachers on a vast scale to meet the EFA goals. Globally, a conservative estimate indicates that at least 10 million more primary teachers are required by 2015, with the most pressing need for additional teachers (1.6 million) in sub-Saharan Africa. Taking teacher retirement into account pushes that figure up to 3.8 million. East Asia and the Pacific need 4 million teachers, and South and West Asia 3.6 million, also taking retirement and other factors into account' (UNESCO, 2008a, p. 22).

Figures for 2006 from the UNESCO Institute for Statistics indicate that China India, Indonesia, Nigeria and Pakistan need to recruit, between them, some 5.7 million primary teachers by 2015. Fifteen other countries will each need at least 100,000 new teachers (UNESCO, 2006c).

Fortunately, the trends are in the right direction. Between 1999 and 2006 the number of teachers in primary schools worldwide increased from 25.5 to 27 million and in secondary schools from 24 to 29 million. Nevertheless, supply is not increasing fast enough to satisfy the future requirements.

The same report gives some revealing data on urban-rural disparities that reinforce the conclusions of Mitra et al. (2008): 'National pupil-teacher ratios (PTRs) often mask large disparities within countries, again associated with location, income and type of school. In Nigeria, PTRs in Bayelsa state were five times higher than in Lagos. Wealthier children often attend schools with better PTRs and a greater proportion of trained teachers. PTRs also vary according to whether the school is publicly funded. In Bangladesh, for example, government schools had average PTRs of 64:1 while non-government schools had PTRs of 40:1' (UNESCO, 2008a, p. 22).

Ensuring that there is an adequate supply of trained and motivated teachers who are deployed where they are needed and discharge their duties conscientiously is a complex challenge that has been analyzed thoroughly in a number of the EFA Global Monitoring Reports (UNESCO, 2004b; 2005b; 2006b; 2007b). Exploring the issues in detail is beyond the scope of this book, but we note the following:

Teachers have to be recruited before they can be trained. Sadly, in most of the world teaching is not a high status profession. Those countries such as Canada, Cuba, Finland and Korea, which come top of international measures of pupil performance such as the OECD PISA surveys, are places where teachers are well respected (OECD, 2009). In the words of the 2005 UNESCO EFA GMR: 'Several common strands emerge in the four high-performing countries. All hold the teaching profession in high regard and support it with investment in training. There is policy continuity over time and a strong, explicit vision of education's objectives' (UNESCO, 2004a, p. 14).

The first step in ensuring a supply of good teachers is to develop policies that enhance their status by addressing issues such as working conditions, salaries, career paths and training opportunities.

Lowering teacher-training admission requirements can increase the supply of teachers but, unless it is compensated by more intensive training, may undermine the quality of student learning.

Increasing class size can reduce the numbers of teachers needed, but may reduce both the quality of student learning and also the job satisfaction of the teachers.

Shortening initial teacher-training can deliver increased numbers of new teachers and may actually raise quality if there are good opportunities for later on-the-job training. However, this requires sufficient support in the schools and an effective system of distance learning.

Many developing countries have employed numerous contract teachers to speed progress towards EFA. In Cameroon and Senegal more than half of all teachers were contract teachers in 2002, although in both countries primary Gross Enrolment Rates increased by nearly one-third between 1999 and 2005 somewhat vindicating the strategy (UNESCO, 2007b, p. 127). Contract teachers have less training, receive lower salaries and enjoy less job security than regular teachers. Obviously, maintaining two groups of teachers on different conditions of service within the same public system is a managerial challenge, and a policy that integrates regular and contract teachers into one career stream is desirable in the long run. Employing contract teachers seems to be more successful when they are hired and managed locally. We note, however, that the private schools in poor areas pay their teachers less than in the public sector and yet get better results from them.

The deployment of teachers to underserved areas is a challenge. Local management may help as well as a system of incentives for serving in remote or unpopular places. One of the weaknesses that threaten progress towards EFA in many countries is the ineffective management of the teaching force, often accompanied by political interference in appointments, promotions and postings.

The increased feminisation of the teaching force in most parts of the developing world is a positive force that encourages parents to send their girls to school. However, female teachers need both pre- and in-service training to be provided in a flexible manner because of their greater family responsibilities—and cultural restrictions on their travel in some societies.

Professional development of teachers is very important, not only for enhancing student learning but also for the motivation of teachers, especially newly trained teachers. How they are supported in their first years in the profession can have a lasting effect on their practice and may determine how long they remain in the profession. Teacher attrition is a major issue in many countries. In the United States, for example, nearly half the teachers leave within five years of entering the profession (UNESCO, 2007b, p. 130).

Our stance on teacher education in this book is that much more emphasis must be put on in-service training, using alternative methods, rather than on the provision of long pre-service programmes. Although there will requirements for teachers in open schools, our primary concern is the teaching force in conventional primary and secondary schools. The demand for training teachers is enormous and the success of the Education for All campaign depends on meeting it.

Summary

In this chapter we have explained why there is general agreement on both the importance of education for all and also on the need for governments to develop policies and take action to see that it is available. We have reviewed the global campaign for Education for All and found that it has achieved some significant successes. Millions more of the world's children are now completing primary school. However, even the primary schooling target will not be met in many countries, and progress on the goals related to skills development and literacy in youth and adults has been limited. Both the successes and the failures of the EFA campaign pose challenges for the future.

The success of the drive for Universal Primary Education is generating a surge of millions of children and young adults who seek to continue their education and training to the next stage. Given the huge numbers, there is no prospect of meeting these needs through the conventional provision of secondary schooling, skills training and adult education. Governments must encourage alternative approaches and providers that can deliver quality learning at scale with low costs. We have suggested that as well as trying to expand public school systems, governments should encourage the expansion of private schooling for the poor and draw lessons from projects involving ICT. This will require governments to look beyond their roles as providers of schooling and establish facilitative and incorrupt legislative and regulatory frameworks within which a multiplicity of providers can work towards EFA goals.

Developing and expanding open schooling is a particularly promising alternative that can also be integrated with these other approaches to make them more cost-effective and cost-efficient. This integrated approach also holds the promise of providing education that is better adapted to the needs of the 21st century by promoting the transition from rote learning to self-directed learning. It can also blur the unhelpful distinction between formal and non-formal education; build bridges between knowledge acquisition and skills development; and reduce the inequalities of access that blight conventional provision in most countries.

The likelihood of failure to reach the goal of UPE in many countries by 2015 requires governments, with the support of the international community, to redouble their efforts at least to get all children through primary school. A key obstacle for most of those countries is a shortage of teachers. Distance learning also offers the most promising solution to the challenge of providing on-the-job training to millions of new teachers and enhancing the skills of those already in service. These methods can deliver, at scale, the kind of school-based training that will make those teachers effective in the classroom and also comfortable and competent with the new approaches to teaching and learning that technology now makes possible.

2
Seeking a Silver Bullet

Everyone from Bono to UNESCO is searching for a silver bullet to bring schooling within reach of the poorest children on Earth.

From the dust jacket of *The Beautiful Tree* by James Tooley, 2009

There is no alternative to primary schools. Technology-based alternatives have not thrived.

UNESCO, 2001c, p. 48

It often happens that the universal belief of one age, a belief from which no one…could be free without an extraordinary effort of genius or courage, becomes to a subsequent age, so palpable an absurdity that the only difficulty is to imagine how such an idea could have appeared credible.

John Stuart Mill, *Principles of Political Economy*, 1848, p. 3

Introduction

In the previous chapter we set the scene by insisting on the importance of achieving Education For All (EFA), reviewing progress towards this goal, and listing the unfinished business to be accomplished. Completing the task of giving all children and adults the learning opportunities that they need to achieve fulfilment as free people in their societies will require action on many fronts and a multiplicity of approaches. This chapter examines the potential of three approaches to scaling up secondary education and the challenges that they face.

First, governments will naturally devote much effort to expanding their public school systems. Data presented in the previous chapter indicated that without new approaches this will be a very expensive proposition. Even if funds were not a constraint, however, expanding schooling of quality is not straightforward.

Second, it has become clear in the last decade that private schools play an important and growing role in the education of poor people. At present this provision operates mainly at primary level. Can private secondary schooling be expanded to help cope with the surge of pupils now moving to this level?

Third, various forecasters, egged on by vendors of information and communications technology (ICT), claim that putting computers in the hands of children can advance their education and reduce, or even eliminate, the roles of teachers and schools. We shall test this claim by examining examples of ICT projects in the developing world.

Reviewing these three approaches will indicate that something more is needed—some element to support all these efforts and integrate them into a wider whole. The development known as open schooling could provide the missing component for expanded and cost-effective secondary schooling systems. Open schooling is an application of technology in education. We shall examine the contribution that technology can make to open schooling—and to schooling more widely—in chapter 3, before reviewing the reality of open schools in chapter 4.

Expanding Public Schooling

Whatever the success of alternative approaches, the drive to expand networks of conventional public secondary schools will continue. Since this will be an expensive process, it is vital that its outcome be an expansion of quality education. Yet public education is suffering a crisis of confidence in many developing countries. This crisis has been presented in a telling manner by recent studies such as those of Phillipson (2008) and Tooley (2009). Although the aim of these authors was to research low-cost private education, their comparative survey of enrolments in the public and private sectors revealed that the public sector is often losing ground. Interviews with parents revealed why this is so, and reports of the personal choices that teachers in the state system make for the schooling of their own children brought the issue into sharp relief. In India, for example, 37% of government schoolteachers are choosing to send their own children to private schools (Muralidharan & Kremer, 2007). As Phillipson (2008, p. 21) notes: 'This represents a damning loss of confidence in public schools'.

This loss of confidence is already a staple of reports of international development agencies, although it has not yet led them to downplay the promotion of public schooling in favour of other routes to achieving EFA. The World Bank called public schooling a 'government failure' with 'services so defective that their opportunity costs outweigh their benefits for most poor people' (World Bank, 2004). The UK's Department for International Development reported that: 'Many children, particularly those from the poorest households, drop out of school or fail to enrol as a direct result of poor quality schooling. Parents will be unwilling to invest in their children's education unless they are convinced of its quality and value' (DFID, 2001, p. 23). Action Aid did not mince its words either, calling government basic education in many of the world's poorest countries 'a moral outrage and a gross violation of human rights' (Tooley, 2009, p. 139).

What are the problems behind these stern criticisms, and can we share the optimism of the development agencies that they can be successfully addressed? From the perspective of the poorest people in those countries that still have a long way to travel to achieve EFA, there are four main issues. All have been documented in UNESCO's series of Global Monitoring Reports (GMRs).

Absentee Teachers

Absentee teachers are the most serious problem. According to the 2005 GMR, 'random surveys in many countries confirm that teacher absenteeism remains a persistent problem' (UNESCO, 2004b, p.18). The UNDP reported that in India and Pakistan teacher absenteeism in the public schools was the main reason that poor people choose private schools. Glewwe, Ilias, and Kremer (2003) reported that in two districts of Kenya teachers were absent nearly 30% of the time and that children would not expect to be taught by public school teachers for over 40% of their time in the classroom. Teacher absenteeism is so much a part of the landscape that UNESCO considers that when teachers leave children to fend for themselves in the classroom it is merely 'graft'. The term *corruption* is reserved for more serious breaches of trust such as stealing textbooks for resale, taking bribes to give better grades, and teaching poorly so as to increase the demand for their business of private tutoring after hours. In short, concluded the World Bank (2004), 'corruption is rife and political patronage is a way of life'.

Social Distance

One of the reasons for this absenteeism, particularly in the poorer areas, is that teachers and principals, usually middle-class people from the richer parts of town, have little respect or understanding for the children in their charge and no knowledge of the slum environments in which they live. The long commutes that some teachers have to make to the poorer areas from their richer suburbs are given as reasons for lateness and absenteeism. The informal categorisation that the teachers apply to the children sometimes leads them to assign the poorer children to cleaning tasks around the school instead of teaching them.

Poor Conditions

In researching *The Beautiful Tree* Tooley (2009) visited many public and private schools serving poor communities. His account of the state of the buildings and sanitation that he saw in public schools in India and Nigeria makes harrowing reading and is corroborated by reports from the World Bank, DFID and others.

Most of the schools he visited were primary schools, but secondary schools do not escape the scourge of decrepit and unmaintained buildings. He had this to say about a public secondary school in Lagos State, Nigeria: 'The secondary school, if anything, was even worse. Its roofs…had been ripped off by the rain and wind. It had a huge classroom block, open plan you might call it, with only blackboards dividing the classes from each other. There were 125 students per class; the noise was deafening; the incentive to learn—or to teach—nil. The senior block, where children 15 years and older tried to learn, had 150 children per class, no walls, again classes divided only by blackboards. The heat under the tin roofs was deadening; there were no fans to cool the children, nor even any electricity' (Tooley, 2009, p. 137).

Low Standards

It is hardly surprising to find that children learn little in decaying buildings where the teachers, whom they see infrequently, are not interested in teaching them. The World Bank (2004, p. 112) referring to a study in Tanzania, noted that: 'the vast majority of students learned almost *nothing* that was tested in their seven years of schooling'. DFID (2001, p. 23) noted that in sub-Saharan Africa 'up to 60% of children leave primary school functionally illiterate. This is a waste of human potential, and also a waste of scarce resources'.

Can Governments Address These Problems?

Our focus is on ways to expand secondary schooling cost-effectively to reach the unreached. The public school systems that we have described are hardly the basis for doing this. Moreover the fundamental problem, which combines lack of accountability and supervision with corrupt administrations, is extremely dif-ficult to solve—and certainly beyond the powers of international development agencies. Were governments to make the necessary reforms many good things would become possible. Without them the schools have no reasons to innovate and other organizations have no incentives to provide equipment and learning materials because they will be filched before they reach the children.

Lewin (2008) has researched the economics of the expansion of public sec-ondary schooling. He found that no country has achieved universal secondary schooling if the cost per pupil of secondary schooling is much more than double that of primary schooling. In the countries that now aspire to expand secondary schooling the ratios are far greater than this. In much of sub-Saharan Africa unit costs of lower secondary education are three times those of primary, a factor that increases to six for upper secondary and to ten or more for specialised technical and vocational education (2008, p. 66).

Lewin devotes a whole chapter (2008, pp. 127–148) to options for the afford-able expansion of secondary schooling. Some of the policy options with most economic leverage are: reducing teacher salaries; increasing pupil-teacher ratios and class-teacher ratios; and increasing teachers' time on task. Inevitably, such policy reforms are most pressing in those countries with the lowest enrolments. The least one can say is that such policy reforms will take time to promulgate and implement.

The irony is that the private schools for the poor, about which Lewin and the development agencies are generally dismissive, seem to have implemented these policy changes already.

Private Schools: A Poor Choice or the Choice of the Poor?

On a visit to Hyderabad, India, in 2000, James Tooley (2009) stumbled serendipitously on what was then a little known—or at least rarely acknowledged— phenomenon: extensive networks of private schools in the poorest communities of the developing world. Since then he and his colleagues have researched this phenomenon thoroughly in China, Ghana, Kenya, and Nigeria (Tooley, 2005, 2009). Meanwhile others have begun to take an interest in this development and the Commonwealth Secretariat has published studies of low-cost private schools in India, Nigeria and Uganda (Phillipson, 2008). These schools, some recognised by governments but most not, enrol large numbers of pupils and often outperform the public sector.

Tooley estimates that the proportion of children out of school in Lagos, Nigeria, drops from the official figure of 50% down to 26% if children in the unrecognised private sector are counted. Furthermore, in the case of India these schools often teach both primary and secondary programmes, making the transition to secondary easier for children and parents than in the state sector where primary and secondary schools are separate entities.

The personal odyssey that led Tooley to discover low-cost private education in some very poor communities has made him a passionate protagonist of this approach and his book, *The Beautiful Tree,* is an engaging read. To avoid the accusation that his enthusiastic advocacy has swayed my judgment, I shall summarize the account of private schooling in Nigeria written by Abdurrahman Umar (2008), who is now my colleague at Commonwealth of Learning (COL) where he heads our teacher education programme. He carried out this research on low-cost private provision before he joined COL, when he was the academic director of Nigeria's National Teachers Institute (NTI), which is a pillar of Nigeria's public education establishment and one of the world's largest teacher education institutions.

Private Outperforms Public

Umar worked from official Nigerian data and admitted that these data from three states, which put enrolment in private schools at 7.25% of the total in 2005, is 'a gross undercounting of private schools and the children enrolled in them' (Umar, 2008, p. 103). These data included only recognised private schools, which are greatly outnumbered by unrecognised schools. He corroborated Tooley's finding that private schools outperform their public counterparts on every criterion except the size of the playground. They have better pupil-teacher ratios—including pupil-to-qualified-teacher ratios—and get better results in all subjects tested. He concluded that in Nigeria, one of the countries most challenged by the EFA goals, private schooling will continue to expand even if public schooling improves.

Umar also talked to Nigeria's National Union of Teachers (NUT) which, perhaps surprisingly, was very positive about the contribution that private schools could make to the attainment of the EFA and MDG goals. Less surprisingly, the NUT assumed that the quality of private education must be inferior to public provision since the teachers had fewer qualifications and were paid much less than their counterparts in the public system.

This attitude, which is not supported by the research data and the views of parents, suggests that if the public teachers' unions want to avoid a steady hae-morrhaging of pupils to the private sector, they should mount a campaign to get their members to show up at school and teach their classes in a committed manner. Umar's study showed that the private schools engaged the parents more thoroughly in their activities, giving them the opportunity to make judgments about what really determines quality in education.

Schooling is Never Free

Umar also found that although private schools charge fees, public schools are not free either. The fees in the private schools fell in the range of $8 to $25 per term and the parents paid nearly $20 per year on top of the fees for uniforms, textbooks, exercise books and writing materials. However, parents of children in the public schools also paid these additional fees, somewhat reducing the cost differential between the two sectors.

It is significant, given our focus on expanding secondary education, that Umar found that many of the private primary schools were eager to add a secondary stream. If they do this, it will make the transition from primary to secondary easier for the children than in the public sector, where they have to change schools.

Looking ahead, Umar (2008, p. 128) pointed to the dangerous inconsistency between rhetoric and reality in governments' treatment of the private schools. Nigeria's declared National Policy on Education 'regards private participation in education as a way of providing variety and allowing for healthy competition between private and public sectors'. Yet 'the implementation of this policy has in practice violated its spirit. Government has so far focused not on supporting low-cost private schools (e.g. through matching grants, provision of instructional materials) but on intimidating their owners and threatening them with closure on the grounds that they do not meet the prescribed minimum standards for the establishment of schools and are therefore of poor quality. This approach is unhelpful and even hypocritical, since many government-owned schools are also of very poor quality but are not threatened with closure'.

Private Schools as Partners for EFA

Umar (2008) recommended that these attitudes must change. Private schools should be seen as partners in the efforts to attain the EFA and MDG targets. School inspections must cease to be a punitive exercise and rather seek to improve all schools by being 'advisory, facilitative and formative'.

Private schools are here to stay. Indeed, they are simply making a comeback. We noted earlier that private schools drove the early expansion of popular education in the 19th century. Tooley ends *The Beautiful Tree* with an audacious analogy. Watching a total solar eclipse in Ghana in 2006, he drew a parallel between the moon obscuring the sun for a period before light returned and the way that private schooling in developing countries was displaced by public provision for half a century but is now re-emerging (2009, p. 270).

Orthodox thinking is still reluctant to catch up with this trend. The 2009 EFA GMR does address the role of private schools for the poor (UNESCO, 2008b, p. 164). However, it tiptoes around the issue, clutching at straws as it goes, to conclude that expanding public systems is the only way to achieve EFA: 'the bottom-line obligation for all governments is to develop publicly financed and operated primary schooling of good quality for all children' (UNESCO, 2008b, p. 168).

Similarly Lewin, in his major study of financing secondary education, is sceptical of the contribution of nongovernment providers and dismissive of their role in relation to the poor: 'Non-government schools can contribute to expanded access. Although it will remain difficult to run effective secondary schools that are affordable to poor households, increased enrolment in non-government schools by wealthier students may free up resources in the public school system' (Lewin, 2008, p. 88).

Improving Private Schooling

Nevertheless, although low-cost private schools outperform public schools in poor areas and seem to give a better service to poor parents and their children, there is still enormous room for improvement. Tooley (2009, p. 247) identifies three problems with which the private schools could benefit from outside help: reaching all children; improving quality; and giving parents better information for making their choices.

Most low-cost private schools already make the poor subsidise the very poor by charging zero or nominal fees to the poorest families or those who have fallen temporarily on hard times. Although well aware of the risks of fraud and corruption in any voucher scheme, Tooley believes it could be made to work if done at a very local level through NGOs.

Schemes to improve quality must start from the fact that most low-cost private schools operate in a very competitive environment and aim to make a profit. Their owners are keen to gain a competitive edge by improving the physical or IT infrastructure and they would take out loans for this if they could get title to their property and operate in a fully legal manner. The larger problem is to introduce forms of pedagogy that break with the deadening tradition of rote learning in both private and public schools. Despite much effort by the development agencies, attempts to introduce child-centred teaching methods have not proved sustainable. Tooley believes that the best route is to take advantage of the competition between owners and encourage widespread experimentation with new methods such as the use of ICT (2009, p. 258).

Finally, noting that consumers often rely on brands to help them choose between competing products, he suggests the creation of chains of private schools that could develop distinctive brands, share resources and even develop new assessment and examination systems. The International Baccalaureate, a highly prized global qualification that is not an emanation of governments, could provide a model.

In striving to make these improvements, the private schools could benefit from the existence of a facilitative body that could help them scale up their efforts to provide quality education by sharing resources and tackling common problems. In chapter 4 we shall ask whether open schools could play this role and under what conditions.

Children and Computers: What Works?

Head teachers of both public and private schools are keen to bring computers into their classrooms, not only because it impresses parents, but also from the belief that ICT have the potential to improve pedagogy and outcomes by engaging the children more fully in their learning. In this section we examine ways that computers have been used at reasonable scale in developing countries to see what lessons can be learned about how to use them most effectively.

Even in the days of mainframe computing, there were enthusiasts for computer-assisted instruction. The most widely used system was PLATO, developed by the Control Data Corporation. It lasted from 1980 to 2006, included courses at all levels from primary to university, and was used extensively in South Africa as well as in industrialized countries (Wikipedia, 2009).

With the arrival of personal computers and laptops, the interest in using computers to enhance children's learning became more intense. In exploring examples of this development we focus not on the use of computers for learning computing skills, but on their application to the wider learning agenda. We shall assess three projects: One Laptop Per Child; the Hole in the Wall; and NEPAD eSchools.

One Laptop Per Child

The One Laptop Per Child (OLPC) programme generates such strong emotions among its protagonists and opponents that it is hard to adopt a neutral style in presenting it. OLPC is the brainchild and very personal project of Nicolas Negroponte, founder of the MIT Media Lab (Negroponte, 2006). He began from the premise that children could teach each other through experiential and trial-and-error learning on a rugged yet cheap educational tool: 'He believes that if he can enable children to learn the very skill of learning, he can leverage education as a force to eliminate global poverty… He wants children in the developing world to 'learn learning' through a controversial learning methodology called "constructivism" in which the learners construct new knowledge from their experiences… Negroponte believes knowledge is constructed by the learner through activities not supplied by the teacher' (OLPCNews, 2009a).

After a brief experiment with standard laptop computers in a Cambodian village school, Negroponte concluded that he needed a new computing platform. The Media Lab then built the OX-1 laptop with specifically designed software and hardware to enable constructivist learning in the dusty, hot, un-electrified schools of the developing world. It was meant to be cheap enough to be purchased in the massive quantities required for a one-to-one distribution ratio, and so child-centric that adults would not be tempted to appropriate it.

To launch a visionary project like this it helps to have friends in high places. At the 2005 Davos World Economic Forum, UN Secretary-General Kofi Annan joined Negroponte to present the new design as the children's "$100 laptop". It was an instant international sensation, and the developing world presidents attending the Forum were 'captivated by Negroponte's dream that they could revolutionize education, the very act of learning, with an inexpensive yet rugged laptop specifically designed for children that negated the need to construct schools or hire teachers' (OLPCNews, 2009a).

With the benefit of hindsight, the launch at Davos now appears to have been the high point of the project. Since then the difficulties have multiplied. One critic who left the project claimed that the operating system was a botched job (OLPCNews, 2009c) and that: 'there are three key problems with one-to-one computer programmes: choosing a suitable device, getting it to children, and using it to create sustainable learning and teaching experiences. They're listed in order of exponentially increasing difficulty' (Krstić, 2008).

Regarding the device, perhaps the most significant but unintended consequence of the OLPC project was to spur other computer manufacturers to produce reliable cheap laptops. Before Negroponte made his announcement at Davos, the industry had not been interested in this market. But, 'this heretical bombast and sales coup upset the longstanding computer manufacturing tradition to keep adding functions to maintain high prices in the developed world, while ignoring the developing world' (OLPCNews, 2009a). Today a wide range of inexpensive laptops and netbooks are available to satisfy the demand that OLPC awoke and some are selling at lower prices than the $200 real cost of the XO-1 machine.

The task of deploying the XO-1 to tens of thousands of children, some in very remote regions, seems to have been left largely to chance. According to Krstić (2008): 'Peru's first deployment consisted of 40 thousand laptops, to be deployed in about 570 schools across jungles, mountains, plains and with total variance of electrical availability and uniformly no existing networking structure… Laptop delivery was going to be performed by untrusted vendors who are in a position to steal the machines en masse'.

In the coy language of OLPCNews, which calls itself an independent blog of record for the project, 'OLPC is experiencing its own learning opportunity as it tries to distribute the XO-1 laptop to children'. OLPC had originally planned, on the basis of the eager response at Davos, 'to convince the presidents of countries to buy laptops by their millions through their national education systems and to pass them out like, or in lieu of, textbooks. Unfortunately, OLPC overestimated the power of presidents to purchase goods directly or even to stay in office. To great fanfare, OLPC announced agreements with presidents in Argentina, Brazil, Libya, Nigeria and Thailand for one million laptops each in 2006, only to have all those orders cancelled' (OLPCNews, 2009a).

Zittrain (2008, p. 326) calls OLPC 'an enterprise of breathtaking theoretical and logistical vision'. It also appears to have been planned and implemented with breathtaking incompetence. It is not hard to understand why responsible governments backed off once they looked at the proposition more closely.

First, the technology and education ecosystem was incomplete. While the XO-1 device was technologically brilliant, it did not have a functional user interface, or supporting technology (e.g. school servers) or significant educational content.

Second, OLPC dismissed the need for pilot testing, claiming it had already been done. But the earlier experiment in Cambodia had really shown that the project needed a complete rethink. Krstić (2008), noting an epitaph in MIT's *Technology Review* magazine, described an earlier test of the concepts conducted by Seymour Papert and Negroponte in Senegal in 1982 as 'a spectacular flop due to management and personality conflicts'.

Avoiding pilot testing when rolling out large-scale projects that depend for their success on economies of scale can be a good strategy. The UK Open University (UKOU), for example, ignored the advice of civil servants to do a pilot test with a few hundred students and launched in 1971 with a first intake of 25,000 students (Perry, 1976). However the UKOU engaged in much more systematic planning than the OLPC project, although it too was a leap in the dark.

Third, as Zittrain (2008, p. 236) notes, 'the XO dissemination plan is remarkably light on both student and teacher training… Students are expected to rely on each other and on trial-and-error to acquire most of the skills to use and re-programme the machines. Content also seems a calculated afterthought. The XO project wiki—haphazardly organized as wikis tend to be—featured a "call for content" in late 2006, mere months before millions of machines were to be placed in children's hands…'

Zittrain goes on to identify the nub of the problem, which is that the OLPC is a generative technology that, like the Internet, invites users to do it for themselves. Negroponte's avoidance of normal planning processes was integral to this "suck it and see" approach. 'XO embraced the procrastination principle that is woven through generative technologies. To the chagrin and discomfort of most educational academics following the project, there is little focus on specific educational outcomes or metrics. There are no firm plans to measure usage of the laptops, or to correlate changes in test scores with their deployment and use. Instead, the idea is to create an infrastructure that is both simple and generative, stand back, and see what happens, fixing most major substantive problems only as they arise...' (Zittrain, 2008, p. 237).

So where are we now? By February 2009, 750,000 XO laptops had been distributed, compared to Negroponte's earlier ambition to place 150 million annually by 2007 (OLPCNews, 2009b). This was because despite a warm reception in Peru, Rwanda and Uruguay, the large population nations of Brazil, China and India had opted not to take part. The bankruptcy of Nortel Networks, a major sponsor, was another blow to the OLPC project, which laid off half its staff in early 2009 and restructured its operations with new software options, including (to the fury of some open source extremists) Microsoft's Windows XP operating system, a new laptop design and a new implementation focus with distribution outsourced.

The project made recipient countries responsible for creating an educational environment around the XO, and their success has been mixed. It is clear the project will only have a lasting and measurable impact when classroom teaching methods and administrative practices are modified to take full advantage of the technology.

Yet the most striking aspect of the evolution of the project is the change of discourse. In the early days Negroponte insisted the OLPC initiative was about 'learning not laptops'. It was presented as a generative technology that would foster constructivist learning. But by 2009 the focus of OLPC project had changed to selling the XO—and selling it in a market that was now replete with cheap laptops that make no claim to be generative technologies promoting constructivism.

What light does the OLPC throw on the wider ambition of scaling up schooling by combining children and computers? The answer, unfortunately, is very little. The OLPC idea is still unproven because the project has shied away from any systematic evaluation. The Australian Council for Educational Research has tried to produce a literature review of the evaluation of OLPC programmes globally but the authors' frustration is palpable (Nugroho & Lonsdale, 2009). Since the XO deployments in over 30 countries 'vary in almost every respect', 'it is difficult to build up a global picture of impact across such different agendas and circumstances'. There was no overall evaluation plan for the XO roll out and at the local level 'formal evaluation mechanisms are rarely embedded in the earliest stages of project planning'. 'Only projects that included formal evaluation measures right from the start of the project had access to baseline data that would allow comparison with subsequent data'. Against this background, 'the findings from existing evaluations are largely anecdotal and positive in nature; and recommendations arising from the evaluations generally relate to training needs and technical matters'.

Zittrain (2008, p. 239) points out that several earlier attempts to bridge the digital divide with computers in schools have fared poorly. He asks: 'Will XO fail like the others? Development experts view it as sceptically as education experts do, seeing XO as yet another risky heaving of hardware at problems that are actually political, social and economic in nature'.

Finally, the OLPC provides no real answers to the six questions we pose in chapter 3 (p. 63) because, although it is based on the principle that knowledge is not supplied by the teacher, it does not attempt to substitute capital for labour in any systematic way. Buying the XO machines is an add-on cost to the participating education system that is not offset by any savings elsewhere. This is the fundamental reason why countries backed out of the project once the enthusiasm of their presidents returning from the Davos World Economic Forum had to be translated into budget proposals within ministries of education.

The Hole in the Wall

It is fascinating to juxtapose the OLPC initiative with an Indian experiment, the Hole in the Wall (HITW) project, that also puts children in front of computers. This one was the brainchild of Sugata Mitra when he was chief scientist at the National Institute for Information Technology, a large IT training organization. Mitra is now known affectionately as the 'slumdog professor' because the HITW project inspired the novel Q&A by Vikas Swarup (2005) that was the basis for the Oscar-winning film Slumdog Millionaire.

Mitra and Negroponte began with similar assumptions but then went in different directions. The common starting point (Inamdar & Kulkarni, 2007) was Seymour Papert's book Mindstorms: Children, Computers and Powerful Ideas (1980). This was a stage in Papert's development of Piaget's constructivist learning theory into constructionism, which combined the ideas of constructing knowledge from experience, and learning by constructing objects in the real world. The relationship between individuals and knowledge goes through three phases: self-directed, experiential learning in early childhood; 'teaching' and 'being told' in schools; and experiential learning again in creative adults.

Papert wanted to bring experiential learning back into the school stage by providing complex exploratory opportunities with computers. He found, however, that in schools computers were put in labs and hijacked by the school curriculum and timetables. He saw the proliferation of computers in homes as a promising development, although the home environment does not offer many social opportunities for interactive learning with others in peer groups.

To this point Mitra's and Negroponte's thinking ran along parallel tracks. But rather than conceiving a massive project like OLPC, Mitra moved the computers out of both homes and schools into local playgrounds—starting with a single computer embedded in the brick wall of an informal playground next to a residential slum in Delhi in 1999. The results surprised everyone: 'Slum children were able to use the computer to browse, play games, create documents and paint pictures within a few days. Children aged 8–14 worked together in groups at the computer, making exploratory discoveries, generalising their learning, describing it in a local context and teaching each other. The press called the experiment "Hole in the Wall". Researchers called it "Minimally Invasive Education" (MIE).

Research showed that groups of children could learn how to use public computers on their own, without adult intervention' (Inamdar & Kulkarni, 2007, p. 170).

Sceptics were slow to accept that these results were genuine. They suspected that adults were involved until evidence from hidden video cameras showed the children were doing it on their own. They supposed that some of the children had previous knowledge of English until the experiment was repeated in a rural setting where that was impossible.

Realising that he was on to something and helped by the fact that he was working in his own country with ready access to researchers, Mitra initiated a substantial research programme that continues. Meanwhile, the HITW project was being reproduced in other countries such as South Africa, where it is called the Digital Doorway (SouthAfrica.info, 2009).

In the beginning the HITW research focused on observing the behaviour of the children and making generalisations about it. It then focused on what they were learning and later on the impact of working with the computer on their performance in school and their attitudes. Dangwal and Kapur (2008) reported on the learning processes based on close observation of behaviour at the HITW computer and interviews with 250 children from 17 locations across India in both rural and urban slums. Ages ranged from 8–14 years with an average age of 10–11 years.

The most fundamental finding is that learning happens in groups. It would not be fair to say that the One Laptop Per Child focuses on learning solo, because the XO laptops are configured to communicate with each other. Nevertheless, Negroponte holds that every child must have one, whereas Mitra has found that having numbers of children working on the same computer is the key to success. It is also, of course, less expensive. Typically, 300 children can achieve computer literacy in India in three months with only one machine.

Groups are normally heterogeneous with three to six children actively engaged, although a wider group of ten or more may gather behind them and offer advice (often wrong). In rural areas there is no differentiation by gender. Children aged 8–14 work together. The lower end of the age range, around eight, is the age at which children have the readiness and preparedness to learn. The upper end, around 14, is when adolescents feel that they are too old to visit a public space with younger children, although some then say they miss the HITW experience. The visits that children make to the HITW last between 5 and 30 minutes. Most of the children are enrolled in local elementary schools, usually government schools. Presumably their freedom to come and go to the HITW reflects the rather sporadic demands of attendance at these establishments that we noted earlier.

The success of HITW is a combination of children's preparedness to learn and the novel and varied stimuli provided by the computer. Piaget (1952) noted that surprise is a determinant of attention, which in turn has an important role in cognitive achievement. Children assimilate by attending to the novel situation.

'The attractions of HITW computers, such as novelty and surprise as attention getting, are also reinforcing in the sense that they instigate, mediate and maintain behaviour; stimulus complexity and reactions to it in terms of multi-sensory channelling; affective fall out in terms of joy, excitement and the desire to master the challenge provided by the new stimulus by adopting varied learning strategies and collaborative networking. These are salient features that go on to play a relevant and crucial process in learning' (Dangwal & Kapur, 2008, p. 346).

Learning at the HITW occurs in stages. The starting point is intense excitement. All children reported that they liked working with computers, using the words 'fun, enjoyment, pleasure, and feeling good'. This nurtures the emotions and motivation needed for learning. Getting started is a challenge. 'For example, during the first week the computer hangs because all the children are pressing on the keyboard simultaneously. Gradually a fluid and flexible group emerges that operates on the computer and learns through…trial and error, exploration, incidental learning, observation, or seeking computer knowledge from others… Any new discovery leads to the next stage' (Dangwal & Kapur, 2008, p. 347).

Certain key features emerge in all groups. They are open to learning from outside and membership of the group around the HITW changes constantly while maintaining the same function and structure. A reliable social network is established. Children rehearse activities, which besides fostering permanent learning lead to more discoveries and more information. This information seeps out in all directions, giving a snowball effect that includes the observers in the outer circle. This, and the heterogeneity of the groups, also has the effect of making each child both a learner and a teacher at different times. The authors comment: 'This process of self learning and teaching is unique and distinctive to HITW computer learning, and can be said to be the core strength of the continuing learning process' (Dangwal & Kapur, 2008, p. 349).

HITW seems to have found the secret of effective multi-grade teaching and self-directed learning. The gap between experts and learners disappears because all participants are considered experts in some capacity. It is the sharing of knowledge by everyone that drives the evolutionary development and continuous progress of the learning environment. The group becomes self organizing as individual members become self regulating. The study concludes that children prefer to learn from their peer group because peers represent a more helpful and attainable competence model than adults or teachers. The HITW evokes curiosity that makes them active learners. The computer allows them to do things without being afraid of making mistakes, which simply contribute to their learning.

The HITW appears to be a cost-effective way of extending computer literacy among children and the learning processes that it stimulates correspond neatly to the skills, such as teamwork, communication and self-directed learning, which are considered important in the 21st century. But what is the impact of engagement with the HITW on the wider learning agenda? Is HITW an option for expanding schooling at low cost? It is not surprising that children can use computers to learn about computing, but what about other subjects?

To their credit Mitra and his colleagues have conducted research on many aspects of the HITW project and its impact. These are summarized on their website (Hole in the Wall, 2009). These studies have to confront the familiar challenge of all research on the impact of adding a new element to an educational ecosystem. Most of the 40,000 pupils who had been involved in HITW activities by 2007 were enrolled in local government schools. This presented both the opportunity to assess how visiting the HITW affected children's school and examination performance, but also the challenge of distinguishing between the impact of schooling, the HITW and other factors.

Inamdar and Kulkarni (2007) tried to assess the impact of participation in the HITW on pupils' achievement in English, Science and Mathematics, using a control group and controlling for relevant variables. Their conclusion was that frequent visitors to the HITW significantly increased their achievement in Mathematics, even after controlling for the fact that frequent users scored higher on intelligence tests than infrequent users. But no effect was found for English and Science. One hypothesis to explain these results is that school examinations in these subjects are based on 'answering textbook questions in a prescribed manner and format from memory'. The software on the HITW computer may not influence scores on such tests. The Mathematics examinations, on the other hand, are based on problem solving, for which the self-directed learning encouraged by HITW is more relevant.

Other research results indicate that involvement in the HITW does develop intellectual maturity, even if this does not improve children's capacity for the rote learning favoured by Indian schools. It also shows that communities believe that HITW computers are beneficial for children—an important finding given that parents are usually sceptical about educational technology. Another significant result is that out-of-school children benefit from the HITW.

The HITW approach does give some answers to the questions on p. 63 in chapter 3. While it does not substitute technology for labour in a significant way, the HITW gives children access to computers at minimal cost without the necessity of hiring additional people. Nevertheless, before it can provide an answer to the scaling of secondary schooling it needs to be embedded in a wider educational ecosystem.

Children and Computers in Africa

Identifying effective roles for technology in achieving EFA is a central theme of this book. Africa is of particular interest because EFA remains a serious challenge for most of its countries. Although there is already an impressive amount and range of activity, the use of computers for education in Africa is still in its infancy. This may allow educators across the continent to draw lessons from the effervescence of experimentation in the rest of the world and integrate ICT into education in a purposeful fashion.

To assess this possibility we shall first examine the overall situation of ICT in education in Africa and then summarize the lessons from a major pan-African initiative, the NEPAD (New Partnership for Africa's Development) eSchools Demonstration Project.

After surveying ICT and education in Africa, Farrell and Isaacs (2007, p. 1) noted that the process of adoption and diffusion of ICT is in transition from a decade of experimentation focused on projects to 'a new phase of systemic integration informed by national government policies and multi-stakeholder-led implementation processes'. Most African countries now have national ICT policies in place and half of them have ICT policies for the education sector. Do these policies influence the development of ICT infrastructure and give clarity of purpose to the integration of ICT into education?

A 2006 survey of ICT infrastructure in African universities found that it was 'too little, too expensive, and poorly managed' (Gakio, 2006). Farrell and Isaacs (2007, p. 3) concluded from their country reports that this is true for all parts of national education systems but forecast that usage will now become more mature because of the emergence of policy frameworks, the evolution of networks and 'perhaps most importantly, the growing commitment to ICT in education on the part of government leaders'. Our earlier account of the enthusiasm of country presidents for the OLPC project at Davos in 2005 (p. 3) suggests a caveat here. It is easy to impress politicians about the potential of ICT but translating their eagerness into coherent policies and implementation is more difficult.

Nevertheless, Farrell and Isaacs (2007) judge that 'the progress being made in the adoption and diffusion of ICT in education throughout Africa, particularly in these early years of the 21st century, is remarkable. The formal schools sector has historically led the way in ICT in education in most African countries, often before national policies have been adopted...much of the emphasis is on secondary school access' (p. 17).

The evolution of the content of policy is particularly encouraging. The aim of the early policies on ICT was to make people computer literate. Later the focus shifted to the role of ICT in development. Although some countries still emphasise the development of ICT infrastructure as the 'silver bullet' for achieving socio-economic development, a recent study shows that investment in ICT does not foster human development without parallel investment in education and health (Morawczynski & Ngwenyama, 2007).

It is encouraging that African policies now try to integrate ICT into education, rather than treating it as merely a subject to be taught. Meeting in Nairobi in 2007, African ministers of education echoed the theme of this book: 'ICTs are seen as one key solution that will allow African countries to meet the needs in rural and underserved areas and bring education to their citizens rapidly and cost effectively' (Morawczynski & Ngwenyama, 2007, p. 4).

In the context of this wider role for ICT in education, political interest is expanding beyond the issue of access to equipment to include content creation, the necessity of staged implementation and the need to manage ICT policy coherently. Policies also provide for the provision of ICT facilities to the wider public through local centres. But there is still a long way to go, especially in rural areas where electricity, telecommunications and trained people are often lacking. In South Africa, for example, while 6,000 schools had access to PCs In 2007, only 2,500 had Internet access. Countries realise they must interpret ICT broadly and continue to use 'old' ICT like radio, audiocassettes and print where appropriate.

In contrasting the enabling and constraining features for ICT development, Morawczynski and Ngwenyama (2007, p. 8) note that 'unlike many parts of the developed world, (African) staff and teachers appear to be more welcoming to the prospect of ICT in education'. This translates into some 60 ICT-related teacher education programmes where the focus goes beyond computer literacy to enabling teachers to use ICT as a teaching and learning resource. In-service training came first but ICT is now part of pre-service programmes too. Africa will be ready with a trained cadre of teachers by the time that expanding connectivity makes it truly possible to integrate ICT into education.

This was the promising context into which the NEPAD eSchools Demonstration Project was introduced. A major aim of the NEPAD is the development of ICT infrastructure. The NEPAD eAfrica Commission (eAC) is the task team responsible for ICT projects, one of which is the NEPAD eSchools initiative. It is a multi-country, multi-stakeholder continental initiative that is intended: (a) to teach ICT skills to young Africans in primary and secondary schools; and (b) to improve the provision of education in schools through ICT applications and the use of the Internet. The Demonstration Project was intended to identify working models for the large scale implementation of the initiative, which aims to equip 550,000 African schools with ICT and connect them to the Internet by 2020.

The Demonstration Project involved six diverse schools in each of 16 countries through partnerships that included private sector consortia, the country government and eAC. The consortia were to provide an eSchool model that included equipment, networking, connectivity, training and curriculum relevant learning materials. A public report on the project was commissioned (Farrell, Isaacs, & Trucano, 2007).

Shafika Isaacs of SchoolNet Africa wrote: 'Amidst this myriad of interventions, programmes, experiments and innovations taking place in almost all African countries, sits the NEPAD eSchools initiative… Never before has there really been a programme that mobilised national government participation and leadership at the official government level in the way the NEPAD eSchools vision has. Further, it has brought the private sector into partnerships that, while experiencing growing pains, have mobilised resources in a way that few other projects have been able to do. And there is much yet to learn about doing this in an optimal way' (Farrell et al., 2007, p. 21).

The public report captured some of the lessons that had been learned, stressing that because NEPAD eSchools was a work in progress it was too early to assess impact. A first lesson was that the roll out occurred more slowly than planned. The project was meant to last a year and the first NEPAD eSchool was launched in Uganda in October 2005. However, by December 2006, 4 of the 16 countries had not yet started. The authors note: 'it is an ambitious, even audacious, undertaking…without precedent in its international scope…expectations of the Demo phase may well have exceeded the practical bounds of its reach within the intended time frame' (Farrell et al., 2007, p. 1). All parties underestimated the complexity of the project.

Other lessons were:

- The eAC had neither the funds nor the people to provide effective leadership, which limited communication between project partners and sparked complains about limp management. The recommendations from interim reports on progress were not followed up. (In this respect there were parallels between the NEPAD project and OLPC, although in the latter case the *laissez-faire* approach was adopted more as a matter of principle than because of lack of funds.)
- The Demonstration Project assumed, as its name implies, that there was little previous experience of ICT in schools in Africa to build on. The earlier work of Farrell and Isaacs (2007) showed that this was a faulty assumption. In some countries the project was dwarfed by existing country initiatives. A greater awareness of existing projects and earlier experiences in the target countries would have made planning easier.
- A related point was that NEPAD failed to include civil society organizations in the project, even though they had extensive experience of introducing ICT in schools in Africa. This deprived the project of valuable support and resources.
- The Demo had a major impact in making governments aware of the importance of adopting ICT in their strategic educational plans and the public/private partnership model used by the eAC has been replicated by some countries. However, the failure even to attempt cost-benefit analyses was a weakness.
- Using local partners has greatly facilitated the implementation of the project and given support to teachers. Indeed, the impact of the Demo school in each community has been greater than anticipated, notably by drawing in teachers from other schools and involving community groups.
- Although a full assessment of the outcomes and impact of the project on pupils was not possible, there was little evidence of integrated use of technologies to enhance pedagogy across the curriculum and create student-centred learning environments, even though the ability of pupils and teachers to use basic computer programmes improved significantly.

The overall lesson from the Demo project was that attempting to roll out a standard model across Africa for integrating computers into schools was not appropriate and would not have worked well even with much stronger leadership and management from the eAC. An eSchool model has to be flexible and adapted to the local context and must build on what is already there. The various consortia involved in the Demo project imagined that they were in competition to create the best model, which would then be the chosen standard for the post-Demo roll out. It quickly became obvious that this one-size-fits-all model would not be appropriate, but the decision to back away from it was not communicated to participants. As of this writing the major roll out of the NEPAD eSchools programme that was originally planned has not begun.

Summary

Achieving EFA will require a multiplicity of approaches and the bringing together of the efforts of many players. In this chapter we have examined the contributions that might come from three areas. First, although most governments and the international development community consider that it must be the principal answer, the expansion of conventional public schooling at the secondary level faces major challenges of both cost and effectiveness in developing countries. Not only is it much more expensive than primary schooling, but the public sector is losing credibility—and often pupils—as parents choose alternatives to schools plagued by decrepit facilities, uncommitted or absent teachers and a general lack of accountability.

Second, the steady expansion of private schooling, even in the poorest areas, is causing a painful re-assessment of conventional development wisdom. For two decades development agencies have assumed that the right to free basic schooling should have priority over the right of parents to choose their children's schools. It is hard to sustain this assumption as the evidence accumulates that some of the poorest parents are choosing private education because they find it better.

Third, given the widespread assumption that information and communications technology has the potential to expand quality education cost-effectively, we have examined three major ICT initiatives in the developing world: One Laptop Per Child; the Hole in the Wall; and the NEPAD eSchools demonstration project. Our review suggests that while computers do enrich children's lives and encourage self-directed learning, they need to be embedded within a wider framework if they are to make a systemic contribution to achieving EFA.

This chapter has also introduced us to two original and iconoclastic educational action researchers, James Tooley and Sugata Mitra. They have now teamed up to explore the practical implications of their findings. The Hole in the Wall project inspired the film *Slumdog Millionaire,* which in turn has inspired these researchers to formalise the HITW somewhat by letting children challenge secondary examinations after working quasi-independently with computers.

We conclude that while each of the approaches to EFA examined in this chapter will have an important contribution to make, something more is needed to integrate these efforts within national education systems. Later we shall ask whether open schooling could be a mechanism for creating synergy and making the overall enterprise of achieving EFA more powerful than the sum of its components. First, however, since open schooling brings technology to centre stage, we must understand the essence of technology and its strengths.

3
Technology Is the Answer
What Is the Question?

This great increase of the quantity of work which, in consequence of the division of labour, the same number of people are capable of performing, is owing to three different circumstances; first, to the increase of dexterity in every particular workman; secondly, to the saving of the time which is commonly lost in passing from one species of work to another; and lastly, to the invention of a great number of machines which facilitate and abridge labour, and enable one man to do the work of many....

Adam Smith, *The Wealth of Nations*, 1776c

Technology and EFA

Previous chapters have detailed the unfinished business of EFA and explored some of the contributions needed to complete the task. In order to take advantage of all useful inputs, governments should conceive their role in education systems as that of regulator and facilitator as much as provider. They must embrace all effective methods of schooling and teacher education and foster innovative ways of making learning opportunities available to their people.

The key requirements for new methods and innovative approaches are to operate at scale, to offer quality, and to cost less than current systems. In the previous chapter we examined three approaches against these criteria: expanding public schooling; encouraging private schools for the poor; and deploying information and communications technologies (ICTs). Chapter 4 will explore the potential of open schooling, which not only has a major contribution to make in its own right, but could also help to reinforce other responses to the challenge of EFA and create synergies between them.

In this chapter we explore the principles and practical experiences that underpin open schooling in particular and technology-mediated education more widely. Open and distance learning (ODL) is the basis of both open schooling and teacher education at scale. We shall show what makes it different from conventional classroom education and how, by achieving wider access, higher quality and lower costs simultaneously, it contains the seeds of the revolution that is needed. Later chapters and appendixes address the practice of open schooling and teacher education through ODL more fully, drawing on examples from around the world.

Conventional school systems, public and private, will continue to play a major role in the expansion of schooling. Over the years the series of EFA Global Monitoring Reports have proposed many strategies for expanding and improving those systems. We shall not add to the analyses in the previous chapter except to note, with four examples, that many innovations and applications of technology can strengthen particular aspects of schooling.

Attitudes to Technology: Irrational Exuberance or Instinctive Scepticism?

Hype about the potential of new technologies to solve the world's educational problems is a staple of popular news stories and futuristic books. "Is technology dazzling everyone?" asked an article reporting on the 2008 Conference of Executive Heads of the Association of Commonwealth Universities (ACU) (Kubler, 2008). *How the Net Generation is Changing Your World* is the subtitle of a breathless recent book about how young Americans use technology (Tapscott, 2009).

Unfortunately, the application of technology to education has created so many false dawns that it provokes cynicism among development specialists, although they disguise this view to avoid being labelled as Luddites. Agencies such as the World Bank have occasionally espoused technological solutions themselves, but the spotty record of projects such as the African Virtual University (AVU) (Kigotho, 2006) has merely reinforced the cynicism.

The discreet but widespread scepticism within the development community about the application of technology to education is one obstacle to the implementation of the proposals implicit in this book. Another is the huge investment that development agencies and their consultants have made in conducting policy research within the framework of conventional classroom models. We shall try to dispel the scepticism, much of which derives from unhappy experiences (like that of the early AVU) of imposing inappropriate technological models from the rich north on the poor south. The growing body of research on the effectiveness of open and distance learning shows that new educational frameworks are not only possible, but necessary.

What Is Technology?

Equipment vendors and hi-tech enthusiasts too often claim that technology is the answer without pausing to ask what the question was. The data and arguments in chapter 1 pose clear challenges for the expansion of secondary schooling and teacher training. Can we find ways to educate people at secondary level and to train teachers that: (a) can be conducted at scale, (b) are inexpensive, (c) deliver acceptable quality consistently, and (d) can be adapted to diverse needs? Similar questions drove the quest for producing more, better and cheaper goods in the industrial revolution.

Division of Labour and Specialisation

We set the tone for this chapter with another substantial quotation from Adam Smith, whose famous description of pin making celebrated the new technologies of his time:

> The greatest improvement in the productive powers of labour, and the greater part of the skill, dexterity, and judgment with which it is anywhere directed, or applied, seem to have been the effects of the division of labour.... To take an example, therefore, the trade of the pin-maker; a workman not educated to this business, nor acquainted with the use of the machinery employed in it, could scarce, perhaps, with his utmost industry, make one pin in a day, and certainly could not make twenty. But in the way in which this business is now carried on, not only the whole work is a peculiar trade, but it is divided into a number of branches, of which the greater part are likewise peculiar trades. One man draws out the wire, another straights it, a third cuts it, a fourth points it, a fifth grinds it at the top for receiving, the head; to make the head requires two or three distinct operations; to put it on is a peculiar business, to whiten the pins is another; it is even a trade by itself to put them into the paper; and the important business of making a pin is, in this manner, divided into about eighteen distinct operations...

He then emphasised the dramatic increase in productivity that was achieved:

> But if (the workers) had all wrought separately and independently, and without any of them having been educated to this peculiar business, they certainly could not each of them have made twenty, perhaps not one pin in a day; that is, certainly, not the two hundred and fortieth, perhaps not the four thousand eight hundredth part of what they are at present capable of performing, in consequence of a proper division and combination of their different operations....

He then summed up the radical changes that had occurred:

> This great increase of the quantity of work which, in consequence of the division of labour, the same number of people are capable of performing, is owing to three different circumstances; *first*, to the increase of dexterity in every particular workman; *secondly*, to the saving of the time which is commonly lost in passing from one species of work to another; and *lastly*, to the invention of a great number of machines which facilitate and abridge labour, and enable one man to do the work of many.... (Smith, 1776c)

In this last statement Adam Smith provides analogies for application of technology to the expansion of education. First, the 'dexterity of every particular workman' translates to the creation of teaching-learning systems that bring together a range of specialised functions in an integrated and effective manner. Second, 'the saving of time…lost in passing from one species of work to another' implies that different specialists can make their inputs simultaneously, which both scales up and speeds up the overall impact. Third, rapid developments in information and communications technologies and other media provide us with a 'great number of machines' to facilitate the tasks of teaching and learning.

Technology-Based Innovations in Conventional Schooling

We shall show in chapters 4 and 5 and appendixes 1 and 2 how these principles are applied in programmes that already deliver secondary schooling and teacher education at scale to millions of students and teachers. However, they are also behind many small innovations that can help to make conventional schooling systems more effective. Here are four that were in the news in a single week in April 2009.

Extending the School Day

The first example is based on the principle of using existing infrastructure more intensively. The World Bank announced an investment of $US120 million in the reform of secondary education in Jamaica. To expand access and improve quality and equity the funds will cover the construction of new schools, public financing of private secondary education and *the extension the school day in selected schools*. School hours vary widely around the world and extending the school day is one way of improving learning outcomes.

Free School Meals at Scale

Adam Smith would have recognised the second example. The Iskcon Sri Radha Krishna Chandra Temple in Bangalore has developed a sustainable delivery model for school meals. 'The temple provides 200,000 local schoolchildren with free meals every day. It achieves this miracle of abundance by a combination of mechanization and careful management. The temple's 250 employees use giant machines to clean rice and prepare chapattis. They then pack the food into steel containers and load it into a fleet of custom-made vans which keep the food warm as they crawl through Bangalore's traffic-clogged streets' (*The Economist*, 2009a, p. 19).

Lapdesks

The same article in *The Economist* reported a project by Shane Immelman that involves innovation through lateral thinking to bring education to poor children in South Africa. 'Appalled that 4m children did not even have desks, let alone schoolrooms, he invented a "lapdesk" that sits on the child's lap and provides a stable surface. The desks are covered in advertisements, so he is able to hand them out free, but they have proved so popular that better-off people have started to buy them, and some of them are now being exported to other developing countries' (2009a, p. 19).

Bouncers to Keep Order

The final example is based on division of labour. It reminds us that expanding secondary education can present new challenges. A report from the UK said that 'bouncers are being employed by schools to take classes when teachers are not available'. One teacher said that his school had 'full-time security on the corridors and on call for classroom and playground fights. These security were actually nightclub door staff, topping up their income with daytime hours—and believe me they were needed' (TimesOnline, 2009).

This random selection of innovations suggests that imagination and entrepreneurship could find many other ways to make conventional schooling more cost-effective. But conventional schooling is not enough.

The Imperative of Scale

We presented Adam Smith's analysis of the scaling up of industrial processes in full for two reasons. First, much current advocacy for educational technology over-emphasises the role of the machines and downplays the vital role of division of labour and specialisation. Worse, it entirely ignores technology's greatest virtue, which is to provide quality at scale.

For example, the 2008 conference report of the Association of Commonwealth Universities states that: 'At the most fundamental level, technology is making the delivery of education more flexible, interactive, collaborative and mobile' (Kubler, 2008, p. 4). ICT can indeed change secondary and teacher education in these ways. However, the first challenge for technology in educational development is to achieve scale. The report continued: 'technology is much more than a tool; it is a transformative development that has the potential to open access to…education to many more people'.

The second reason for having a correct understanding of the innovations of the industrial revolution is that much commentary about the impact of new technologies on education wrongly assumes that classroom teaching is based on the principles of the industrial revolution. Tapscott displays this misunderstanding when he writes that 'the model of education that still prevails today was designed for the Industrial Age' (Tapscott, 2009, p. 122). While it is true that the industrial revolution generated a strong demand for the expansion of education, it is *not* true that methods of schooling were based on the principles of the industrial revolution. Those methods derived—and still do—from the earlier craft tradition. They are analogous to Adam Smith's craftsman creating one pin a day.

The craft tradition of classroom teaching is so rooted in our thinking that even those writing about the impact and potential of technology usually fail to see that the classroom is a pre-industrial artefact that is unlikely to provide a good framework for applying technology to education at scale in cost-effective manner. For example, Palfrey and Gasser, in their otherwise thoughtful book *Born Digital,* never pause to wonder whether the school or the university campus should remain the framework for education in future (2008, pp. 244–253).

A telling example of this old way of thinking occurs in Bill Gates' book *Business @ the Speed of Thought: Using a Digital Nervous System* (Gates with Hemingway, 1999). Tooley (2000) comments: 'What I find most depressing about this book is epitomised when you turn to the Index and look up 'education'. You find:

> Education, *see* Schools
>   But this isn't just laziness on the part of the lexicographer. For Gates' book, like so many others in this mode, is just about how schools can use computers to do what they are doing already, in a slightly modified way, without any sense that perhaps the information revolution can do far more than that'. (p. 6)

If Bill Gates, one of the leaders of the information revolution, thinks this way, then it is perhaps not surprising that of the three projects involving children and computers that we reviewed in the last chapter, only one, Mitra's Hole in the Wall, had the imagination to see how computers could contribute to children's education outside the school environment.

The fixation that education is the same as schooling helps to explain why development specialists question the use of technology in learning and why most educators are uncomfortable with the concept of scale. The notion that in education quality and exclusivity must go together is deeply rooted in the public mind. People can accept the idea of expanding education by multiplying the craft workshops of classroom teaching but they have difficulty imagining entirely different approaches to scaling up learning. Yet new approaches are vital because the resources available simply will not allow many countries to satisfy the learning needs of youth, adults and teachers just by building more classrooms.

We shall show that it is the *combination* of division of labour, specialisation and equipment that can deliver quality education at scale, not the equipment in isolation. A proper understanding of technology integrates these three concepts.

Defining Technology

The UK Open University defines technology as the application of scientific and other organized knowledge to practical tasks by organizations consisting of people and machines (Open University, 1978). This definition is broad—drawing on tacit knowledge, business processes and even common sense as well as science—and reminds us of the role of people.

At the global level the practical tasks to which we seek to apply scientific and other organized knowledge are to provide tens of millions of youngsters with schooling and to train millions of teachers. This means identifying technologies that can, at a minimum, increase scale (i.e. widen access), lower costs, and deliver consistently good quality. If, at the same time, technology can further educational reforms and create new capabilities, so much the better. However, the first imperative is scale.

How does technology achieve scale in education? Representing the three vectors of scale, cost and quality as a triangle (as in Figure 3.1A) helps us see what needs to be done to transform education from a cottage craft into a cost-effective mass enterprise of quality.

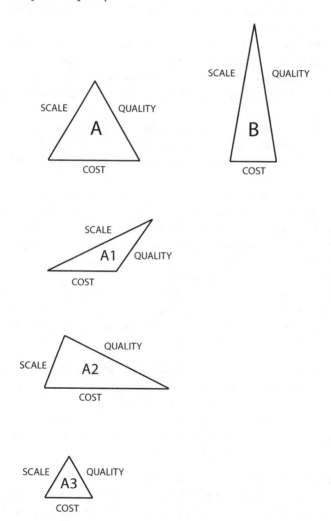

Figure 3.1 The Iron Triangle: Scale (Access), Quality, and Cost

Making this transformation requires us to stretch the triangle vertically by increasing the vectors of scale and quality while at the same time reducing the cost vector (as in Figure 3.1B). But this is impossible with conventional classroom teaching.

Trying to increase scale by putting more pupils in each class somewhat reduces the unit cost per child but quality suffers above a pupil/teacher ratio of about 40:1 (UNESCO, 2007 b, p. 75). This is represented in Figure 3.1A1. Achieving scale by multiplying the number of classes does nothing to reduce the unit cost unless cheaper teachers are used, which may also raise quality concerns.

In a similar manner attempts to increase quality, say by offering more learning materials or better equipment, will increase costs and likely reduce scale (Figure 3.1A2). Finally, a determined effort to cut costs will reduce both scale and quality as indicated in Figure 3.1A3.

This iron triangle has been the bugbear of attempts to expand education throughout history. The difficulty of stretching it to achieve wider access, better quality and lower cost all at the same time explains why, if the only paradigm for education is classroom teaching, quality and exclusiveness are indeed two sides of the same coin.

The basic dilemma is that classroom teaching is the economic equivalent of Adam Smith's craftsman making one pin at a time. One person, the teacher, is usually responsible for organizing every step of the learning process with each class: designing the lesson; preparing any study materials or visual aids; instructing the children; answering their questions; testing their achievement; recording and forwarding the results; and finally reviewing the process so as to improve it. The virtue of the process is that it is flexible, because the teacher can, in principle, adapt readily to the needs of different pupils and learning environments. Its vices are that it does not lend itself to economies of scale and that quality is inherently variable because some teachers are better than others.

Can education, like the pin factory, achieve economies of scale and consistent quality by adopting the principles of division of labour, specialisation and the use of machines? The economic purpose of adopting these principles was expressed 30 years ago by Wedemeyer (1974, p. 4):

> As an operating principle the system is capable, after reaching a critical minimum of aggregation, of accommodating increased numbers of learners without a *commensurate* increase in the unit cost of the basic learning experiences: i.e. costs must not be directly and rigidly volume sensitive. After reaching the necessary level of aggregation, unit costs should show a diminishing relationship to total system costs.

Wedemeyer's statement is another way of saying that using technology in education is analogous to industrial production, where the ratio of committed costs to flexible costs is higher than in craft work. Adam Smith's factory had to invest in machines and training, but these quickly paid for themselves in a much lower production cost per pin than the solo craftsman could achieve.

What are the ways in which division of labour, specialisation and technology can be applied to education in general and to our two sectors of interest, secondary schooling and teacher education, in particular?

Two Modes of Learning

Approaching this question from the perspective of the learner allows us to explore the possibilities. Some years ago we made the simple distinction between two modes of learning: independent learning, where you study alone with a book, a computer or some other medium; and interactive learning involving other people (Daniel & Marquis, 1979).

The optimal blend of independent and interactive learning varies widely. It depends on individual tastes, which will also vary with time, and with the nature and complexity of the topic begin studied. The ability to learn independently generally increases with age and previous education. A person studying with a book or listening to a podcast is a simple example of independent learning.

The notion of interactive learning needs a deeper analysis because it can be a very slippery concept. Even independent learning obviously requires some kind of interaction between the individual and the material being studied. Bates expressed it well: 'There are two rather different contexts for interaction: the first is an individual isolated activity, which is the interaction of the learner with the learning material, be it text, television or computer programme; the second is a social activity, which is the interaction between two or more people about the learning material. Both kinds of interaction are important in learning' (Bates, 1995, p. 52).

Today, an explosion of social media and social software allows interaction of the second type to take place through technology, as well as in person. In using technology to design educational systems to operate at scale, we must be clear about how we use the term. As Mason noted: 'The word "interactivity" is currently used in a wide variety of ways. The obvious meaning—communication between two or more people—is by no means the only one... Much of what passes for interactivity should really be called "feedback"—to the organization or the teacher. It would be useful if the term "interactivity" were reserved for educational situations in which human responses—either vocal or written—referred to previous human responses. The educational value of any specific interactive session could then be seen in terms of the degree to which each utterance built on previous ones' (Mason, 1994, p. 25).

In what follows we shall try to make clear how we are using the term *interaction* wherever it is not clear from the context.

Independent Learning

Independent learning is an important element of any education system because learning how to learn is one of education's most desirable outcomes. Ironically, those educational institutions, such as Oxford University, which are often perceived by outsiders as teaching in a very social and interactive manner through college-based tutorial systems, really operate largely through independent learning. The students' key learning task is to prepare weekly assignments drawing on the libraries and other resources, including a schedule of lectures at which attendance is voluntary and questioning the teacher is rare. It is a system for developing self-directed learners.

Independent learning is an especially important component of mass education systems because the technologies that support it lend themselves to economies of scale, reaching across distance or time, and consistent quality. This was first true of print, the oldest medium for independent learning. Using print as a teaching medium enhances access because you can make as many copies as you like. The greater the print run the lower the cost per book, so you achieve economies of scale. Books are durable and easy to distribute, so they can bridge time and distance. Print gives consistent quality, and for a large print run it is worth making the investment necessary to ensure that the text is of good quality.

Some of these qualities of print are even more marked with newer media such as television, radio, and the web. Producing good materials for independent learning requires an upfront investment, but once it is made the material can be reproduced and distributed inexpensively. These newer learning media yield even greater economies of scale than print, although they may transfer some of the costs of learning from the institution to the student. For example, correspondence schools usually send printed learning materials to students by mail. Students who have mail boxes and access to postal services receive them at no cost once they have paid to enrol in the course. If, however, the independent study material is broadcast, cablecast or put on the web, the student must either own the receiving equipment (radio, TV set, computer, mobile phone) or be able to access it. This can still be an obstacle to many learners in the developing world.

From the point of view of the teaching institution each new independent learning medium tends to generate greater economies of scale than its predecessor. Once you broadcast a TV or radio programme, or place material on the web, adding a further viewer, listener or surfer costs almost nothing. Furthermore, making this material portable also costs little. Huge amounts of text, audiovisual material and software can be put on a DVD or a memory stick that costs very little to reproduce. The cost of sending this content through the Internet to many people—or putting it on the web so they can access it themselves—is also very low. Always provided, of course, that people have access to a networked computer.

Another development with the potential to lower further the cost of materials for independent learning is the emergence of open educational resources (OER). We return to this important topic later, but in essence OER are learning materials in digital format that are freely available for adaptation and use. Finding suitable OER and adapting them to the particular approach to a topic that an institution wants to take holds out the possibility of major cost savings. That is because the investment of the time of academics and experts in producing quality learning materials is a major cost item for mass learning systems such as open universities and open schools.

Thus evolving technological media, from print onwards, allow economies of scale to be achieved in reaching people with that part of education that involves independent learning. They also require the introduction of division of labour and specialisation within the educational system that wishes to use them. The production and distribution of learning materials, even in print formats, but especially using audio-visual and computer-based media, require a range of professional skills that academics and teachers do not usually have.

Independent learning, however, is only a part of most educational experiences. Reading a book or watching a TV programme is instructive, but by itself it is not education. Education implies a relationship with an institution that attests to what you have learned and usually helps you with your learning along the way. This relationship is a vital part of schooling.

Interaction in Primary School

The simplest, most flexible and most common form of educational interaction is face to face with other people. Children in primary school may do some independent learning with toys, books and games, but most of their time is spent interacting with the teacher and with classmates. Quite apart from facilitating learning, this interaction is fundamental to the process of socialization of children—one of the key purposes of early schooling. By interacting with others in school children begin building each of the four pillars of their future learning: learning to know; learning to do; learning to live together and learning to be (UNESCO, 1996).

Interaction with others is so vital for young children that we see only a limited role for scaling up learning with technology in primary schools, whether to support independent or interactive learning. In the previous chapter we reviewed computer-based initiatives for children and noted that, apart from the Hole in the Wall (HITW) experiments, which tended to engage children aged 8 and over, these projects were intended for a classroom setting. The basic purpose of the campaign for Universal Primary Education, which is to get younger children into classrooms and put teachers in front of them, is vital.

Interaction at Secondary Level

At secondary level, however, the requirements are somewhat different. There is a greater focus on subject matter, and secondary pupils carry out more independent learning from books and other resources. Yet they still need to interact with others for various purposes. First, most pupils will, from time to time, need help in understanding the subjects they are studying and in preparing their assignments. Second, they require feedback on those study assignments so that they are aware of their own progress and performance. Third, they should be able to seek advice on the general course of their studies and the study choices that they should make in the light of their personal aspirations. Last, and by no means least, they will be helped by contact with members of their peer group, not only as a means of gauging their own progress, but to continue building the four pillars of their learning. The attraction of learning from peers accounts for much of the success of the HITW initiative.

In principle, if not always in practice, all these forms of interaction are generally available in conventional secondary schools. The essential challenge in scaling up secondary schooling is to develop alternative and cost-effective ways of giving pupils opportunities for interaction on all these dimensions without having to create expensive networks of school buildings. We shall see, as we examine open schools and mega-schools around the world, how they have responded to these challenges in the past and what opportunities changing technology offer them for the future.

Interaction in Teacher Education

School teaching is the most interactive of professions. Acquiring the skills needed to interact effectively with a class to enable children to learn to know, to do, to live together and to be, is the essence of teacher education. The most common criticism of teacher education programmes is they focus too much on subject matter and theories of pedagogy and not enough on the skills needed to be an effective classroom teacher. Pre-service teacher training programmes give students the opportunity to learn these skills through teaching practice in real schools, but to be effective this requires good organization and skilled supervision by experienced practitioners.

One of the biggest challenges in completing the drive to give all children a primary education of quality is, as we have seen, the availability of good teachers. Unfortunately, even where teachers are available many of them are inadequately trained, and even fully-trained teachers both require and desire regular in-service training. In-service teacher training has a long history of being conducted at scale through distance learning in many countries. Often the schools themselves are used as study centres, ensuring that teachers continue their professional development in a collegial manner in close contact with the day-to-day reality of the classroom.

Providing opportunities for interactive learning at scale in both secondary schooling and teacher education also requires division of labour and specialisation. The experts who designed the materials for independent learning may not be the best people to help students who are having difficulty understanding them, quite apart from the challenge of serving the numbers involved. Counselling students also requires special skills, as does supervising trainee teachers in the classroom.

Designing Learning Systems to Operate at Scale

Blending opportunities for independent and interactive learning in an optimal manner is the key to creating systems that can operate cost-effectively at scale. While the requirements of teacher education and secondary schooling are different—and will vary further by country and circumstance—such learning systems must, to be successful, operate three sub-systems effectively: administration; courseware development; and student support. These sub-systems express, within the organization, the principles of division of labour and specialisation that underpin the application of technology to achieve scale. Although the computer set ups used in large-scale systems sometimes blur the distinction between these functions in day-to-day operations, it is helpful to keep them separate conceptually. We shall describe these elements here in a very general way and note later, in appendixes 1 and 2, how they are implemented in particular circumstances.

Administration and Logistics

All educational systems require some administration, but organizing learning at scale requires more extensive arrangements that also include logistics. We begin with this element not because it is more important than the pedagogical aspects of the system, but because it is often neglected in planning even though it is crucial to the success of the system as a whole.

The systems of open schooling and teacher education that we shall examine later involve large numbers of learners who are usually not in regular physical contact with their institution. This means that the administrative processes of registration, course choice, the organization of examinations and the communication of results must be done reliably and at a distance. The student on campus can go and make a fuss in the appropriate office if an administrative process is not satisfactory—whereas the student at a distance may not even know that the process is meant to be occurring.

In earlier days of technology-mediated learning these processes were handled manually using the mail service. I have a lasting memory from the 1980s of visiting the University of Madras Correspondence School, which then enrolled over 100,000 students, and being taken to a vast hall near the sea front. Inside a veritable army of clerks worked at desks stacked high with files and dozens of mail bags were being prepared for shipping.

Today very few administrative operations are not computerised. If properly organized, they allow great economies of scale with consistent quality. Furthermore, the Internet and web technology now allow students to do many administrative operations themselves, something that most of them greatly appreciate. For example, after it introduced online registration in 2007, India's National Institute for Open Schooling (NIOS) found that within two years 30% of its students were enrolling online.

Such examples lead Du Vivier and Ellis (2009, p. 28) to remark: 'Ironically the advantage brought by new technology may come more from its capacity to enable greater efficiency in the organization and administration of education rather than improved communication between tutors and learners, though that will come later'.

Closely allied to the administrative functions—and preferably using the same data-processing system—is a logistics function that is largely absent in conventional schooling. While some open schools and teaching education institutions are able to distribute all their material online, most institutions, especially those in developing countries, need systems to ensure that course material (books, DVDs, etc.) reach students in a timely manner. Such material may be sent directly to students' homes, or distributed for collection at study centres or at the schools where the teachers meet for group work as students. Whatever the distribution channel, it is essential that the right material reaches the right people at the right time.

Understandably, few things upset students as much as the impossibility of beginning or continuing their studies because course materials have gone astray or were mislabelled. One of the many good memories of my time at the UK Open University was the tremendous care taken by the packers in our warehouses to ensure that the parcels that they made up contained the right material and carried the correct names and addresses of the students.

Course Materials Development

The second specialised function of education at scale is the development of course material. Today this is almost always prepared in digital format, no matter what the final form of the learning materials when they reach the students. Just as the functions of administration and logistics need to emphasise reliability in a scale operation, so course materials for students in an open learning system need to have higher quality and greater clarity than handouts that might be acceptable in a classroom where the teacher is on hand to explain any shortcomings.

Experience has shown that developing courses in multi-specialist teams improves academic and presentational quality while also ensuring that students are given a balanced perspective on the topic. However, course teams are more costly than individuals and the economics of course development need careful consideration because, since courseware is prepared by experts and skilled people, this is an inherently expensive part of the operation.

The growing pool of open educational resources has the potential to reduce costs by removing the need to develop all material *ab initio*. Indeed, the Asian eUniversity finds that it is no longer necessary to develop any courses from scratch since good OER are available for adaptation for all the topic areas in which it plans to teach (J. Phillips, personal communication, 2008).

The offering of an increasing number of courses in eLearning formats is both an opportunity and a threat to the operation of large-scale systems. eLearning gives institutions the opportunity to distribute course materials inexpensively, to update them frequently and to integrate independent and interactive learning by operating online. However, we shall see when we explore the economics of large-scale operations that this is also a threat to the cost-effectiveness of the system. There is a temptation to change the course material frequently and to add more and more online tutorial support. Both raise costs and may even reduce quality.

Student Support

Large-scale learning systems can be thought of as three-legged stools. The third leg is the student support system. Nearly all students, even at tertiary level, need some direct personal support from other human beings to succeed in their studies. In this book we are seeking to scale up learning opportunities for secondary age children and for a great variety of young people and adults, many of whom are not well prepared for study. In the case of trainee teachers, where a vital focus of learning must be the reality of the classroom, feedback on their behaviour and performance with classes is obviously vital.

Charles (2008, p. 172) gave this advice to the planners of the National Open University of Nigeria, quoting Glennie (1999, p. 90): 'Spend at least 30% of the institutional recurrent budget on tutors who will support students through tutoring of various kinds, teaching on assignments and face-to-face tutorials'.

The learning systems that we shall examine later provide this support in a great variety of ways, ranging from study centres run in partnership with other organizations to direct electronic support from the institution. Support to students is essential and failure to provide it adequately is the most common Achilles heel of technology-based learning systems. However, it is important to design support systems with an eye to the evidence on what is most cost effective.

An important programme of research by Bernard and his colleagues at Concordia University, Montreal (Bernard, Abrami, Lou, & Borokhovski, 2004; Bernard et al., 2009; Abrami et al., 2008) explodes a persistent myth about the primordial importance of face-to-face support. They carried out a meta-analysis of hundreds of studies in which distance-education students were treated in different ways. They distinguished three types of interaction: student with content; student with student; and student with teacher. They then analyzed all the studies to find which type of interaction made the greatest difference to student performance when it was increased. The results showed clearly that increasing student-content interaction had much the greatest effect, with student-student interaction coming next and student-teacher interaction last.

These conclusions have important implications for both designing and improving large-scale learning systems. Previously, when challenged to increase completion and success rates, such systems have tended to increase the amount of personal tutorial support. This appears to be the least cost-effective way of helping students. Facilitating student-student interaction through self-help groups and meetings is also common and is more cost-effective than student-teacher interaction. But much less effort has been devoted to enriching student–content interaction, although this is potentially the most cost-effective strategy. eLearning provides new and inexpensive ways to do this—websites with answers to frequently asked questions being a simple example.

The Economy of Learning Systems

Since our purpose is to increase access, improve quality and reduce cost, understanding the economics of large-scale learning systems is essential. The economics of open and distance learning is well-tilled ground and a study by Rumble (2009) is directly relevant to the design of open schools and other attempts to use technology in support of EFA. When Wedemeyer (1974) first addressed the economic characteristics of open learning systems the distinction was made between fixed and variable costs.

Committed and Flexible Costs

Today a more accurate and helpful distinction is made between committed and flexible costs. Costs arise from acquiring and using organizational resources. Most of these costs result from the commitment to create systems for administration and logistics, courseware development and student support. These committed costs cover most full-time personnel, ICT and knowledge management systems, and depreciation on physical plant. The key point is that committed costs are unaffected by how much the committed resources are used, because they reflect the level of activity that was planned. Therefore, if patterns of demand fail to match forecasts, the organization will bear the cost of unused capacity. This underlines the need for good design and planning for such learning systems.

Flexible costs, on the other hand, are paid for only when those resources are used. They cover payments to people who are brought in temporarily and paid for tasks performed, such as course development, tutoring, responding to peaks in workload in administration and logistics and so on. Administration and logistics costs such as telecommunications and postal service also fall into this category. Costs can be adjusted to meet demand.

The implementers of the learning system must commit costs in the light of their plans. There will be basic business-sustaining expenses and initial capital costs to reflect the scale of operation envisaged. Setting up the administration and logistics systems will call for committed costs and some flexible costs as business develops. Decisions on the curriculum to be offered will engage committed costs for the staff who anchor the curriculum and flexible costs for commissioning particular courseware. Presenting the courses and supporting students will, in a similar way require a core of committed costs and considerable flexible costs.

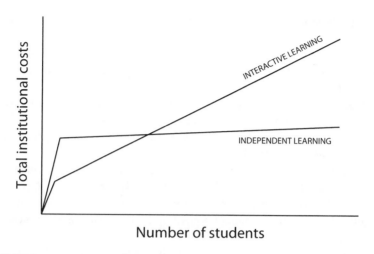

Figure 3.2 Cost Curves for Independent and Interactive Learning

Cost Structures and Cost Factors in Distance Learning

In our earlier book on mega-universities (Daniel, 1996, p. 62) we stressed the sharply different cost curves of independent activities, where the flexible cost per additional student is small, and of interactive learning, for which, if it involves human intervention, flexible costs per additional student are higher. This is shown schematically in Figure 3.2.

This is still a useful distinction, at least insofar as it encourages institutions to be aware of the cost curves of their different interventions with students. If, inspired by the work of Bernard and his colleagues, designers of learning systems put more emphasis on student-content and student-student interaction using ICTs than on student-tutor interaction, the cost curve for interactive activities could become much less steep. However, the reverse trend seems to be the reality because eLearning makes it possible for teachers to interact more frequently—and expensively—with their students (Gauthier, 2009).

In his treatment Rumble (2009, p. 58) summarizes the cost structure of a distance learning system as:

Total Annual Costs =
Business Sustaining Costs +
Committed / indirect common course development costs +
(Flexible course development costs ÷ life of the course) +
Committed / indirect common course maintenance/presentation costs +
Flexible course presentation costs +
Committed / indirect common Student Support Costs +
Flexible Student Support Costs.

From this equation it follows that the following are particularly important cost factors:

- The total number of students: larger numbers spread the committed costs more widely.
- The number of course options: offering more courses drives costs upwards, especially if some courses attract small numbers of students. There is a difficult trade-off between offering a credible and broad curriculum and operating cost-effectively.
- The number of years that a course is presented without significant changes: the longer the course is offered the lower the annual cost. Again there is a trade-off between keeping courses up-to-date and operating cost-effectively. By encouraging frequent updating eLearning risks increasing system costs.
- The choice of learning media and technologies, because each one has its own cost structure (Bates, 1995): when operating at scale print, audio and pre-recorded video are inexpensive whereas face-to-face tuition and computer-based communication are much more costly.
- The type of learner support offered: if large-scale learning systems, whether designed for secondary schooling or teacher training, try to mimic conventional approaches by adding more face-to-face teaching they risk undermining their cost and quality advantages.

Looking at the other side of the coin, Rumble suggests the following ways of keeping costs down:

- Avoid copyright fees by using open educational resources.
- Limit the size of course teams and wrap courses around textbooks instead of developing them *ab initio*.
- Pass costs on to students, which will happen anyway when materials are distributed in electronic form.
- Adopt human resource policies that contain costs by hiring specialists as casual labour with contracts for service rather than as full-time employees.
- Use IT to make academics and administrators more productive.
- In general substitute technology for labour wherever it can be effective, rather than making it an add-on.

Costs and ICTs

This book is about scaling up learning opportunities. There will be many occasions when choices have to be made between investing in technology and spending the money in more conventional ways. A key point is that these trade-offs are not at all the same in rich and poor countries because relative costs are very different. Orivel (2000) noted that since ICTs operate in a global market costs are similar around the world—although communications costs (e.g. broadband connections) are often higher in developing countries—even in absolute terms. The costs of face-to-face teaching, however, vary greatly. Comparing costs in 1999 he estimated that in industrialized countries using a computer for an hour cost between 15% and 40% as much per student as an hour of face-to-face teaching, making the computer very competitive. But in developing countries, where teachers' salaries and other costs are much lower, the cost advantage is reversed. Computing can cost more then ten times as much per hour per student as classroom teaching.

In the light of this work on costs there are six questions we should ask about proposals to use technology in scaling up schooling and teacher education:

- Does the technology substitute capital for labour in ways that reduce costs?
- Are the learning materials being used cost effectively (i.e. they reach large numbers of students and remain in use for some years)?
- Is the personal support that the secondary pupils need provided in a cost-effective manner that does not wipe out the cost advantage of substituting capital (technology) for labour in delivering the course material?
- Is cost-effectiveness the key criterion for choosing the technologies that are used?
- Are cost calculations and comparisons made in the context of the local environment?
- Are the school or teacher education curricula relatively stable?

These are demanding criteria but Rumble (2009, p. 63) concludes on a positive note: The encouraging thing is that we know enough about what makes distance education, and hence open schooling, more or less expensive to be able to control costs. We also know that, properly designed, open schools can work; delivering a quality of education that is at least as good as traditional schools. We can therefore design open schooling systems that will deliver a significant increase in the number of school places available at a reasonable cost per place, compared to the alternative strategy of expanding traditional schools.

Summary

Amid the hype and excitement about the potential of technology to transform education it is important to identify the nature of the transformation we want to make and the problems that we are trying to solve. We concluded from chapter 1 that the essential challenge is to develop learning systems that: (a) can be conducted at scale, (b) are inexpensive, (c) deliver acceptable quality consistently, and (d) can be adapted to diverse needs.

Given the absolute necessity of operating at scale, we examined the industrial revolution through the eyes of Adam Smith and concluded that technology allows processes to be scaled up by combining division of labour with specialisation and appropriate machines. The successful application of technology requires the application of scientific and other organized knowledge to organizations consisting of people and machines.

We suggested that considering learning as a blend of independent and interactive activities is a useful way of analyzing the requirements of large-scale learning systems and understanding their economics. However, interaction in education is a slippery concept that needs to be defined in the context within which it is used.

In large-scale learning systems specialisation and division of labour are usually identified as three sub-systems: administration and logistics; course materials development and student support.

Finally, we summarized the economics of technology-based learning systems in order to identify the cost drivers and to suggest how expenses can be kept down in order to operate cost-effectively at scale.

4
Open Schools and Mega-Schools

Open and distance learning is regarded by students and ministries of education as a second-rate system used to offer a shadow of education while withholding its substance. It is an efficient but cheap way of containing educational demand without meeting it. Through its existence it helps to insulate the elite system from pressures that might otherwise threaten its status or ways of working.

Perraton, 2000, p. 199

Introduction

Previous chapters have stressed the importance of achieving Education for All (EFA), examined how conventional schooling and the use of computers might contribute to this goal, and explained how distance learning systems can operate effectively at scale. In this chapter we examine how open schooling can help to expand secondary education. The next chapter reviews the challenge of scaling up teacher education.

Here we shall look first at the contribution that open schooling can make to the achievement of the EFA goals in its own right and then extend the discussion to explore how open schools could usefully act in synergy and symbiosis with the rest of the educational enterprise. A government contemplating the introduction or expansion of open schooling has to choose between several models. Positioning open schooling as a central element of national education systems could improve the quality and effectiveness of these systems as a whole as well as enabling them to reach larger numbers.

The criteria for choosing a model for an open school have changed significantly since, in the quotation reproduced above, Perraton (2000, p. 199) could refer to open and distance learning as offering 'a shadow of education'. Attitudes to open schooling have evolved because distance learning has achieved greater legitimacy worldwide and is now closely linked to the use of information and communications technologies in education. Large open universities whether public, such as the UK Open University (UKOU) and the Indira Gandhi National Open University (IGNOU), or private like the Open University Malaysia and the University of Phoenix Online, have used their economies of scale to create innovative and high quality applications of ICT in higher education. In the case of the UKOU much of the study material is freely available to the world on its OpenLearn website (Open University, 2009) giving yet another meaning to the concept of openness in education.

What Are Open Schools and Mega-Schools?

The basic principles of distance learning that underpin open schooling were presented in chapter 3. Here our focus is more practical. How can governments maximise the benefits of open schooling through appropriate policy? In answering this question we shall draw on the examples of open schools that are provided in appendix 1. These have been chosen to represent a range of approaches in both developing and developed countries. To situate these examples a selection of open schools is listed in Table 4.1.

A short definition of open schooling is 'the physical separation of the school-level learner from the teacher, and the use of unconventional teaching methodologies, and information and communications technologies to bridge the separation and provide the education and training' (Phillips, 2006, p. 9). This definition focuses on one important feature of open schooling: its use of distance learning. We examined the dynamics of distance learning in the previous chapter to show why they allow educational systems to operate at scale. Introducing the term *mega-school* is one way of designating open schools that have exploited this possibility.

When I coined the term *mega-university* for large distance-teaching universities, I set the threshold at 100,000 active students (Daniel, 1996, p. 29). This figure was significantly higher than the enrolments on any single conventional university campus and distinguished such institutions from the rest of higher education. Secondary schools are usually much smaller than universities, so we shall define a mega-school as an open school with more than 10,000 active pupils. In the school sector this is an indication of useful scale, even though some open schools in high population countries (Table 4.1) have much larger enrolments, exceeding a million in several cases. However, using the figure of 10,000 rightly identifies an institution such as NAMCOL (p. 129) as a mega-school. The total population of Namibia is only 2 million, yet NAMCOL's 28,000 students account for 40% of the country's secondary enrolments.

Furthermore, setting the threshold for a mega-school at 10,000 students does appear to distinguish usefully between open schools that operate with lower unit costs than the conventional system and those, usually in the richer jurisdictions, that do not achieve—or indeed aim for—a significant cost advantage, such as the Open Access College of South Australia with 1,500 students (Schocroft, 2009).

Most of our focus here is on mega-schools and on those open schools that aim to reach a significant proportion of the secondary school population, even if they do not achieve large numbers in absolute terms because they serve small countries.

Table 4.1 Open and Mega-Schools (Partial List)

Country	Name & Date Established	Enrolment (approx.)	Curriculum (category)	Media & Technology
Australia (NT)	Schools of the Air (1940s)	120	Complementary	HF radio transceivers
Australia (SA)	Open Access College 1991	2,500	Complementary	Print, phone, online
Bangladesh	Open School, 1992	163,000	Complementary & vocational	Print, audio, broadcast, contact
Botswana	BOCODOL*, 1998	6,000	Complementary, secondary, vocational	Print
Brazil	Telecurso, 1995 Bahia State,1995 Minerva, 1995	200,000 8,000 120,000	Complementary, basic & skills	Television
Canada*	Contact North 1986	13,000	Programmes of other providers	Teleconferencing, eLearning
France*	CNED 1939	95,000	Complementary	Print, DVD, online
India	NIOS*, 1989	400,000	Alternative	Print, contact
	Andhra Pradesh, 1991	600,000	Complementary	Print, contact, telecast
	Haryana, 1994	130,000	Alternative (NIOS)	Print, contact
	Karnataka, 1996	5,000	Alternative (NIOS)	Print, contact
	Kerala, 1999	90,000	Alternative (NIOS)	Print, contact
	Madhya Pradesh, 1996	350,000	Alternative (NIOS)	Print, contact
	Punjab, 1991	80,000	Complementary	Print, contact
	Rajasthan, 2005	220,000	Complementary	Print
	West Bengal, 1997	38,000	Complementary	Print
Indonesia*	SLTP Terbuka, 1976	1,200,000	Complementary (Junior secondary)	Print, contact, broadcasts
Malawi	Correspondence Study Centres 1978	17,000	Complementary (Secondary)	Print
Mexico*	Telesecundaria 1968	1,200,000	Complementary (Secondary)	Television, print (in schools)
Namibia*	NAMCOL, 1997	28,000	Complementary (Secondary)	Print, contact
New Zealand	Correspondence School, 1928	18,000	Complementary (Senior Secondary)	Print, online, teleconference
Papua New Guinea*	Open College, UPNG, 2001	20,000	Alternative (Vocational & skills)	Print, contact
South Korea	Air & Correspondence High School	20,000	Complementary (Secondary)	Print, radio
Trinidad & Tobago	National Open School, 2007	1,250	Complementary (Secondary, adult)	Print, radio, TV, online
United Kingdom	National Extension College, 1963	20,000	Complementary (Secondary, adult)	Print, online
Zambia	Correspondence Study Centres 1964	1,200	Complementary	Print, contact

Notes: See this chapter for discussion of the designations 'alternative' and 'complementary'.
* See profile in appendix 2.

Parallels with Higher Education

Although some open schools are rooted in decades of practice, most are recent creations. Few of them existed in their current form when I wrote *Mega-universities* in the mid-1990s (Daniel, 1996). While we cannot assume that the evolution of open schooling at the secondary level will follow the same pattern as ODL in higher education, we may expect—and should prepare for—at least five parallels.

First, the expansion of ODL through the growth of open universities and the introduction of distance learning programmes in conventional universities (dual-mode provision) has stimulated research on ODL in higher education. Open schooling has attracted much less research, which has been a handicap in writing this book. I hope that the increasing importance of open schooling will give future authors more data to work with and encourage practitioners to be more reflective and analytical.

Second, private provision of higher education has increased steadily in recent times to the point where it is now the fastest growing component of the sector worldwide. It was the public sector, notably through the UK Open University, that first modernised and scaled up higher distance teaching (Perry, 1976), but the private sector has now joined in through institutions such as the Open University Malaysia and the University of Phoenix Online. At present governments are the main driving force behind the expansion of open schooling in the developing world, but this is a promising area for private investment and provision. Private sector correspondence schools have a long history.

Third, across much of the world governments are gradually—albeit sometimes reluctantly—accepting that universities contribute more effectively to the public good if they operate fairly autonomously within a clear regulatory framework. Our profiles of open schools suggest that the same principle applies to these institutions too: they could serve the public better if governments eased up on day-to-day control.

Fourth, the rapid development and penetration of online technologies, at least in the richer parts of the world, has given distance learning, in the form of eLearning, a more glamorous image. Compared to older approaches to distance learning, online instruction also fits more readily into the cottage-industry tradition of university teaching, whereby academics act as what Bates (2004) calls 'lone rangers' in developing and offering their courses. This trend is already influencing secondary provision in jurisdictions in industrialized countries, which should take seriously his warning that: 'The main mistake is just to drift into eLearning through keen Lone Rangers. This will just add cost and frustration'.

In the Canadian provinces of British Columbia, Quebec and Saskatchewan open schooling has been decentralized to school boards. The Vancouver Learning Network is a good example (Gauthier, 2009). Whether such decentralization improves or reduces cost-efficiency overall, either in universities or schools, may be a minor concern in rich countries but is a very important issue for poorer countries confronting the challenges of EFA with few resources.

Finally, the rapid expansion of distance education in higher education has given it greater respectability and credibility. This gain in reputation is a slow process because—rightly in my view—the public changes its perceptions of education only gradually as evidence and experience of the effectiveness of new approaches accumulates. However, as iconic distance learning institutions such as the UK Open University have risen towards the top of national quality league tables and millions of people have come to enjoy the convenience and empowerment of distance learning, paradigms are shifting. Open schools can take advantage of this trend—but only if they give their own students a good experience.

Open Schools: Means and Ends

We have defined open schools in terms of the means that they use for teaching and learning: namely distance education. Most of the open schools profiled in appendix 1 deploy distance learning methods in similar ways. They carry out the three functions that we described in chapter 3 (administration and logistics, course materials development, and student support) and discharge these functions in much the same manner, even where they use different technologies (Commonwealth of Learning, 2009).

Administration and logistics take advantage of electronic data systems, even in less ICT-rich countries, although they may differ in the extent to which they use regional offices and study centres, rather than their headquarters, in managing the system. All use systematic instructional design and some elements of course teams in developing course materials. Student support is provided in local study centres, usually located within the facilities of other institutions and sometimes operated by them (e.g. the accredited institutions of India's NIOS).

Differences between open schools become apparent, however, when we examine the ends or purposes that they pursue through these means. Open schools can achieve various purposes. An authority seeking to establish an open school must decide on the priorities that it wishes to pursue.

Rumble and Koul (2007, p. 234) point to three significant differences between open schools and conventional systems: mode, markets and curriculum. *Mode* refers to the use of distance learning already captured in our earlier definition. *Markets* indicate the clientele that open schools can serve. Conventional schools are not usually open to adults aged more than 20 years whereas open schools can serve people from a wide age range. *Curricula* may or may not differ greatly between open and conventional schools. Among the profiles in appendix 1 for example, Botswana's BOCODOL offers exactly the same curriculum as the conventional schools and prepares its pupils for the same national exams. By contrast India's NIOS, which is its own examining body, has worked hard to develop a set of curricula suited to its particular market, with a special emphasis on vocational education. Much the same is true of the CTSC programme in Papua New Guinea, which also sets its own examinations and has put a special focus on life skills.

We conclude that just as the adjective 'open' may designate different types of openness when used in the term 'open university', so it is with open schools. The degree and type of openness is a decision for those designing a particular open school. Admission may be decided on exactly the same criteria as that of conventional schools or it may be more liberal. The curriculum may be exactly the same as in the conventional system—as it must be if both open and conventional schools prepare pupils for the same examinations—or more specifically adapted to the clientele.

However, at a time when there is considerable dissatisfaction with conventional secondary school curricula, open schools present the opportunity to do something different. Too often the regular curriculum is geared to preparing a small proportion of pupils for access to tertiary education, rather than giving the majority a basis for lives and livelihoods in the 21st century. Because open schools usually reach out to those who do not have ready access to a conventional school they may serve them better by offering something different from the conventional curriculum. Rumble and Koul (2007, p. 235) conclude that open schools may be either a complement or an alternative to formal education.

Which Model: Complementary, Alternative or Integrative?

Complementary Open Schooling

Complementary open schools offer the same curriculum as do conventional schools to children who never had a chance to attend a regular school or had to drop out because their grades were too poor. Of the institutions profiled in appendix 1, CNED (France), BOCODOL (Botswana), NAMCOL (Namibia), SLTP Terbuka (Indonesia) and Telesecundaria (Mexico) are complementary open schools. Each reaches a significant proportion of the national secondary-age population and enables its pupils to study for the same certification as those in the conventional schools. This is an important function.

Moreover, because they teach the national curriculum at scale, these open schools are able to invest in the production of better learning materials, whether as print, audio-visual media or software, than the conventional schools could expect to develop. It is clearly desirable to share these materials across the whole education system because lack of good learning materials often undermines the quality of conventional schooling in developing countries.

What are the challenges facing complementary open schools? How can they improve their performance and contribute more fully to their national education systems? The answer appears to lie in what may seem a paradoxical combination of closer integration with the wider educational system accompanied by greater autonomy in governance and management.

Closer integration—or at least better communication with ministries of education—is particularly desirable in the area of curriculum. Complementary open schools teach to the national curriculum by definition. But since good distance learning courses require significant lead times and investment to develop and produce, governments should involve their open schools in all curriculum revision processes from the earliest stages. CNED, BOCODOL and NAMCOL have all had to scramble to react to curriculum changes—and sometimes to scrap quantities of learning material rendered obsolete by them.

Governments should regard open schools as helpful allies in national curriculum development in the era of ICT. We describe later (p. 75) a programme whereby open schools from five countries are working together to create secondary curricular materials in the form of open educational resources. These can readily be versioned for each country and at the level of individual schools. As it exploits its new status as an online academy, for example, CNED will greatly expand the usefulness of its curriculum materials to children, parents and schools.

There is also a case for harmonising regulations, for example by removing the time restraints on study that make it difficult for BOCODOL students to get better grades. This would be consistent with the general trend in education to assess topic mastery rather than the time taken to acquire it. For both CNED and BOCODOL improving coordination with national examination systems is also desirable. For its own performance management CNED needs better information about how its students perform in national examinations, whereas BOCODOL students should be offered an inclusive package of course and examination so that they do not complete their studies only to find that they cannot afford to take the examination.

All the complementary open schools are engaged in the development of vocational education as a growth area. CNED already operates to a national curriculum, the *lycée professionel,* but the other open schools are opening up the area of work-related studies as they go. Here again better coordination with ministries of education seems desirable so that relevant vocational curricula can be developed for the benefit of the countries as whole.

Along with closer coordination, however, complementary open schools could serve their nations more effectively if their boards were given greater autonomy, especially in financial management and the setting of fees. Currently these supposedly independent bodies are so hemmed in by government controls on fees that strategic planning is practically impossible. In a time of rapid change the principle of subsidiarity, whereby decisions are made at the lowest appropriate level, is also a factor of efficiency and innovation. We describe later, as a possible model (p. 81), the new legislation governing tertiary education in Alberta which, having defined the missions of institutions, gives them wide latitude in fulfilling those mandates.

Finally, none of this relieves the complementary open schools from doing everything possible to improve the performance of their pupils. Since they teach to the same examinations as the conventional schools, the performance of the two systems can be compared directly. Open schools must continue to gain credibility by showing good results even though—or especially because—their pupils have a background of educational disadvantage.

Alternative Open Schooling

Alternative open schools may cater to some of the same children as complementary open schools, but they also aim to engage older youths and adults by offering programmes that are more vocationally oriented and have a greater focus on life skills. Of the institutions profiled in appendix 1, India's NIOS, the PNG Open College and, to some extent, SLTP Terbuka can be considered as alternative open schools although they have very different national contexts, mandates and governance structures.

Alternative systems that break new curricular ground are steadily becoming more attractive in comparison to complementary systems that simply extend the conventional programme at a distance. Clearly, however, adapting the school curriculum and the school year to meet the needs of youth who could not access the conventional school system—and who may be employed—poses a dilemma. How far should the system aim to produce the same results as the conventional secondary schools? Few parents and students wish to contemplate studies that do not hold the promise of certification.

Some years ago Figueredo and Anzalone (2003, p. 2) wrote: 'In most countries, the formal system, even when its curriculum is acknowledged as lacking relevance to the real world, casts a long shadow on aspirations and expectations. Curriculum developers for alternative models who start down the road to producing a more relevant curriculum are often roped back into traditional subject-matter content as students and parents become more vocal about passing examinations'.

Since that time, however, both India's NIOS and the PNG Open College have shown that programmes that focus on life skills and work-oriented content are attractive to students and their parents. In these two cases, of course, the institutions provide their own certification, which is accepted at par with certification from the conventional system by employers and tertiary institutions. That is a key criterion with implications for the status and governance of open schools to which we shall return.

Notions of certification are evolving. Few now dispute the value of certification from private companies such as the Cisco Networking Academy and the Microsoft IT Academy. Indeed, in India, to judge by the advertisements that parents place to find suitable spouses for their offspring, diplomas from the (private) National Institute for Information Technology (NIIT) are greatly prized. An older and quite different example is the highly esteemed International Baccalaureate (IB), which is managed and certified by an international non-governmental body. Indeed, the IB organization is discussing how it might offer its diploma in an alternative manner through some sort of open international college and there have been successful experiments with open admission (Mayer, 2008).

Governments may wish to establish or facilitate the creation of an open school that offers an alternative curriculum geared to 'ensuring that the learning needs of all young people and adults are met through equitable access to appropriate learning and life-skills programmes' (Dakar Goal 3). If they do, they must arrange for the new entity to have appropriate powers of certification.

The alternative open schools that we have reviewed can claim considerable success. NIOS is not only drawing many school-age youth into its alternative route (74% of its secondary students are aged 15 to 20) but also has achieved parity of enrolment between male and female students in its vocational courses. To the extent that these young women see a greater sense and purpose in education that promises economic independence and a better life, NIOS is acting as an important agent of social change (Rumble & Koul, 2007, p. 244). These authors also point out that over time the conventional school system is increasingly more costly relative to open schooling (2007, p. 255).

Integrative Open Schooling

We now explore a third model, the integrative open school. This is an open school which, instead of operating on the margins of a conventional secondary system, is placed at its heart in order to improve and strengthen the quality and reach of that system and to be a source of innovation for it. This is not a new idea. A review of the contribution that distance education could make to the quality of primary schooling suggested cautiously 'a move towards greater complementarity between distance and regular education, a far more judicious, rationalized use of distance education. This would depend on a greater integration of distance education approaches into the mainstream educational system, where once it was only an alternative or emergency system' (IRFOL, 2004, p. 11).

We note below that integrating the notion of open schooling into conventional provision could also be a catalyst for reform. However, for most educational authorities more pressing issues than reform are making the conventional system more effective and improving its quality. Can open schooling help? The EFA GMR for 2005 conducted a thorough review of what makes for effectiveness and quality in schooling. If we conflate its conclusions on the key elements that determine educational effectiveness (UNESCO, 2004b, p. 66), and the important factors in a policy for quality (2004b, p. 142) we can construct two lists. The first gives those aims that could be achieved more readily if an open school acted as a resource for the whole school system:

- good learning materials
- focus on the curriculum
- regular, reliable, and timely assessment of learning
- pedagogical materials for teachers
- an inclusive learning environment with special attention to AIDS orphans,

children with disabilities, those living in conflict zones, those obliged to work and those disadvantaged by gender, race and ethnicity, culture and language, religion, social status and migration

- relevant content
- teaching of reading and writing
- structured teaching: direct instruction, guided practice and independent learning
- appropriate language of instruction
- larger classes *if* accompanied by better inputs (assistants, materials, etc.).

The second list includes those items that depend to a large extent on more and better training of teachers and school heads:

- school leadership
- better teachers
- appropriate educational aims and values
- school-based in-service training for teachers
- structured teaching time
- using instructional time well
- keeping pupils focused on learning activities
- focus on basic skills
- a secure environment
- high expectations
- attention to the health and nutrition of children.

It is clear from both these lists that having a source of good learning and assessment materials and an adequate capacity for regular in-service teacher education are important foundations of effectiveness and quality. We shall take up the issue of teacher education in the next chapter. Here we argue that open schools, as well as addressing the issues of inclusiveness comprehensively at the national level, can be a prime source of good learning materials focused on the curriculum. We shall first describe how learning materials can be produced and shared in a very modern way as open educational resources and then explore wider ways in which open schools can be leaven for a national school system.

The Collaborative Creation of Learning Materials

Open schools—and indeed all approaches to pedagogy that involve distance learning—have to produce learning materials, usually in a variety of formats. These materials have always been useful to the conventional schools which, at least in the developing world, often have neither the money to buy materials nor the critical mass of teacher time and expertise to develop materials of quality themselves. Fortunately, two developments have made the learning materials produced by open schools potentially even more useful to the wider school system.

First, most learning materials are now developed in digital formats, even though they may eventually reach students in the form of printed materials. However, holding materials electronically has three advantages: they are easy to move around; they can readily be adapted and revised; and they can be converted to eLearning formats when online learning becomes a possibility.

Second, there is now a growing movement, inspired by the ideal that knowledge is the common wealth of humankind, to create a global intellectual commons in which learning materials are shared. This movement involves many thousands of teachers, at all levels, creating open educational resources (OER), which are learning materials in digital format that are freely available for adaptation and use.

OER Africa defines them as: 'educational resources that are freely available for use by educators and learners, without an accompanying need to pay royalties or license fees. A broad spectrum of frameworks is emerging to govern how OER are licensed for use, some of which simply allow copying and others that make provision for users to adapt the resources that they use. OER is not synonymous with online learning or eLearning, and indeed, in an African context, it is anticipated that many of the resources produced—while shareable in a digital format (both online and via offline formats such as CD-ROM)—will be printable. Thus, we anticipate that a very high percentage of resources of relevance to African higher education will be shared as RTF or similar files (for purposes of adaptation) and packaged as PDF files (for purposes of printing)' (OER Africa, 2009).

The William and Flora Hewlett Foundation has done much to foster the OER movement in higher education by supporting the OpenCourseware project at MIT, which shared instructors' course outlines (MIT, 2009); the OpenLearn website of the UKOU, making available self-study material (Open University, 2009); and the Virtual University for Small States of the Commonwealth, through which teachers in small states around the world develop courses through online collaboration (VUSSC, 2009).

The Foundation is now encouraging similar work in open schools by supporting a programme that combines the professional development of teachers with the development of OER. Twenty sets of self-instructional learning materials on the secondary curriculum will be produced in six developing countries: Botswana, Namibia, Trinidad & Tobago, Lesotho, Seychelles and Zambia (a set of material refers to the complete syllabus for one subject at Grade 10 or Grade 12 level in each of the six countries with the possibility of adapting it to the curriculum of any other country).

This material will be suitable for use in both open and conventional schools and will permit open schools to offer current and new subjects through print and online teaching. The programme will create a pool of 100 trained and experienced master teachers, who can train other teachers in their countries and support online materials development once the formal project is complete. These master teachers will also have been trained in the use of the Commonwealth of

Learning's instructional design template and will have the skills to develop learning materials collaboratively online, thus creating a new network of expertise in developing countries.

However, the fact that learning material is available does not mean it will be used. Educational technologists have learned the hard way not to make the assumption 'build it and they will come'. Hatakka (2009) examined the use of open content in developing countries and found that eleven factors inhibited its use: educational rules and restrictions, language, relevance, access, technical resources, quality, intellectual property, awareness, computer literacy, teaching capacity, and teaching practices and traditions.

Hatakka's (2009) survey focused mainly on the use of open content from developed countries in universities in developing countries, notably Bangladesh and Sri Lanka. Without underestimating the challenge of introducing any new approach it does seem that the COL/Hewlett project will avoid these difficulties, mainly because these OER are being created in developing countries for developing countries by organizations (open schools) that have the authority to develop curricular material and will use it in their own teaching.

It is too early to claim that OER will transform the availability of learning materials in the secondary schools of developing countries. However, if open schools engage with this movement in a spirit of sharing OER with the entire national school system, public and private, it holds out great promise.

It is clearly desirable to associate the development of OER by open schools with curriculum development in ministries of education. Because open schools are preparing materials for use by students they have to pay close attention to pedagogy and instructional design, whereas curricular authorities focus on purpose and content. These approaches are complementary. By working together curriculum designers and open schools can develop material that is of wide usefulness to teachers and pupils in the conventional schools. Some years ago, for example, the Commonwealth of Learning helped the Caribbean Examinations Council to create self-instructional material, based on their curricula, for out-of-school adults. This material was eagerly sought after by the schools (Stephens, 2005).

Open Schooling to Strengthen the Conventional Schooling System

In a report for the 2005 EFA GMR (UNESCO, 2004b), IRFOL (2004) concluded that the areas in which distance learning could increase the quality of primary schools were teacher education, the special needs of rural schools and the general enrichment of learning resources. Although our focus is on secondary schooling, much of what they recommend is directly applicable to the contribution that open schools could make to strengthening conventional schooling generally.

Their prescription for under-resourced primary schools was a 'form of highly structured whole school approach' and they gave a number of examples. In Columbia the Escuela Nueva project provided self-study learner guides that 'expose both pupils and teachers to new educational resources and practices but also offer support, respite and training to hard-pressed inexperienced teachers dealing with multi-grade classrooms' (IRFOL, 2004, p. 12). Interactive radio instruction (IRI) has been successful in Haiti, Guinea, South Africa and Zambia. Schoolnets have been an effective way to introduce an element of computing in various African countries. The report noted that there is multiplier effect if learner guides, interactive technologies and teacher training through distance learning are used together to address the needs of the whole school, as BRAC has done in Bangladesh.

The benefits that an open school can bring to the secondary school system as a whole will depend on the precise nature of the open school and how it addresses its primary audience. Figueredo and Anzalone (2003) distinguish four ways in which alternative models of schooling can be distinct:

- policies that favour the participation of students unable to enter conventional schools;
- organizational arrangements that provide flexibility for the time and place of learning;
- an instructional system that operates at lower costs than conventional schools; and
- learning and curricular materials designed for especially for the country, the community or the learners.

They conflate the range of alternative models into three broad approaches based on their profiles in relation to three factors: distance education, open learning and group study.

We explored the contribution of *distance education* in the earlier section on the complementary approach to open schooling and through the examples in appendix 1. The authors give further examples of the cost advantage of open schooling that are not included in appendix 1. Thus in Malawi correspondence education with tutorial support through study centres operated at one-fifth the recurrent cost of the regular secondary schools and the cost per pass in the Junior Certificate examination was about half that of students in the regular system. The National Correspondence College in Zambia has costs for secondary education of between one-quarter and one-twentieth those of the regular schools (Figueredo & Anzalone, 2003, p. 16).

Their definition of *open learning* corresponds broadly to our alternative approach to open schooling, and Figueredo and Anzalone (2003) too cite India's NIOS as a prime example. Other examples are South Korea's Air Correspondence High School, a highly successful and cost-effective programme in the 1970s, which operated at one-fifth the cost of the regular schools while maintaining rigorous academic standards. Given the focus of this book on achieving EFA, South Korea is a particularly interesting example of the use of open schooling to increase access to education rapidly. Today South Korea is a world leader in participation rates and student performance at all levels.

Also relevant to our argument is the Philippines Non-Formal Education Project which had the effect of institutionalising non-formal education in the conventional sector in the last decade by creating a highly flexible system which, like the Philippines tertiary sector, made extensive use of private providers (2003, pp. 18–19).

Their discussion of the *group study* model shows that it is risky to categorise these systems in a hard and fast manner since one can evolve into another. Figueredo and Anzalone (2003) report that the Malawi College of Distance Education (MCDE) began as an open learning model but changed to group study when administrators 'realised the individual home study was not suitable for adolescents, who needed more face-to-face support'. By operating through community-supported study centres, the MCDE reached more students than the regular secondary schools. However, the experience also demonstrated the need for achieving the right mix of learning materials and support (Daniel & Marquis, 1979) because after a while printed learning materials were of poor quality and in short supply.

Finally, Indonesia's SLTP Terbuka, described in appendix 1, is a mega-school that is closely integrated with the conventional system and has organized group work on a very large scale with good results in places with little infrastructure for formal schooling.

Open Schools as Catalysts for Reform

Open schools could also facilitate a number of reforms proposed for conventional educational systems—or act as a safety net if they go wrong. There is no shortage of proposals for changes in school systems. Here we focus on just three that were proposed in the UK a decade ago. Without judging their merits as reforms we simply note that open schooling could complement them usefully.

First, in *All Must Have Prizes*, Melanie Phillips (1996) argued for revisions to the UK National Curriculum and more selection and streaming by ability. The challenge with such streaming is that even with the best intentions of allocating pupils flexibly it is not straightforward to re-sort them at a later stage to correct bad decisions. By offering easy entry to a wide range of courses, open schools can help to convert ladder-like curricula into climbing frames on which pupils can move in various directions to the courses they need. Open schooling can also contribute to the rapid implementation of curriculum changes. By working alongside the curriculum authorities during the revision process, an open school can have new materials ready as soon as the curriculum is introduced— materials that have good instructional design and can be used throughout the entire school system.

Second, the title of Tom Bentley's *Learning Beyond the Classroom* (1999) resonates nicely with the concept of open schooling, as do his proposals. He wanted to get away from the notion that schooling is the same thing as education and to create 'a system of networked learning, connecting neighbourhood learning centres with a wealth of learning resources and opportunities' (1999, p. 182). He gives many examples of the type of learning opportunities that he means—some created by non-governmental bodies not unlike NIOS' accredited institutions. We shall return to the idea of local learning and resource centres in chapter 6.

Third, Michael Barber, formerly a close advisor to the UK's Labour Government, proposed in *The Learning Game* (1996) a similar loosening up of the education system relying on the creativity of individuals and communities. This assumes that the interaction of such initiatives creates a self-organizing system that generates spontaneous order. Such systems benefit from having some network structure behind them to give stability and an open schooling organization—not necessarily operated by government—might provide this.

Barber also sees changes in the role of teachers, who 'might work in schools, but increasingly schools will open for longer hours, providing a much wider range of learning options. Teachers might work in an out-of-school study centre. They might provide individual tuition to pupils and their families... Groups of teachers might work in the equivalent of consulting companies, and put together a portfolio of activities' (1996, p. 236). This notion of the role of teachers has parallels with the concept of the integrative open school and we again have here the notion of local learning and resource centres.

We conclude from this summary review of three reform proposals from a single country that open schools could backstop a range of educational reforms by acting as glue to hold a diverse system together and providing an alternative when things do not turn out as planned—as usually happens!

Computing and Children: Can Open Schools Help?

Open schools could act as organizing elements for the expansion of ICT in secondary schools generally. Politicians and parents are two groups that are particularly eager to associate computers with education: the first because computers symbolise a country's evolution towards a knowledge society; the second because computer literacy will improve their children's chances in life. In chapter 2 we examined three projects that put computers in the hands of children. The One Laptop Per Child (OLPC) and the NEPAD eSchools demonstration project placed computers in schools, whereas the Hole in the Wall (HITW) experiment put them in playgrounds and public spaces.

Although the two projects involving schools gave disappointing results, especially to those who expected a revolution in teachers' pedagogy and students' performance, there continues to be a strong drive in most countries to get more computers into the schools. India, for example, is now planning to make ICT a major plank of their programme for universal secondary education, *Rashtriya Madhyamik Shiksha Abhiyan*. The plan is to put computers directly into the classrooms rather than in computer labs because 'the fact that the impact of ICT use to date on learning outcomes is negligible in most places, or at least a matter of much debate, is…at least partially attributable to the fact that, in most places, computers are only used to teach ICT literacy' (Trucano, 2009).

The mounting evidence that the benefits of computers in the classroom are elusive should not lead to abandonment of the idea but ought to encourage educational authorities to plan their introduction carefully. Just one example of the pitfalls is a list of ten problems with teaching science online that includes slower reading speeds, lower comprehension (30% lower than paper), erroneous information on websites, broken links (linkrot), and the costs of infrastructure renewal and software updates (Schrock, 2009).

Open schools seem well placed to help whole school systems implement computing. Collaborative projects in OER curriculum development can help to create locally adapted eLearning materials of quality that are always in short supply. Moreover, since open schools have to be technologically savvy to take advantage of new developments for their own students they are a natural source of expertise for wider use.

Student assessment is an area of special relevance in this context. Regular, timely and reliable assessment is an important tool in securing students' attention to content and the curriculum. It figured prominently in UNESCO's summary of determinants of quality and effectiveness (UNESCO, 2004b), a list that is consistent with the results of Bernard and his colleagues (Bernard, Abrami, Lou, & Borokhovski, 2004; Bernard et al., 2008; Abrami et al., 2008) that we noted on p. 59. Interaction with content is the most important way of promoting learning. Although reliable and regular assessment encourages students to focus on content, assessment is the element of their role that many teachers like least. Moreover, designing effective instruments for student assessment is a challenging task calling on skills that many teachers do not have.

Because of their scale and flexible entry requirements open schools have to operate with large banks of assessment instruments (quizzes, examinations, etc.) for both formative and summative assessment. These are held as databases on computers so that they can be made available on demand. By strengthening this function of open schools, governments could create an extremely valuable resource for their entire school systems.

The Governance of Open Schools

A government that decides to place an open school at the centre of its plans for expansion, quality enhancement, technological updating and general reform of secondary education faces a dilemma. On the one hand, since such a move means giving the open school organization considerable influence over the implementation of its educational policies, governments will be tempted to keep the integrated open school tightly bound to the education ministry. However, government administrative structures are unlikely to offer the flexibility required for an open school to operate effectively in a fast changing world. Ashby's cybernetic principle of requisite variety expressed this by stating that the larger the variety of actions available to a control system, the larger the variety of perturbations it is able to compensate (Ashby, 1956).

Acknowledgement of this principle is leading governments to re-arrange their relationships with tertiary institutions, in particular, so as to give them greater freedom to adapt to change—but within a clear statement of mandate. The Government of Alberta, for example, has passed a new tertiary education act that gives the boards of colleges, universities, and technical institutes the powers and privileges of natural persons. This allows them the flexibility to conduct business in the same way as regular citizens, provided that they stay within the mandate laid down in the act for their category of institution (Government of Alberta, 2009; University of Alberta, 2009). The purpose of the new legislation was to increase access, affordability and quality: aims identical to those for the expansion of secondary education that is our principal theme.

This could provide a model for a new type of governance of open schools. The task of drawing up the mandate for an integrative open school would be a useful exercise in its own right and a way of making expectations clear to all parties.

Summary

Drawing particularly on the examples of open schools provided in appendix 1, this chapter has shown that open schooling can add value to national school systems in many ways. Some open schools are large, particularly those in developing countries, and we have used the term mega-school to designate those with more than 10,000 students that constitute a significant element of secondary provision.

Although analogies are imperfect, we noted some likely parallels between the development of open schooling and the earlier development of open and distance learning in higher education. In both cases institutions use a variety of means to serve various ends and we have explored how open schooling, using some of the methods of distance learning, can serve a wide variety of purposes.

Open schools can be embedded in national education systems in essentially three ways. Complementary open schools offer the same curriculum as regular schools in order to allow pupils, who may have difficulty accessing those schools, to prepare for the same examinations. Alternative open schools usually serve a somewhat older clientele and design their own curricula and certification with more emphasis on vocational education and life skills. An integrative open school not only has its own student body but also strengthens the entire school system. It can do this by acting as a source of quality learning and assessment materials, a mechanism for introducing innovations, such as computing, and a catalyst for reform.

Finally, noting the trend to give educational institutions greater autonomy in governance within a clear statement of mandate, we suggest that governments could get greater value from their open schools by giving them more autonomy in strategic planning, financial management, and routine administration.

Integrative open schools can also have synergistic links to teacher education, which is the topic of the next chapter.

5
Teacher Education at Scale

Our ability to realise the goal of Education for All is dependent upon our ability to address the worldwide shortage of teachers. Higher education must scale up teacher education, both pre-service and in-service, with curricula that equip teachers to provide individuals with the knowledge and skills they need in the 21st century. This will require new approaches, including open and distance learning (ODL) and information and communications technologies (ICT).

Communiqué, World Conference on Higher Education, UNESCO, 2009a

The attention has shifted, or is in the process of shifting, from 'we need schools' to 'we need good teachers', and at the heart of this is a desire for teaching and learning of the highest quality.

Leach & Moon, 2008, p. 167

Introduction

In chapter 1 we reported that at least 10 million additional teachers will be needed worldwide by 2015 if Education for All (EFA) is to be achieved. This is a substantial proportion of the current global teaching force of around 73 million (UIS, 2009). However, the number of teachers has increased by some 1.5 million annually since 2000 so progress is being made, although many of these new teachers have little or no training before they join their schools.

Expanding open schooling, as recommended in the previous chapter, could somewhat reduce the demand for fully-trained secondary teachers and use the better ones to reach larger numbers of pupils. At the primary level, however, there is no substitute for the teacher in the classroom. Shortage of primary teachers is a worldwide problem. California, for example, has to employ thousands of untrained teachers in order to staff its schools.

Here we shall focus particularly on the challenge in the developing world while noting strategies in richer countries that may be relevant to developing countries. As a backdrop to this discussion, appendix 2 provides profiles of diverse approaches to teacher education and retention. An early example was PERMAMA, an innovative Canadian in-service programme for mathematics teachers conducted nearly 30 years ago that still seems to be having an impact where it really matters, i.e. on the performance of today's pupils. Other profiles report on large scale programmes in Nigeria, Pakistan and Malaysia and examine the use of newer technologies for teacher education in the UK, California and a number of African countries. In these countries large-scale in-service training by ODL is a current reality.

The aim of training teachers is to raise educational effectiveness and quality. A Quality Assurance Toolkit for Teacher Education Institutions (TEIs) has been produced through international collaboration and tries to address quality issues in all forms of teacher education (NAAC, 2007). We also recall the list developed by the 2005 EFA GMR (see p. 73) of those elements of school improvement that depend on more and better teachers (UNESCO, 2004b, pp. 66, 142). Important items for this discussion are the calls for: structured teaching time; using instructional time well; keeping pupils focused on learning activities; and more school-based in-service training.

Despite its crucial importance, teacher education seems to be a confused mess in much of the world. Robinson and Latchem (2003) brought together a collection of papers under the title *Teacher Education through Open and Distance Learning*. The challenge the authors faced was that ODL, to be effective, requires clear tasks and objectives whereas the goals of teacher education are too often incoherent.

Moon (2008) has pointed out, however, that if teacher education still needs major reform it is not for want of policy initiatives. He noted that 'more policy attention has been given to teacher education in the 1990s than in the hundreds of years of history that preceded it. And most of the activity has focused around quality'. Unfortunately much of this 1990s policy has proved to be ill-matched to the realities of the 21st century for three reasons: it failed to address the crisis of teacher recruitment; it was poorly coordinated with school systems; and it did not take account of the potential of technology to do things differently.

First, long programmes of pre-service training received most policy attention. These are an object of increasing scepticism and we shall cite examples later of new teachers making a good start with little training. Today's main need is for properly focused programmes of continuing professional development (CPD)—some prefer the term *continuing professional learning*—for those already teaching. These both improve classroom effectiveness and motivate teachers to stay in the profession.

Second—a related point—too much teacher education, both pre- and in-service, fails to focus on the schools and the children that it is meant to serve. Lewin (2002) has argued that because the continuing professional development or upgrading of primary teachers is carried out without reference to school needs—often without the knowledge of the school head—it encourages them to move to other jobs rather than improving their effectiveness in their schools. We explore the wider issue of the relationship between teacher education and the schools in a later section.

Third, policy usually ignored the gathering momentum of distance learning and its enhancement by ICT and open educational resources. Today ODL cannot be ignored because it provides the only way of addressing the two central requirements of teacher education just identified: the emphasis on continuing professional development and the focus on the teacher in the classroom. These requirements complement each other. Any form of continuous professional development (CPD) that involves bringing teachers regularly institutions in the towns is inherently expensive and inconvenient. More importantly, to judge by a report on CPD in teacher resource centres in Africa (DFID, 1999), it seems to have little impact on their performance as teachers. The locus of CPD must be the school and its focus must be the classroom. This has always been the strength of ODL systems for teacher education.

Teacher Supply and Retention

The general shortage of teachers in the developing world has long been recognised, but perhaps because much of the early analysis of the challenge of achieving EFA was done by economists, it was assumed that supply would rise to meet demand. There is no mention of recruitment and training of teachers in the EFA goals formulated in Dakar in 2000, nor in the Millennium Declaration. By 2005, however, the Report of the Commission for Africa (2005, p. 186) commented: '...the push to achieve EFA will certainly never succeed without substantial investment in teacher recruitment, training, retention and professional development'.

Today governments have realised that teacher supply is a complex equation and that the shortage will not solve itself. The three variables in the equation are recruiting people who want to be teachers, training them appropriately, and then retaining them in the profession. Situations vary widely from country to country and are always in a state of flux. We shall first comment on retention then discuss teacher recruitment and education together.

A century ago the playwright Bernard Shaw (1903) made the catty—and oft repeated—remark 'those who can do; those who can't teach' (to which Laurence J Peter [1977] later added 'and those who can't teach, teach the teachers'). One cause of today's teacher shortage is that the knowledge economy has stood Shaw's remark on its head—today those who can teach can also pursue many other knowledge-based occupations. The training and skills that teachers acquire are highly valued in the contemporary labour market.

These are qualities such as analytical capacity, critical thinking, teamwork, empathy, intergenerational/intercultural awareness and communications skills. This list has become a commonplace in statements of the desired outcomes of higher education—and there is a growing awareness that experienced teachers possess these qualities to a high degree. In the UK the secret intelligence service, MI5, has advertised for teachers, seeking their 'relationship-building skills' (*The Week*, 2009, p. 13).

Most countries have stories about public school teachers moving to other sectors and doubling their salaries. The Teach for America and Teach First programmes described in the next section take advantage of this phenomenon to get top graduates into teaching, if only for a short time.

As well as those teachers who move into other employment sectors within their own countries, there is considerable migration of teachers between countries. Europe and North America actively recruit graduate teachers in Africa and the Caribbean, and the best and most experienced teachers are usually the first to go. In appendix 2 we describe the Protocol for the Recruitment of Commonwealth Teachers. This is an attempt to bring some degree of order and predictability to the phenomenon, given that there is no way of preventing either the legal migration of teachers or the right of countries to recruit wherever they can find candidates.

In Africa many teachers leave the profession involuntarily because of the HIV/AIDS pandemic. In the early years of the 21st century in Kenya and Zambia, the annual deaths of teachers from AIDS were greater than the output of the teacher training colleges. Other countries, such as Namibia, predicted large shortfalls of teachers for the same reason by 2010 (Moon, 2007, p. 4). In South Africa the startling headline 'a teacher dies every two hours' brought the gravity of the problem home to ordinary people (Education in Labour Relations Council, 2005).

Finally, there will be large numbers of teachers retiring in many countries in the coming years, which also exacerbates the teacher supply problem. In the richer countries statutory retirement ages were set when life expectancy was lower than it is today. Yet many teachers retire earlier than the statutory age. In Germany, where the official retirement age is 65, only 6% of teachers work to that age—most leave in their early 50s. The UK is particularly worried about the age profile of its head teachers—60% of them are due to retire by 2017 (Moon, 2007, p. 3). These trends reflect the greying of the population that challenges many governments. Some already have proposals to increase the official retirement age or abolish it completely.

This discussion of teacher retention suggests actions that governments can take. Although education authorities cannot stop either the greying of the population or the HIV/AIDS pandemic, they can do much to enhance the status and attractiveness of the teaching profession by offering teachers decent working conditions and managing the teaching force effectively. They must keep in mind the crucial finding that they will never achieve universal secondary education if its cost per pupil is more than double that at primary level (Lewin, 2008). The OECD countries operate their education systems within this ratio and developing countries must aim to do likewise.

Reforming the overall management of developing country education systems is beyond the scope of this book. One of the main obstacles to reform is that there is often little consultation with teachers during the change process, which has led to the failure of a number of reforms (VSO, 2006). Another is the lack of management training. Head teachers are often promoted from classroom teaching into school management positions with no training except their experience of observing other heads at work. Sometimes there is not even that opportunity: 'In the more remote districts (of Ghana) where there are few trained teachers, the head, as the only qualified teacher, may in fact be fresh out of teacher training college' (VSO, 2006, p. 3). Management training and professional development programmes for head teachers and other education managers are an important component of the wider teacher education agenda on which we shall concentrate here.

Radical changes to the organization of teacher education that emphasised local school-based on-the-job training could also favour retention by giving teachers more professional pride in their work and deeper roots in their communities.

Teacher Recruitment and Education

In some developed countries such as Austria, Canada, Finland, France, Germany and Ireland teacher recruitment and retention is not a major issue. These jurisdictions have, in different ways, managed to maintain teaching as a high status profession (in Ireland only medicine attracts more highly qualified recruits (Moon, 2007, p. 2). In most countries, however, the social standing of teachers is in decline. Not surprisingly, the status of teachers correlates positively with the performance of their pupils. Those countries which rank most highly in the PISA surveys (PISA, 2009) tend to be those where teachers enjoy high status.

In most developing countries the status of teachers is not high. Teachers have sometimes brought this loss of reputation on themselves by unprofessional behaviour, notably the habit of absenteeism discussed in chapter 2. A 5% rise in teacher absenteeism can reduce pupil learning achievement by between 4% and 8% of average gains over the year (Moon, 2007, p. vii). Presumably parents notice this. But the problem goes wider. Reporting on education in South Africa's rural communities, the Nelson Mandela Foundation (2004, p. 107) noted a 'deep rift between teachers and the guardians of children in their care' adding that: 'criticisms of teachers encompass a complex set of issues related to their lack of qualification, subject knowledge and sense of vocation'.

Yet in many places rural teachers are doing heroic work. In the profile of the TESSA project in appendix 2, we cite an inspiring study of female teachers' experiences of living and working in rural sub-Saharan Africa entitled, rather appropriately, *Pride and Light* (TESSA, 2009).

Governments must also take part of the blame for the decline in teacher status. Teachers' salaries in Africa have declined relative to those of comparable professions (Colclough, Al-Samarrai, Rose, & Tembon, 2003) and corrupt administration of teacher deployment has further undermined the notion of teaching as a profession. The 2006 Global Corruption Report of Transparency International reported rampant bribery around teacher placements and transfers in Kenya. Such corruption can also encourage absenteeism since a teacher who has obtained a rural teaching post by bribery may feel under little obligation to move to the village and do the job that he or she is being paid to do.

But even incorrupt governments are in a bind. In order to put adults in front of children in their school classrooms, there is a strong temptation to recruit untrained people with a vague promise of training them on the job. Obviously, the presence of large numbers of untrained teachers further lowers the image of the profession and makes it less attractive to those who might wish to undergo the official course of pre-service training.

Yet this notion of a full course of pre-service training is increasingly anomalous. A better policy for many developing countries would be to hire the brightest and best educated local people as teachers and devote all the resources now allocated to teacher education to training them on the job. Focusing on on-the-job training would fit naturally with another key trend in teacher education which is to favour school-based programmes. The 2005 EFA GMR stated: 'Training models for teachers should be reconsidered in many countries to strengthen the school-based pre- and in-service training rather than rely on traditional, institutional pre-service training' (UNESCO, 2004a, p. 3).

It is time to make necessity the mother of invention by taking a more positive attitude to the recruitment of people who are sent into classrooms to teach with minimal initial training. It is, of course, imperative that this be done in good faith and that ongoing on-the-job training be available. We are not advocating the general dumbing down of teaching through cost-cutting that was excoriated by the Global Campaign for Education:

> Para-teacher schemes are large expansion schemes where pre-service training is compressed or abandoned completely, wages are lowered, working conditions are poorer and career paths are limited. They are being used by many governments to cut the costs associated with expanding educational access to all children. The price such governments are forced to pay is the quality of training. This massive recruitment is often accompanied by the mandatory early retirement of more experienced and often more expensive, teachers in order to cut costs even further. (Nock, 2006, p. 27)

Such a strategy will not lead any country towards a viable and sustainable education system. What is required is the establishment of large-scale school-based training systems that can, over a reasonable period, impart the knowledge and skills required for certification and give teachers the status and working conditions to match. This is not a new reality. The CalStateTEACH programme described in appendix 2 does exactly this and elements of it are found in the PERMAMA, UKOU and OUM programmes also described there. What is needed in developing countries is to focus the work of all existing TEIs on this task. This will be a wrenching adjustment for some of them, although many campus-based TEIs are already adding an ODL stream in order to cope with demand.

The example of the University of Fort Hare, South Africa, that we discuss later shows that this can be highly successful.

ODL school-based programmes have additional advantages. As in the case of distance learning routes generally, they open up access to the teaching profession to people, especially women, who are not able to attend a conventional training programme for either financial or cultural reasons. The large-scale teacher education programmes of AIOU, described in appendix 2, are playing this role in Pakistan.

With the major focus now on expanding secondary education, subject knowledge becomes relatively more important. Putting teachers into the classroom with minimal pedagogical training is not necessarily a bad thing. New graduates, who master their subject, can communicate it with enthusiasm and are not much older than their pupils may do better than trained teachers with no specialisation in the subject—and half of all history and science classes in the US are taught by non-specialists. This is the basis for the Teach for America programme and its UK equivalent, Teach First, which recruit top graduates who are prepared to commit to teaching for two years.

Teach for America (TFA) began in 1990, and by 2004 10,000 graduates recruited under the scheme had taught 1.5 million pupils. TFA recruits talented liberal arts graduates from prestigious colleges, offers them some condensed training, and then places them in some of the toughest US public schools. TFA is not itself an alternative certification programme, but it uses such programmes to help promising young professionals become teachers.

Evaluations of the TFA programme are positive, and it has stirred up controversy by questioning the value of conventional approaches to initial teacher training: 'The TFA programme, we learn from this study, proves that it's not necessary to spend an extended period in a (teacher education institution) in order to be effective in a K–12 classroom. It reinforces the view that there's no single path to excellent teaching. To us, this presents a strong argument for letting many flowers bloom when it comes to teacher preparation. Perhaps learning to be an effective teacher can best take place on the job rather than in a university classroom. Surely it is premature to impose anybody's pet regimen on the entire education system. What's needed now is experimentation with different modes of teacher preparation, accompanied by rigorous evaluations of these experiments' (Raymond, Fletcher, & Luque, 2001, p. ix).

The main difference in the UK programme, Teach First, is that this does provide training during the first year for the graduates to acquire Qualified Teacher Status. Here again, evaluation of the programme is very positive, and almost three-fifths of the graduates elect to stay in teaching once their two-year commitment is over (Hutchings, Maylor, Mendick, Menter, & Smart, 2006). This is despite the fact that during those two years they receive further training to prepare them for careers in other areas such as management. Applicants to Teach First are impatient to tackle challenges. The Economist (2009b, p. 49) reported:

'Teach First describes the job as tough and demanding because the right people are those who are attracted by the most daunting tasks'. Such people seek a rapid route to the classroom and consider the standard one-year postgraduate course as 'too slow', 'too theoretical' and 'boring'.

Similar reflections on conventional pre-service teacher education are heard in the very different context of the private schools for the poor that we described in chapter 2. Noting that that the owners of these schools were disparaging about the government teacher-training certificate, Tooley (2009, p. 11) quoted an Indian owner as saying: 'government teacher training is like learning to swim without ever going near a swimming pool;…our untrained teachers learn to teach in the well'. From Tooley's account it seems that these owners and school heads take the training of their teachers seriously and do it well. Neither these teachers nor those in the Teach for America and Teach First programmes have teaching certificates although they usually have bachelor and sometimes master degrees.

Balancing Pre-Service and In-Service Teacher Education

These very different examples of the recruitment of teachers without formal training suggest that the balance between the pre-service and in-service components of teacher education needs rethinking for four reasons.

First, in many countries significant numbers of teachers begin their careers with no training at all or only the most rudimentary preparation. The CalStateTEACH programme in California was set up to enhance the professionalism of the 30,000 untrained teachers in the schools of that state. In Nigeria there are over 100,000 teachers who are candidates for immediate training. In 2000 one-third of existing primary teachers in 11 eastern and southern African countries were untrained (UNESCO, 2000). Worldwide the children in the classrooms of these untrained teachers number in the tens of millions and come disproportionately from disadvantaged groups. It makes no sense to give long pre-service training courses to teachers that many children will never see while leaving the untrained teachers—who are usually eager to learn their way into the profession by developing their skills—to fend for themselves.

Second, especially given the current importance of expanding secondary education, pre-service education should focus particularly on subject knowledge. No amount of pedagogical training or educational theory is going to make people with little knowledge of physics into good physics teachers in conventional classrooms—although they might be good at facilitating study in an open school learning centre where the pupils have quality self-instructional materials.

Furthermore, the evaluation of the UK's Teach First programme showed that while those brand new to teaching were often bored by courses in pedagogy and educational theory (The Economist, 2009b), they understood and valued this material once they had gained experience in the classroom (Hutchings et al., 2006). This result likely applies to most teachers and most professions. This is strongly corroborated by the rural women teachers in Africa interviewed for the report

Pride and Light (TESSA, 2009). Most of those who had gone through formal pre-service training found much of it irrelevant to their working situations. However, they were effusive about the role of mentors in their schools—often their head teacher—and local opportunities for professional learning. Some stressed the importance of using telephones to keep in touch with colleagues.

Third, effective programmes of in-service learning help to make teachers feel that they belong to a real profession and encourage them to remain in it. Although in-service learning is a difficult way to impart basic subject knowledge because of the range of subjects in the school curriculum, it is an excellent way of updating teachers on new developments in their discipline—as in the case of the PERMAMA programme—if they already master the basics of their subject.

Fourth, planning the professional development of teachers and other staff can be a valuable element of school management. Good organizations make the planning of professional development part of the annual performance management cycle. Discussing the balance between collective and individual professional learning opportunities in the school's annual training plan can be an important factor in fostering teamwork and creating cohesion among the staff.

In summary, most professional learning for the majority of teachers will have to take place in the schools. The old model of campus-based training followed by occasional short courses—for those fortunate enough have access to them—cannot meet current needs and is ineffective anyway.

Teacher Education and the Schools

Teacher education prepares people for work in schools and most pre-service teacher education programmes have always included teaching practice. Historically the partnerships between TEIs and schools for this activity have been rather unequal, with the academics from the TEIs assessing their students' classroom teaching, sometimes in a cursory manner on the basis of little recent school experience themselves.

The UK, which is often a useful laboratory for other governments to watch because it likes to test various alternative solutions to educational challenges, has explored different ways of rebalancing the power relationships between TEIs and schools in teacher training. Brooks (2006) has reported on the 'quiet revolution' in the UK 'aimed at unseating TEIs and supplanting them with school-led training' through the Training Schools project.

Brooks (2006) concluded that policies for pre-service training based on the dominance of either the schools or the TEIs run counter to research showing that teacher education is most effective where students 'are able to benefit from the collaboration of those in schools and the TEIs who seek to train them'. She also found that the Training Schools project was in danger of leading to an 'ever-expanding patchwork of small-scale initiatives devoid of a strategic overview and coherent planning'.

It is important to bear these conclusions in mind in emphasising the desirability of conducting most teacher education through in-service learning by teachers who are already working in the schools. The TEIs must remain vital partners but will face different challenges. Dealing with teacher-learners in large numbers of schools requires the use of open and distance learning, but this does not mean relying solely on existing ODL providers. The University of Fort Hare, in South Africa's poor Eastern Cape province, is an example of a campus institution that has introduced its own distance learning programme and embraced classroom-based teacher education with considerable success.

The account of the Fort Hare programme by Devereux and Amos (2005) is a compelling read with many pointers for the future. It reveals the care that was taken to embed learning in situations and contexts that make sense to the learner, which required a move from 'instructional materials to those that facilitate and mediate what is learned'. The teachers were very typical of the developing world context that is our focus here. Programme evaluation was based on a sample of 80 teacher-learners 'all of whom were female, worked mainly in rural settings, with two-thirds teaching classes of over 40 children; of these 30% had classes of over 60 children. Within these classes 59% of teachers taught children whose ages differed between two to five years from the norm for that standard...' (2005, p. 282). In this context the teachers worked alongside their pupils in exploring how they themselves learned. The teachers used the term *teacher-learner* for themselves and *learner* for their pupils.

A powerful way of embedding learning was the use of African concepts and words to describe the elements of the ODL approach. The Nguni word *umthamo* was used for the bite-sized chunks of learning in the core areas; the word *siyetyisas* (chewing the cud) was applied to the review units in the fourth year; and the designation of the local tutor as *umkhwezeli* (someone who keeps the fire burning) arose from the strong local story-telling heritage. This strong linkage to the local communities meant that the teacher-learners were able to study without neglecting their learners, their classroom or their wider community and district. Indeed, because some of the content ranged beyond the classroom, villages and communities became involved in some of the changes.

The programme is clearly a success. It has effected the change from teacher-centred to learner-centred education that is the ambition of contemporary thinking such as UNICEF's 'Child Friendly Schools' philosophy. Seventy-five percent of teacher-learners said that understanding how children learn and realising that all children have their own ideas were the most significant outcomes.

The way that the programme was embedded in local needs was crucial to its success but this does not mean that everything has to be developed locally *ab initio*. The University of Fort Hare is a member of the TESSA consortium that provides resources and systems to support the development of school-based teacher education programmes in Africa. It is an 'open content' project providing web- and text-based open educational resources (OER) for use initially with primary teachers but extending eventually to all the secondary subjects. It is not a training programme *per se* but rather provides tools and content to allow local developers to create school-based programmes (Moon, 2007, p. 17).

The TESSA programme is just one example of the use of OER, a development that has profound implications for extending the quality and impact of ODL.

Open and Distance Learning in Teacher Education

ODL is destined to play a vital and dominant role in teacher education not simply because there is no alternative, given the needs that we have outlined, but because new forms of ODL are better value for money. Chapter 3 laid out the basic principles of technology, insisting on the ability of technology to operate at scale, and outlined the economic structure and organizational requirements of ODL. Here we shall comment further on two developments in ODL: OER and ICT, because both can greatly facilitate the transformation of teacher education that we are proposing.

Practitioners of ODL have long enthused about the potential for sharing course materials but until recently it was unfulfilled for two reasons. First, the not-invented-here syndrome was deeply rooted in the academic mind. Google has changed all that. All teachers now know how much useful material is out there and most borrow from it. The second handicap was that before courseware went digital the process of sharing it was tiresome. Adaptation was always required and that meant rekeying long texts and re-editing video and audio material.

OER (see p. 75 for the OER Africa definition) address both issues and have sparked a wave of sharing, some of it between developing countries as in the example of the Virtual University for Small States of the Commonwealth (VUSSC, 2009). OER are the basis of the TESSA consortium. Thakrar, Zinn, and Wolfenden (2009) describe how this works from the perspective of one consortium member, the University of Fort Hare. TESSA's OER are based on the principle that a critical aspect of teachers' professional development is 'consistent engagement on issues of learning and teaching based on what actually happens in the teachers own classrooms, rather than a primary focus on guides, suggestions and theories of what should happen in classrooms'. In other words these OER facilitate the move to school-based professional learning.

TESSA offers a global intellectual resource of materials to support school-based programmes: at primary level there are 75 units designed to improve classroom practice directly. Although the consortium has devoted resources to planning the use of the study units, it is an important principle that implementation of the OER is a dispersed and decentralized process. Each institution decides which selection of OER to incorporate and how. The use of the materials has now spread spontaneously beyond consortium members and their countries.

Some member institutions, notably the large-scale distance learning institutions (NTI, Nigeria and the Open University of Sudan—which between them have over 200,000 student teachers using TESSA materials) employ the materials in a highly structured manner. Others, including Fort Hare, generally use them in a more loosely structured way, but always adapting them to the local context.

A wider exploration of the use of ICT in teacher education in Africa was conducted by Leach, Ahmed, Makalima, and Power (2006) through the Digital Education Enhancement Project (DEEP). The focus was on rural areas of Egypt and South Africa and the results were encouraging. They flowed with the grain of the emphasis on school-based teacher education and showed that teacher development in ICT should not only be integrated with student- and curriculum-focused ICT developments, but also focused holistically on the needs of rural communities more broadly.

Some of the key findings were that:

- Teachers learned to use ICT very quickly, whether they had previous exposure or not, and felt greatly empowered by their new skills. Where support was scarce they worked to solve the problems.
- They introduced ICT into planned lessons in their classrooms with good results and collaborated with fellow teachers in new ways. Men and women were equally successful.
- Hand-held devices were used regularly including for classroom activities.
- Costs of ICT tend to be overestimated and are falling anyway.
- Policy should explicitly recognise the role of ICT, putting the focus on local contexts, classroom relevance and learner achievement.
- Mobile technologies have an important role to play.
- The use of ICT can have a significant impact on the self-image, confidence and professionalism of teachers. It offers the potential to redefine and enhance their status within their communities and society generally.

The report concurs with earlier studies that school-based, computer supported training can be part of the answer to the teacher education challenge and that 'technology could make teacher training experiences better and shorter' (Leach et al., 2006, p. 2).

Since that report was written the penetration of mobile telephones in Africa has continued to increase at 65% annually. The institutional use of mobile telephony is still in its infancy, but there is no doubt that it can make a major contribution to school-based professional learning for teachers. Experimentation is rife. One example is a collaborative project of the Commonwealth of Learning and the University of British Columbia called LIVES (Learning through Interactive Voice Educational System). The aim is to deliver learning materials asynchronously on mobile phones through auditory means with responses by the learner. LIVES uses an open source learning management system and can operate at scale (Commonwealth of Learning, 2009b).

Summary

This chapter has addressed the worldwide shortage of teachers and examined the issues of retention, recruitment and training. The status of teachers has declined in many countries; sometimes as a result of unprofessional behaviour but also because of government action in reducing real salaries and hiring untrained teachers without giving them opportunities for on-the-job education.

The teaching profession suffers from attrition in four ways. In knowledge economies other employers find teachers' skills attractive; richer countries recruit teachers from poorer countries; death rates from AIDS are high in parts of Africa; and a wave of retirements is happening in various parts of the world.

Teacher education must be re-balanced in order to facilitate recruitment and improve the quality of education. Presently too much weight is placed on pre-service education—often divorced from the reality that teachers will encounter in schools. The focus of effort must shift to continuing professional development centred on the reality of the classroom. This will allow new groups of candidates to access the profession and, by being school based will enhance teacher effectiveness.

We have begun to explore how teacher education might be radically reorganized to concentrate on school-based professional development. All TEIs will need to engage with ODL, but new technologies, such as open educational resources, ICT and mobile telephony will make it possible to develop programmes that are rooted in local context while drawing on global resources. Reforming teacher education will be a long and arduous task, but governments could start by conducting root-and-branch reviews of current arrangements in the light of the educational challenges and opportunities facing their countries.

In the final chapter we shall place these conclusions in a wider context and suggest strategies for success in bringing teacher education into the 21st century and maximising synergies with other necessary developments notably open schooling.

6
Strategies for Success

For Forms of Government let fools contest; What'er is best administer'd
is best.

Alexander Pope, *Essay on Man*, 1734

Introduction

Achieving Education For All (EFA) is a challenge of scale and quality. Good
progress is being made but many countries, including some large ones, will
struggle to reach the 2015 target for providing universal primary education
(UPE). Recruiting and training large numbers of teachers are essential if they
are to win that battle. For many of the states that have achieved UPE the challenge is now to expand secondary education. This will require further millions
of teachers as governments exploit every possible means for expanding secondary schooling.

Although improving quality is a multi-dimensional challenge, two elements
that research consistently shows to be essential are expanding the availability of
learning materials and providing in-service professional development for teachers. These relate closely to our two principal themes in this book.

Expanding the public system of conventional secondary schooling will be
difficult because in most developing countries it now costs too much relative to
primary education. The reforms needed to make it less expensive—primarily
deploying teachers more efficiently and making them more accountable—will
be unpalatable. Private schooling can make an important contribution, but to
take advantage of it many governments will need to change their attitudes and
policies towards this sector and collaborate more closely with it.

By themselves, however, such moves will barely scratch the surface of the
problem. The scale of the challenge—training millions of teachers and educating
tens of millions of children—requires responses at scale. Previous chapters have
shown—and the examples in the appendixes demonstrate—how open schooling and teacher education can be conducted on the scale needed by creating
mega-schools and expanding in-service professional development using open
and distance learning.

This final chapter shows how such developments could combine to create
an effective educational ecosystem for the 21st century. We shall first revisit the

essential notion of scale and then explore the potential for productive synergies between open schooling and school-based teacher education. A third section will show how this could work as a national system reaching from governments to communities. Finally, we shall explore practical strategies for achieving the ultimate objective of a quality education for all and suggest how the international community could support these next steps in the EFA campaign.

Scale

Although it has been a refrain throughout this book, we come back to the imperative of scale because many educators reject it instinctively. The insidious link between quality and exclusivity remains a subconscious assumption. Yet technology allows us have both abundance and quality in other areas of life. Technology can and does—as the real examples in appendixes 1 and 2 prove—make possible the combination of quality and mass access in education too.

We do not argue that scale operations should replace existing forms of provision of either schooling or teacher education. The challenge of achieving EFA is so great that all providers will struggle to address the needs it creates and every contribution is welcome. Conventional approaches, however, are not sufficient. Governments must encourage the development of institutions that can operate at scale. Furthermore, over and beyond the pupils and teachers that such institutions enrol directly, governments should mandate them to enhance the quality and effectiveness of the whole national educational system. This will present a major opportunity if two common habits of mind can be overcome.

We have the opportunity not merely to reduce costs but to introduce a new cost structure. Chapter 3 showed that although scale operations require an upfront investment to put systems in place, this advance spending is more than recouped in lower operating costs once scale is achieved. This is not wishful thinking: the examples in appendixes 1 and 2 show consistently that open schools and TEIs based on ODL can have lower operating costs per student than conventional provision.

The first challenge to our usual habits is that you cannot demonstrate the benefits of scale operations by conducting pilot projects. Both the economics and the quality of the institution—and its ability to fulfil its mission—depend on scale. So the sponsor of a new mega-school must have the courage to start at scale after undertaking the careful planning required for its success. We noted on p. 34 the example of the UKOU, one of the great educational innovations of the 20th century, which would have been an expensive failure as a pilot project.

The second challenge to common practice is to adopt systems thinking. A system is a group of interacting, interrelated or interdependent elements forming a complex whole. While this is an excellent description of national education systems, there is little evidence of systems thinking in the way that most are currently run. With few exceptions, such as Singapore, the temptation for governments is to create departments for the different parts of the system and let them operate as separate compartments. Donors such as the World Bank are also more comfortable focusing on individual projects rather than thinking in system terms. However, the complexities of the 21st century demand systems approaches that generate higher quality responses to public needs at lower cost.

Chapter 4 gave some examples of the roles open schooling can play in improving the performance of national school systems and promoted the concept of the integrative open school. The most tangible assistance that a mega-school can give is to make learning materials available to all schools, public and private, as open educational resources (OER). Another role is as a catalyst for the introduction of ICT because, as chapter 2 demonstrated, it is not enough simply to place computers in the schools. We explore the implementation of these roles in the next section.

Chapter 5 demonstrated the system implications of large-scale school-based teacher education. One example was how OER allow institutions and teachers to adapt global resources to make them authentically local. Another was that school-based teacher education, particularly where it involves ICT, can extend its influence and make the wider community part of the system.

What are the synergies between open schooling, teacher education, school systems, ministries of education, and the wider community?

Synergy

Synergy is the interaction of two or more agents or forces so that their combined effect is greater than the sum of their individual effects. That is precisely what governments should expect from mega-schools and school-based teacher education programmes. Ministries of education have a determining role in creating that synergy particularly as it concerns the curriculum. We noted on p. 71 that even mega-schools have been blindsided by curriculum revisions that came without warning.

True synergy, however, requires more than simply giving advance notice of changes. Ministries should treat open schools as vital partners in conceiving and implementing new curricula. Such collaboration should be a two-way street, because the wider school system can greatly benefit from the curricular innovation in vocational education and life skills that is being conducted by alternative mega-schools such as NIOS and the Open College of UPNG. In Botswana there already appears to be good synergy between the national school system and BOCODOL, which is now proposing to offer teacher education.

The relationship between the units in the ministry of education responsible for curriculum and teacher education presents a similar opportunity. Ministries should encourage the trend to school-based teacher education because it has the potential to improve teachers' ability to mediate the official curriculum with their pupils. To make this process fully effective teacher education institutions (TEIs) must also be brought into the curriculum development loop so that learning materials for teachers mirror the learning materials of their pupils.

This implies that a further productive step would be to formalise the links between TEIs and mega-schools in the interest of making fully congruent the learning materials that they develop. As more teachers get involved in developing OERs for open schooling this is likely to happen informally anyway. We noted on p. 75 that one result of the six-country COL/Hewlett project to create OERs for open and conventional schools was the creation of a pool of 100 master teachers with skills in instructional design and collaborative content development online. Ministries of education should take full advantage of such people in both schooling and teacher education.

Joint learning and resource centres could be another important expression of such synergy and major assets to the education system as a whole.

Local Learning and Resource Centres

The notion of teachers' centres—also called teacher resource centres (TRCs)—goes back to the 1960s and was popular with donors in Africa in the 1990s. The idea is to create, equip and maintain centres where teachers can have access to a wider range of resources than they would expect to find in their schools. They were also used as venues for in-service training. Although the notion seems plausible, an evaluation conducted at the end of the 1990s concluded that the TRCs had not had the desired impact (DFID, 1999). First, apart from taking teachers out of the classroom for in-service courses and thus contributing to absenteeism, the training undertaken in the TRCs did not seem to have much effect on their subsequent classroom teaching. However, teachers liked the idea of a local resource centre even if they did not often use it.

Chapter 5 showed that the most effective teacher education is not only school based but effectively classroom based. The TRC evaluation suggests that even moving in-service training to a local centre diminishes its useful impact. So in outlining a role for a 21st century version of local learning centres we are not suggesting that they displace school-based teacher education by ODL. However, a local learning hub (LH) could have other valuable roles in a modern educational ecosystem.

First, an LH could have a level of broadband connectivity that was inconceivable for the TRCs in the 1990s and is still unlikely to reach most rural schools in the developing world for some years yet. Connectivity transforms the notion of a learning resource centre. Its primary usefulness to teachers would be giving them access to online and other resources rather than to formal training.

Second, LHs could be local study centres for the open schooling system. This would give the open school pupils better access to ICT than in most of the conventional schools, following the principle that educational technology should go first to the most disadvantaged.

Third, an ICT-rich LH could be the locus for experimentation with applications of ICT in the classroom by larger groups of teachers than would be found in any one school. They could pursue further the promising advances recorded in the DEEP project (Leach, Ahmed, Makalima, & Power, 2006) and exploit developments in mobile technology in particular.

Fourth, the LH could also be a facility for the community. Multipurpose community tele-centres have been an important strand of UNESCO's strategy for increasing access to ICT for a decade (UNESCO, 2009b). Linking them explicitly to the formal educational system by giving them roles in open schooling and teacher education would strengthen the system's link with local communities and help to create the critical mass of users needed for sustainability. However, the most important community aim should be to involve the local people in participatory content creation for their local media, such as community radio. This is the key to real empowerment. Mozambique has made community access to ICT centres an integral part of all its development policies (Massingue, 2006).

Fifth, the exterior yard of the LH would be a good place to install a Hole in the Wall computer facility, in order to juxtapose 'minimally invasive education' and mainstream education and create synergy between the children's spontaneous activity with computers and the work of the teachers on ICT applications in classrooms.

Systems

This potential for much greater synergy between ministries of education, schools, communities, mega-schools and TEIs suggests a set of interacting systems that we present schematically in Figure 6.1.

We refer to systems rather than a system for two reasons. First, this is an interlocking set of systems rather than a single entity. Second, the danger of representing systems as diagrams is that it makes them look monolithic, which is not the intent. The purpose of the diagram is to capture some elements of the interactions, interrelationships and interdependencies of the systems without implying that the whole is driven or controlled from any central point. The most effective systems have a high degree of self-organization.

The systems described in earlier chapters show some good examples. The accredited institutions (study centres) of NIOS conduct their business and their interaction with pupils in a variety of ways. The teacher-learners in the University of Fort Hare's school-based teacher education programme ensured that it became fully indigenous to their schools and communities. Similarly the LH would allow the community members to organize and create their own content for a website and community radio.

In the wider educational system competition is another process of self-organization. While taking advantage of common resources, such as learning materials and OER, public and private schools will work to maintain their distinctiveness and promote their comparative advantage to parents. Similarly donors and vendors will want to encourage projects and experimentation in particular schools. Other parts of the system will review the results and may change their own practices based on their observations.

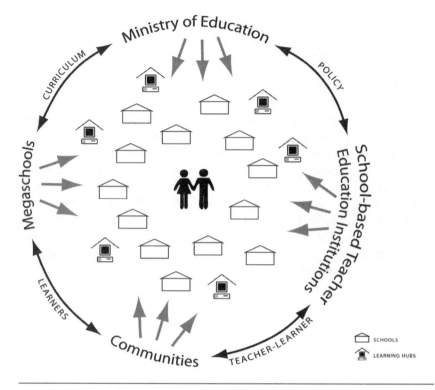

Figure 6.1 An Educational Ecosystem for the 21st Century

The diagram shows that there is a national school system, including public and private schools and a network of LHs, under the authority of the ministry of education. The ministry is also linked to the open schooling sub-system, particularly through its curriculum and examinations function, and this sub-system also relates to the schools, notably as a source of learning materials, and to the LHs where it locates its study centres.

Also linked to the ministry, through its teacher education unit in particular, is the TEI sub-system. All TEIs have links with the schools and these are particularly strong for school-based teacher education. They will also relate to a national higher education system and to international groupings such as TESSA.

The LHs act as resource centres for teachers, giving them access to a richer ICT infrastructure than they have in their schools. Finally, intersecting with all these systems and subsystems is the community system, which has a highly complex set of sub-systems of its own.

Strategies

Strategies are the means by which objectives are consciously pursued and obtained over time. The overall aim, which is to achieve EFA, will generate a set of specific objectives for each country depending on its current profile with respect to the EFA goals and its national priorities. This discussion of strategies is for those jurisdictions that either have already developed—or propose to develop—a scale response to the challenges of either secondary schooling or teacher education—or both.

Although we write as if countries were starting from scratch in scaling up institutional responses for EFA, many already have such structures in place. In our organizational profiles in appendixes 1 and 2, we comment on the strategic challenges facing those institutions; some of which may also be relevant in other countries. For example, appendix 2 reports on the choices facing CNED, which is both a mega-school and a TEI and has recently undertaken a major strategy review.

Countries have various legislative arrangements, diverse cultures of leadership, and different traditions of management and administration so we shall not try to prescribe ways of implementing EFA at scale. ODL in higher education and teacher education already has an abundant literature and research on open schooling is developing. Here we simply outline some general principles before concluding with some comments on how the international community might help.

Legislation and Policy

An open school or ODL-based TEI will develop into a significant element in any education system. As such it must have a legislative basis to be sustainable. The clarity, consensus and national ownership achieved during the process of reviewing and passing legislation is worth any delay.

Similarly, a growing number of countries have put in place policies for the development of ODL nationally, which also contribute to institutional robustness by assigning roles and managing expectations. Some countries may need to review their existing policies on teacher education in order to offer it through ODL.

Governance and Leadership

ODL institutions that operate at scale become influential players in national education systems. There is therefore a natural tendency for politicians and civil servants to anchor them within the government administrative structures. They should resist this temptation because such institutions function better with considerable autonomy. On p. 81 we recommended the approach taken by the Government of Alberta, which gives institutions considerable operational latitude within a clear statement of mandate.

Research shows that good institutional leadership is essential to educational quality. Leaders of large ODL institutions should be chosen with special care. Paul (1990) stressed the importance of value-driven leadership, which in this case must include commitment to inclusiveness and widening access—qualities that are not automatically found in educational leaders from the conventional sector. Furthermore, managing large-scale ODL is different from running a conventional institution. It is helpful for the leader to have some experience of the difference.

Management and Administration

The challenge of conducting ODL successfully at scale is as much organizational as pedagogical. In chapter 3 we identified the three components of ODL systems: administration and logistics, course materials development, and student support. We shall not dwell on them further here except to note that an institution will falter if any one of these functions performs badly.

Three special challenges in managing ODL operations, which do not have the same acuity in conventional institutions, are managing relations with government, making sound choices about technology, and sustaining a strong commitment to students among all staff.

How Can the International Community Help?

We have laid out an agenda that includes both challenges and opportunities. While many countries will strive hard to maximise their achievement of the EFA goals by 2015, the reforms and initiatives that we have proposed should be seen in a long-term perspective. The same applies to the role of the international community.

In chapter 1, after describing the global campaign to achieve UPE, we forecast that the international community is very unlikely to mount a similar campaign to help countries move toward universal secondary education and the attainment of the other Dakar goals. But this does not mean that the international community will be idle. Intergovernmental agencies such as the World Bank, bilateral donors and foundations will continue to encourage the development of education and may increase their support as economies improve.

Technology-based innovations such as mega-schools and large-scale school-based teacher education are attractive to donors because they present the opportunity to invest in creating systems that lower operating costs once scale is attained. Other parts of the ecosystem presented in Figure 6.1 will also attract support. For example, an effervescence of experimentation will be necessary to support the evolution of an optimal design for local learning hubs.

UNESCO has made an invaluable contribution to the EFA campaign through its impressive series of Global Monitoring Reports—without which it would have been difficult to write this book. There is an adage that 'if you can't measure it, you can't manage it', and the data and analyses in the GMRs have strongly supported national and international efforts. The GMRs should continue to focus tightly on the Dakar goals until 2015. After that there is a strong case either for giving them a broader focus, like the earlier series of World Education Reports, or focusing on post-basic education. Already countries that have the EFA goals in sight are placing a new emphasis on tertiary education. We suggest that regular monitoring reports focused on all the inter-related components of the complex world of post-basic education, from senior secondary through skills training to postgraduate, would be more useful than a narrower focus. Just as the GMRs have done, such reports could single out one sector for special treatment each year.

Summary

In this final chapter we have stressed the three principles of scale, synergy and systems thinking that must underpin national strategies to complete the drive to EFA by expanding secondary education and training many more teachers. Governments responding to challenges of scale must have the courage to implement responses at scale without doing pilot projects first. They will be rewarded by reductions in the cost of schooling and training. Mega-schools and large-scale in-service teacher education programmes should not be viewed in isolation but as part of new educational ecosystems for the 21st century that exploit the synergies with the wider school system, governments and communities. A new type of local learning hub could be a useful element of these ecosystems and link schooling and teacher education more closely to the wider community.

Quality and sustainability must be the watchwords of these developments. They should be grounded in legislation and policy but governance arrangements should recognise that institutions having operational autonomy within a clear mandate perform better. Scale operations for mass access have special requirements for leadership. Finally, although arrangements for international support will be different from those put in place for Universal Primary Education, technology-based scale operations are inherently attractive to donors as are, in a different way the local learning hubs where many elements of the 21st century educational ecosystem will come together. UNESCO must continue to support the next stages in the push towards Education for All by continuing to hold up a mirror, in the form of a sequel to the GMRs, so that stakeholders can assess their progress.

Conclusions

For 20 years there has been an intense international effort to expand primary education. We are not there yet, but the aspiration of seeing all the world's children go to primary school by 2015 is no longer fantasy. This success should be celebrated soberly because it has spawned two new crises. Tens of millions of children and their parents are now looking for secondary education but many countries are ill-equipped to provide it. That is partly because of the second crisis: the shortage of teachers.

Crises combine dangers and opportunities. A danger is that failure to expand schooling beyond primary will not only act as brake on the development of individual countries, but will also create a much larger world population by 2050 than if all girls were to receive secondary education. An opportunity is for developing countries to create new types of community-focused educational ecosystems by developing open schooling and school-based teacher education to enhance existing forms of provision.

Such 21st century educational ecosystems have several special characteristics. First, they take advantage of the principles of technology (specialisation, division of labour, economies of scale and ICT) to operate at scale, widening access to education of quality at low cost. Second, they can be leaven for improving whole school systems by offering good learning materials, bringing teacher education into the classroom and acting as a catalyst for integrating ICT into learning. Third, they are based on the notions of synergy and sharing, both nationally and globally.

People aspire to take part in the life of their communities, to contribute as citizens of their countries and to feel membership of the global community. This vision of full participation in 21st century life is being made achievable as mobile technologies allow poorer countries to leapfrog over conventional developments in ICT. Moreover the blossoming of open educational resources is creating a global intellectual commons to which everyone can contribute and from which everyone can draw.

As developing countries use new methods to achieve Education For All they will not simply be following in the footsteps of the countries that attained the goal in earlier generations. They will break new ground by creating and nurturing the habit of self-directed learning that the 21st century requires.

Profiles

Selected Open Schools and Mega-Schools

Introduction

Chapter 4 showed that open schooling has developed in various ways with different purposes around the world. To provide additional background this appendix gives short profiles of eight open schools, six of them mega-schools. Although our focus is primarily on open schooling for developing countries, we begin by examining the growing trend of home schooling in North America. Home schooling and open schooling might appear to be opposites, because open schooling responds to the absence of regular schools, whereas home schooling expresses parents' dissatisfaction with schools that are available. However, both approaches share the challenge of educating children outside the regular school system.

We next examine the opportunities and challenges facing a long-established mega-school in an industrialized country, France's Centre National d'Enseignement à Distance (CNED) (which also features in appendix 2 on teacher education along with an account of a strategy review conducted in 2008–09). Other profiles present the different approaches to open schooling in the developing world that have been adopted by Mexico, India, Indonesia, Namibia, Botswana and Papua New Guinea. We end with the example of Canada's Contact North. This is not strictly an open school since most of its offerings are at postsecondary level, but it shows how ICT can now be used to offer courses synchronously to scattered populations. Elsewhere Abrioux and Ferreira (2009) provide profiles of more traditional open schools in the developed world: the Open Access College of South Australia (Schocroft, 2009, p. 129) and the Vancouver Learning Network in British Columbia (Gauthier, 2009, p. 173).

These profiles are only a sample of the open schools listed in Table 4.1, but they do illustrate our thesis that depending on the intentions of their designers, these institutions can be complementary, alternative or integrative in relation to the conventional school system.

Home Schooling in North America

Although the trend to open schooling that is our primary interest and the phenomenon of home schooling are quite different, there are some interesting parallels because in both cases children are educated without attending conventional schools. Home schooling occurs worldwide but we shall focus here on North America (Canada and the United States); partly because home schooling is reasonably well documented on that continent, but also because in developing countries where many children do not attend secondary school, it is impossible to determine whether they are simply out of school or being schooled at home.

Even in North America, however, getting accurate figures to gauge the extent of home schooling is impossible because education is the responsibility of 64 district, provincial, state and territorial governments (not to mention thousands of school boards). All North American jurisdictions allow home schooling but not all require parents to notify government education authorities when they elect to educate their children at home.

The Ontario Federation of Teaching Parents (OFTP, 2009) estimates that 1%–2% of all school-age children are homeschooled in North America. This translates to around 20,000 children in Ontario, 60,000 in the whole of Canada and some 1 to 2 million in the United States. However Tooley (2000, p. 236) claims that home schooling 'is growing at an extraordinary rate with perhaps five per cent of parents home schooling children in the USA… As dissatisfaction with state schooling grows, and the potential enhancement of home schooling through technology becomes apparent, more parents will opt for this'.

Why do parents opt for home schooling? Prior to the introduction of compulsory school attendance laws most childhood education occurred within the family or community. In developed countries home schooling in the modern sense is an alternative to the formal schools. Parents cite numerous reasons for educating their children at home. According to a 2003 US Census survey, 33% of home schooling households cited religion as a factor in their choice. The same study found that 30% felt school had a poor learning environment, 14% objected to what the school teaches, 11% felt their children were not being challenged at school, and 9% cited morality (Bauman, 2001). These results were reinforced by a later study (NCES, 2003) which reported that 85% of home schooling parents cited 'the social environments of other forms of schooling' (including safety, drugs, bullying and negative peer-pressure) as an important reason why they have opted for home schooling. Native Americans, who have a tradition of home schooling and apprenticeship, strongly resisted compulsory schooling by the state (Witte & Mero, 2008).

The claim that home schooling is better for the socialization of children may seem surprising, but the OFTP insists strongly on this point: 'Homeschooled children learn their social skills from their parents rather than their peers, so they are learning from adult role models. Because they don't spend much time in peer-intensive environments like school, but do interact with other children in smaller or more supervised groups, homeschooled children don't experience too much peer pressure or bullying, so they don't tend to develop dysfunctional bully-survival strategies nor the excessive peer orientation that is of such concern these days' (OFTP, 2009).

One home schooling parent put it like this: 'Once upon a time, school playgrounds were a place to look forward to happy interaction with friends, a place to meet new children and play. Now, it's an arena of conflict. Children must learn to avoid being seriously hurt by students whose behaviour problems are tolerated due to diagnosed conditions and medication. If you consider this to be socialization then your child is in the right place. In a classroom of 26 to 32 students, adult intervention for socialization is minimal at best. Accommodations for behaviour are made daily and cannot include the consistency of moral or fair treatment because there are too many factors at play: from inciting a crisis with a behavioural student, a conflict with parents, and even injury' (Denis, personal communication, 2009).

How do parents who educate their children at home tackle the task? In particular, are they clients of open schools and other bodies that provide learning materials and support based on national curricula? The answer is a qualified 'yes'. The key characteristic of home schooling is the diversity of motives and approaches of the parents, who range from out-and-out anarchists to those who are quite happy with the official local curriculum but do not like the schools. The anarchists—who do not usually stay the course for long—will mostly make it up as they go along, using any resources that appeal to them.

Those who want their children to study the official curriculum can usually find appropriate resources: the courses of the local open school; curriculum materials on the web; and books designed for the curriculum. However, government curriculum materials designed for teachers may not be particularly user-friendly for parents, who may also have difficulty getting their hands on—or even affording to buy—the teachers' handbooks that accompany commercially published textbooks. Parents choosing home schooling for religious reasons are quite well served because faith groups publish affordable and excellent curricular materials with all subjects meshed into their religious studies.

Given the variety of parents' motives for home schooling it appears that no single provider of materials and courses has more than a tiny share of this large market. One indicator of this is that Laurel Springs, a US-based correspondence and online school that advertises aggressively on home schooling websites, has only 3,000 pupils despite charging fees of between $US 1,000 and US$ 2,000, per semester—a reasonable level in North American terms (Laurel Springs School, 2009).

Home schooling in North America inherits a long tradition of thought and a growing body of research. An early classic was Samuel Griswold's *Fireside Education* (1838). A chapter entitled 'Provision of Providence that the Controlling Lessons of Life Shall be Given by Parents' included the passage: 'The seminary is home; the teacher is the parent. What spot on earth so likely to abound in genial influences as the fireside? What schoolmaster so likely to teach with blended wisdom and kindness as the parent?' (Griswold, 1838, p. 64).

Also cited is the work of John Caldell Holt *How Children Learn* (1983) and Raymond, Dennis and Dorothy Moore, *Better Late than Early* (1983). These authors did much to promote the concept of home schooling but stressed that it was neither a response to the badness of schools nor an attempt to bring the school construct into the home. A more radical line of thinking was represented by Ivan Illich's *Deschooling Society* (1971) and Harold Bennett's *No More Public School* (1972). Illich argued that schooling undermined the potential of working-class communities and wanted to replace it with a learning web through which children could access education from a variety of sources.

The notion that schooling needs radical change is now on the agenda again. In his *Reclaiming Education* (2000) Tooley summarizes proposals put forward in the UK at the end of the 1990s in four books by what he calls 'millennial' authors. These were Melanie Phillips, *All Must Have Prizes*; George Walden, *We Should Know Better*; Tom Bentley, *Learning Beyond the Classroom*; and Michael Barber, *The Learning Game*. Tooley finds some merit in all their proposals but argues that their common weakness is to suppose that they can be introduced by tinkering with a state-run school system. For Tooley: 'If we want to promote a learning society…then we don't need the engines of government to steer us on that course. The wind is already blowing in the desired direction, simply by virtue of us being in human society. If government would get out of the way, then we could really set sail unhindered' (2000, p. 208).

We pick up three of these proposals in chapter 4, not to comment on their merits but to show that an open school can facilitate reforms and provide a safety net if they go wrong.

Centre National d'Enseignement à Distance (CNED), France (Mega-School)

History

CNED is one of the older open schools (CNED, 2008a). It was created in 1939 as a small correspondence and radio school for children who were evacuated from French cities at the beginning of World War II. At first it was seen as a provisional, stopgap measure to cope with a sharp increase in the number of secondary pupils at a time when many teachers had been drafted into the armed forces. Later in the war the organization was split in two, one part serving occupied France from Paris, the other serving Vichy France from Clermont-Ferrand. By the end of the war there were some 1,500 enrolments.

As France faced the challenge of reconstruction after the War, this provisional educational establishment became even more necessary and its mandate was extended. However, either because of its origins as an emergency wartime measure, or because of the poor image that often dogs distance learning, CNED was perceived by the press at the time as a 'strange establishment' and a 'silent school'. In 1950 a government budget review even proposed closing it, but Jacques Barraud, CNED's director, fought successfully for its continuation using the arguments of social justice and low cost. Many children and young adults simply could not attend regular schools and the annual cost of a CNED student to the public purse was about one-third that of the conventional secondary schools.

Despite the low cost (1 teacher per 92 pupils) there was strong bonding between teachers and students even though they never met. One pupil remarked that 'an exceptional current of humanity united students and markers'. A student in prison wrote: 'I know nothing of you, you know little of me. I don't know your name and for you I'm just an anonymous pupil. But you have become part of my life, not just as a teacher but as a friend—a friend that I like to meet in a correction in red ink' (CNED, 2008a, p. 21).

Because it was clearly serving important needs, CNED's status became increasingly permanent and it was asked to offer additional programmes. In 1949 it introduced technical and vocational courses and programmes of teacher education. Teaching for the primary years was added in 1951. As a result, enrolments climbed rapidly during the 1950s, reaching 25,000 by 1958 and making it France's largest school. Even this was only a beginning. By 1980 CNED was reaching nearly 200,000 students, a figure that doubled to 400,000 by 2000. Since its beginnings 70 years ago CNED has enrolled some 10 million students in programmes at all levels (CNED, 2008a, p. 5).

Status

CNED is a state institution under the authority of the Ministry of Education. It has eight institutes with national responsibility for particular programmes located in Grenoble, Lille, Lyon, Poitiers Rennes, Rouen, Toulouse and Vanves. The headquarters is also located in Poitiers in modern buildings at the Futuroscope, which include a satellite video transmission and production centre and houses CNED's School for Distance Education Engineering. The status of CNED was reinforced in 2009 when it was designated as France's 31st 'Académie'—the Online Academy (*Le Figaro*, 2009) and a decree was passed reinforcing its status as France's official public distance teaching institution for primary and secondary school level (JORF, 2009).

Programmes

CNED offers a huge range of programmes (CNED, 2008b). Indeed, a recent consultancy on the modernisation of the organization (see p. 143) recommended that CNED prune back its offerings in order to present a sharper market image by focusing on its most legitimate and viable programmes.

At the secondary level CNED offers the following programmes:

- The three years of junior secondary schooling (*collège*) and courses at the senior secondary level that aim to prepare pupils for the various (general, technical, professional) *baccalauréat* school leaving examinations. These programmes are available free to all pupils who cannot attend a normal school, provided they are less than 16 years old or did not interrupt their school studies for more than one year. Others can enrol with the permission of the *inspecteur d'académie*. However, all courses (primary and secondary) are available, as full class courses or selected subjects, for pupils prepared to pay fees.

- Open summer courses to help pupils prepare for the next year of study.
- Refresher courses in languages, science, mathematics, etc.
- Remedial courses for adults.
- Professional diplomas.

Enrolments

CNED's enrolments at secondary level show a downward but stabilising trend. At junior and senior secondary levels the total enrolments in 2007 were 29,507 and 54,564 respectively, representing just over three-quarters of the figures for 2000 in each case. Within these figures, however, the trend in the senior secondary vocational stream (*lycée professionnel*) is upwards, enrolments having risen by 20% from their 2000 level to reach 15,076 in 2007 (CNED, 2008c, p. 60).

The Teaching-Learning System

Like all good distance education systems CNED tries to match its services to individual needs, enabling the student to be an independent learner while providing academic support and counselling as needed, as well as the possibility of face-to-face sessions.

Print, video, DVDs and CDs are the principal independent learning media. These are backed by various online services: virtual classes; electronic resources; tutorials (written or oral) and assignment marking; and language tests.

At 500 centres, run by partner organizations across France, students can buy a range of services, including coaching in study and examination skills, self-assessment and practical work.

Results

CNED does not make its own awards but prepares pupils for the national *baccalauréat* examination. CNED has a 45% success rate in these examinations, which is below Ministry of Education targets for the country as a whole. However, given the open admission policy, the challenge of distance learning and the difficult life situations of many of the pupils this is a respectable figure. As is frequently found in distance education, significant numbers drop out before reaching the examination.

Financial and Staffing

CNED's overall operating budget was €105m in 2007–2008. Student fees, which have to be approved by the Ministry of Education for programmes teaching to national curricula, represented about half of its revenues. Under the new legislation there will be three fee categories:

- no fee for pupils admitted to enrol as school public service pupils;
- pupils taking school level courses on a voluntary basis will pay a subsidised fee;
- fees for other courses will be set at a commercial level.

Staff, in full-time equivalents, numbered 2,641.

Opportunities and Challenges

See p. 143 for a general account of the strategic development of CNED. In its school programmes the main challenge is to adapt to the reforms being introduced in the national secondary curriculum. These reforms place more emphasis on group work and individual projects, which present special, but not insuperable, challenges for CNED.

Telesecundaria, Mexico (Mega-School)

Context and History

Mexico, with a population of 110 million, is one of the 'E9' high population developing countries identified by UNESCO and the international community for special help in achieving EFA. Although Mexico City is one of the world's largest urban agglomerations, much of the country's population lives in 150,000 communities spread throughout the national territory of nearly 2 million square kilometres. One hundred thousand of these communities have populations of less than 100, making them very difficult to serve with conventional secondary schools.

Although the average Mexican adult has 7.2 years of schooling, compulsory schooling is now 10 years and the gross enrolment ratio at the secondary level is 60%. Telesecundaria, which has been in existence for over 40 years, is a mega-school with an enrolment of over one million pupils. Intended as a complement to the conventional system, it was established in 1968 to bring schooling at the junior secondary level, grades 7–9, to communities that were not served by conventional secondary schools. Today it caters to 22% of Mexico's pupils at that level reaching some 17,000 Telesecundaria schools and 1.2 million pupils with 54,000 teachers and para-teachers. Telesecundaria is run directly by the Federal Ministry of Education and in 1999 there were more Telesecundarias than general and technical secondary schools combined (Estrada, 2003).

The Teaching-Learning System

The teaching-learning system is based on the large scale use of broadcast television, delivered since 1994 by the EDUSAT satellite on six channels. Originally the government retained 5% of the satellite capacity for state use, particularly education, but this provision was not retained when telecommunications were deregulated in the 1990s. This has not directly affected the TV delivery for Telesecundaria, but it has created high prices for bandwidth that are a brake on the use of the Internet in the schools.

Some 4,000 TV programmes are broadcast every year, and daily schedules usually include two broadcasts of the same programme because some schools function in the morning and some in the afternoon. Telesecundaria is a nice example of a self-improving and cost-effective use of technology that uses the principles of division of labour and specialisation in an effective way.

The TV programmes have evolved from the original talking-head style to be much more interactive as teachers have become more involved in their design. Each class consists of a 15–20-minute TV programme followed by 40 minutes of discussion with the teacher or para-teacher. The programmes are broadcast live or can be recorded where schools have the equipment.

Telesecundaria is a single-classroom school for all three years of the cycle. In any particular hour the students of one year are watching the TV broadcast, those of another are being tutored and taught directly by the teacher, while the third group are working on assignments. This schedule rotates in accordance with the broadcast schedule.

An important element of the system's cost-effectiveness is that it only requires one teacher per three-grade classroom and the programmes encourage the teachers to adapt them to their own instructional style. The content delivered through the broadcasts and the supporting material provided make up for the disciplinary expertise of the eight or nine additional teachers per grade who would be present in the conventional schools (UNESCO, 2005c).

The programmes follow the national curriculum for the junior secondary school level and are supported by three main didactic aids:

- The *Learning Guide*, a textbook for pupils covering the content of the course and its evaluation.
- The *Book of Basic Concepts* is a thematic encyclopaedia where the pupil can find information given during the TV sessions.
- The *Didactic Guide* is book for teachers to help them plan and facilitate the learning process.

Since the early 1990s an important secondary objective of Telesecundaria is intergenerational learning and community education and action. The aim was to link the community around the teaching method so as to involve it in the organization and management of the school and encourage the pupils to carry out community activities. Telesecundaria is building on the possibility of communities producing their own material, extending the concept of learning beyond the classroom.

Effectiveness

Telesecundaria's approach is well received by the pupils. Research by Estrada (2003) reports that: 'Students found that televised classes present the topic of the class and provide a clear explanation and source of information on that topic. When the TV programme is shown at the beginning of the class session the students value it highly...Students see the book of basic concepts as a permanent reference—one that is often used at home'.

The complementarity of the three key elements of the learning system: television, teacher and *Book of Basic Concepts* appears to be effective: 'the advantages the students attribute to the complementarity of the mediators of their learning, and the comparisons they make with other types of secondary schools, imply that they value Telesecundaria highly, have a feeling of belonging, and identify with Telesecundaria'.

Interestingly, the students also find it an advantage to have only one teacher per grade because it allows for a 'more personal and trustful relationship with the teacher in addition to permitting greater interaction among students'. Estrada (2003) concludes: 'when it functions consistently (Telesecundaria) permits scholastic achievement equivalent to that of other types of secondary schools, in addition to generating student confidence about learning and a feeling of identity with the school'. However, there is insufficient published data to allow rigorous comparisons of Telesecundaria's outcomes with those of the other junior secondary schools.

Telesecundaria is cost effective. It has a high pass rate of 93% (UNESCO, 2001b). Because the aim was to reach areas where conventional schools would be costly, the government did not aim to develop a system that was less expensive than conventional schooling (Perraton, 2000, p. 187). However, given the scale at which it operates, Telesecundaria's cost per student in 1997, at $562 per student, was 32% lower than the cost of the alternative (2000, pp. 126–127).

Altogether Telesecundaria appears to be a good example of the use of technology to increase access to quality secondary education and reduce costs at the same time. Indeed, the agreement of the Mexican government with the ministers of education of the Central American countries of Costa Rica, El Salvador, Guatemala, Honduras and Panama to create Telesecundarias in those countries confirms this view. These countries select and adapt Telesecundaria materials as appropriate and broadcast them through their own stations.

Flores and Albarrán (2007) criticise Telesecundaria for not going far enough and for using the technology badly by simply dressing up old ways of teaching in new clothes. They argue that since Telesecundaria already uses technology it could be an excellent vehicle for bringing Mexico into the era of the knowledge society, but unfortunately there is too big a gap between promise and practice. They conclude that Telesecundaria is stuck in a traditional teaching paradigm instead of cultivating autonomous learners who can teach themselves and construct their own knowledge.

Telesecundaria may also be stuck in a technological rut because the TV infrastructure and equipment are not being updated. Neither it nor the conventional schools are able to take advantage of the Internet, partly because of cost but also because of the government's commitment to a national project, *Enciclomedia*, that puts local multi-media content on PCs without Internet connections. As of this writing, however, new programmes are being field-tested and prepared for deployment.

A more robust judgment was made in an article by Laura Poy Solano (2008) in *La Jornada* newspaper in the year of Telesecundaria's 40th anniversary. On the basis of an evaluation report and interviews with those who founded Telesecundaria, she claimed that Telesecundaria was undergoing a profound crisis caused by underfunding by the government and the stranglehold of the teachers' unions on the organization. She alleged that officials in the Ministry of Education regarded Telesecundaria as an 'ugly duckling' despite its major contribution to extending secondary education in Mexico and the attempts to emulate it in other countries.

National Institute of Open Schooling (NIOS), India (Mega-School)

National Context

With its population of over 1.1 billion and a median age of 24 years, India's progress is a crucial determinant of the success of the global EFA campaign. Since 2001, with the launching of the *Sarva Shiksha Abhiyan* (Education for All) initiative (Government of India, 2009), India has made rapid progress towards universal primary education. The number of out-of-school children decreased from 25 million in 2003 to an estimated 9.6 million in 2007 (World Bank, 2009). Most of those still not enrolled are from marginalised social groups. The challenge now is to reach the millions not yet enrolled and to improve quality. The problem of teacher absenteeism and the other quality challenges described on p. 27 are particularly serious in India.

India now has the major challenge of expanding secondary education, currently accessed by fewer than 40% of adolescents. For this purpose it has launched a campaign for universal secondary education (*Rashtriya Madhyamik Shiksha Abhiyan*). India will be the world's most important test case for expanding schooling at secondary level. Given the capacity challenge, the Central Advisory Board for Education has suggested that 15% of the secondary population be catered for through open schooling.

In addition to expanding capacity, curriculum and teaching practices need upgrading to impart more relevant skills, such as learning to learn, and critical and independent thinking. India is a striking example of the need for students to engage in learning that is more self-directed. Just as importantly, more vocational education is required to prepare youth adequately for current jobs. This would benefit from setting common standards for training and defining goals that ensure learning in fields where there are employment opportunities.

We reported in chapter 2 on the large but relatively unacknowledged role that private education plays in both primary and secondary schooling for the poorer sections of society in India. Any expansion policy needs to recognise and build on this reality as well as make the public system more accountable to parents.

Institutional History and Status

The origins of NIOS go back to 1979 and a desire to introduce more flexibility into the secondary education system. The 1986 National Education Policy proposed that open learning facilities be phased in all over the country and in pursuance of this policy the National Open School was established as an autonomous organization in 1989. It was vested with the authority to 'register, examine and certify students up to pre-degree level courses' (Pant, 2009, p. 111).

In 2002 the organization was re-named the National Institute of Open Schooling and became an apex body for open and distance learning with responsibility for facilitating the development of a network of state open schools alongside its own teaching operations. NIOS has supported 16 states in establishing open schools—three of them in 2008—with the remaining 13 states being encouraged to follow suit. The 10 state open schools created before 2008 enrol around 1 million students between them (see Table 4.1). NIOS itself has a cumulative enrolment over the previous four years of 1.5 million students at the secondary and senior secondary levels and it enrolled over 350,000 new students in 2007–08. A National Consortium for Open Schooling with coordination and clearing-house functions has its secretariat at NIOS.

The legal and regulatory framework of NIOS is provided by the Memorandum of the National Open School Society. It follows the general rules of the Government of India for the terms and conditions of service of staff. The General Body of the National Open School, which is the senior policy instance, is chaired by the Minister of Human Resource Development and includes senior representatives from government and other bodies. An Executive Board oversees operations.

NIOS organizes its work through five departments, 11 regional centres and some 3,260 study centres located in accredited institutions of various kinds. One-third of these study centres specialise in vocational education.

NIOS itself has only 250 staff members, which must make it one of the world's most efficient educational institutions, although there are, of course, many other people contracted to the regional centres and accredited institutions to perform various tasks. In this sense NIOS sees itself as a facilitative institution that makes it possible for much of the work to be done elsewhere. This is a corollary of its other characteristic as a linked institution, working with partners wherever possible and having the role of apex body in relation to the state open schools.

Curriculum

NIOS has developed its own curriculum to serve its clientele, drawing on the National Policy on Education and responding to perceived needs. It offers secondary, senior secondary and vocational education courses. The secondary course is a composite equivalent to grades IX and X in conventional schools, offering 26 subjects (of which 17 are languages). There is a similar composite of grades XI and XII at senior secondary level with 19 subjects (three languages). Students must pass five subjects, including up to a maximum of two languages. They may opt for two additional subjects.

NIOS is more advanced than other open schools in developing its curriculum in vocational education, where it offers 86 courses. To the extent possible it collaborates with leading organizations in the relevant sector in developing and delivering these subjects. Students at the secondary level may combine one from a list of 10 vocational subjects (20 at senior secondary) with their regular curriculum and have the pass credit transferred into their academic programme. Given its commitment to openness, NIOS is particularly concerned to provide more vocational education related to the rehabilitation of people with disabilities.

In the interests of the concurrent development of hand, head and heart, NIOS is now beginning to offer life-enrichment courses such as Music, Painting, Art and Yoga. More generally, NIOS is very concerned to ensure that its curriculum gives appropriate place to the development of life skills and a focus on the world of work, hence its decision to enable students to combine vocational and academic courses in their studies.

Assessment and Results

In each course NIOS offers students the opportunity to submit three assignments for marking by tutors, one of which is compulsory. Summative assessment is by public examination at the end of each course. Whereas the conventional schooling system conducts one examination per year, NIOS offers its examinations twice annually in 1,800 examination centres around the country. It has also developed a computer-based system offering examinations on demand, supervised by closed-circuit television, which 'is experiencing tremendous uptake'. However, this is not yet available in all the regional centres, let alone the thousands of study centres (Pant, 2009, p. 121). A student has nine chances in five years to pass the required number of subjects. More than 400,000 students take NIOS public examinations each year, which requires a highly efficient examination system. NIOS uses the services of banks, magistrates and state boards of education to ensure the security of the system.

NIOS' overall pass rates are 58% at the secondary level and 60% at the senior secondary level. The base for calculating pass rates is all students admitted, so drop-outs are reported as failures. These pass rates are comparable to those of India's other school examinations boards.

Clientele

After reviewing six case studies of open schools, Abrioux noted that NIOS, despite being the largest open school, was also the most open and flexible in its treatment of students (Abrioux, 2009, p. 15). Pant (2009, p. 116) states that: 'Open School is for all learners in society, regardless of any distinction. In fact, Open School offers the promise of becoming the mainstream learning system, like present-day conventional schools, at some point of time in the future'. The majority of NIOS students are in the 14- to 25-year-old age range.

NIOS' commitment to openness is expressed in the following ways:

- No upper age limit (some students are in their 80s).
- Year-round admission to vocational courses and self pacing.
- Free choice within the curriculum (apart from the language requirement).
- Credit accumulation over five years and credit transfer with some Boards.
- Flexibility in examination dates and provision for on-demand examination.

Managing this flexibility relies on having complex yet efficient management information systems, an area of strength for NIOS. For example, some 30% of students use an online enrolment facility introduced in 2008, a remarkably high figure given the nature of the student body. Soon students will be able to use this facility through the common service centres that India is putting into all of its 600,000 villages.

Ferreira (2009, p. 195) commented: 'it is not coincidental that NIOS, the largest open school in the world, is not only the most autonomous of our case studies but also the most open in terms of academic regulations (e.g. time to completion, examination-sitting options, self-pacing) and alternative vocational curriculum'.

Funding and Fees

NIOS is to a large extent self-funding. It collects one-time admission fees (making a substantial reduction for disadvantaged students) and examination fees from students that constitute some 85% of its income. Government funds account for only 8%–15% and there are some miscellaneous revenues from sales of publications, interest and so on.

Course Development

NIOS develops self-learning material using a team approach as well as calling on individual writers and in-house staff. The systematic process employed involves needs analysis, the study of curricula of other boards of education, the development of general and subject specific approaches, the development of curriculum and learning outcomes, the formation of the course team, the development of learning material, support material and audio-visual aids, and production of the material. A comprehensive style guide ensures consistency of formats and layout across the institution. Staff training in issues of quality assurance is also vital and self-instructional packages for this purpose are being developed.

Only one set of materials is produced for each subject, although NIOS realises that given India's diversity it would be desirable to have several versions. This would, however, be very expensive and the state open schools are there to cater more closely to local needs. Since NIOS is a pioneer in the teaching of vocational subjects through open schooling, the development of a national vocational qualifications framework, which is now under consideration, would be very helpful.

Course Delivery and Student Support

The basis of the NIOS system is independent study of self-instructional materials. However, all learners, and especially those attracted to NIOS, need help and guidance from time to time. To provide this NIOS conducts personal contact programmes of 30 hours (35 for science subjects) at the study centres on weekends, holidays and at convenient times during the week. Students must attend at least half of these diagnostic and remedial sessions for their particular course. Considerably more contact is required for some of the vocational courses (e.g. 600 hours in each of the two components of the Diploma Course in Radiography).

In addition to the support available from academic facilitators at these personal contact programmes, NIOS operates a 24/7 call centre at headquarters and also plans to put call centres in its regional centres. Government aims to provide Internet and broadband connectivity to all NIOS study centres by 2012.

To enable students and their parents to keep track of progress, a single-window information system on the NIOS website provides complete information about each learner.

Quality

For a developing country NIOS' systems for administration and student support are impressively rich in the use of ICT. Ferreira (2009, p. 194) notes that the use of ICT tends to centralize student support, but NIOS considers that its study centres will remain the most important sites for the teaching, training and guidance of students for many years to come (Pant, 2009, p. 125). Therefore, improving the quality of the infrastructure and personnel at these centres is the main challenge to quality assurance. Regional academic facilitators are required by contract to visit each study centre (accredited institution) seven times during each academic session and NIOS personnel also conduct inspections. The independent nature of the very diverse accredited institutions, which helps to make NIOS so efficient, does pose a challenge for consistency of practice and quality assurance.

NIOS also monitors its huge examination system very closely and examination answers are sampled as a check to the suitability of treatment of topics in the study materials.

Efficiency, Synergy and Future Prospects

In 2007 the Commonwealth of Learning sponsored a comparative study of the costs and effectiveness of NIOS and the Namibian College of Open Learning (NAMCOL). This showed that between 2002 and 2006 costs per student at NIOS were on average 12.4 times lower than those of the two conventional secondary school systems to which they were compared (Rumble & Koul, 2007, p. 128).

The study also reached the conclusion that with the passage of time NIOS' cost advantage will become even greater. This is essentially due to the intrinsic nature of technology-mediated education described in chapter 3. Systems like NIOS have the possibility of continuing to increase their economies of scale and the inflation of staff costs has much less impact than in conventional systems since they are a small proportion of the total cost of open school operations. This is an important finding, which supports the basis tenet of this book that open schooling has an increasingly important role to play in achieving education for all at the secondary level.

NIOS is now becoming active in teacher education, the second major theme of this book. Some 60% of primary teachers in north India are untrained and will soon be obliged to obtain the necessary qualification to keep their jobs. There are plans for IGNOU, the state open universities and NIOS to work together to provide training to this very large group.

General Implications

Open schooling has much to learn from the example of NIOS. Already a very large system, it is still experiencing 'moderate scaled increases in enrolment of about 10% a year' (Pant, 2009, p. 126), although it has taken the decision to put more energy into its role as an apex organization and foster the growth of the state open schools to handle much of the expansion. Being regional in nature the state open schools are, in theory at least, closer to the clientele.

One conclusion we can draw from the NIOS experience is that giving an open school a good degree of autonomy fosters a more innovative, performing and dynamic institution than controlling it tightly from the ministry of education.

Another is that even poor and disadvantaged students are eager to make use of ICT systems that enhance their studies or make them more convenient.

SLTP Terbuka (Open Junior Secondary School), Indonesia (Mega-School)

National Context

Indonesia's territory of 2 million sq. km. is an archipelago of over 17,000 islands with a population of nearly 250 million people. It has a high level of regional, cultural and linguistic diversity with 300 ethnic groups, 583 languages and 200 dialects spread over the islands. This dispersion and complexity often make conventional educational solutions impracticable, so there have been extensive distance education programmes to offer alternative learning pathways to those who simply cannot attend school, either because there are insufficient places or because they live in remote areas. In 2002 gross enrolment rates were 93% in primary school, 65% in junior secondary and 42% in senior secondary (World Bank, 2007). Indonesia has used distance education programmes both to support the work of regular schools and to create a network of institutions for out-of-school children, principally at junior secondary level. Broadcasting, especially on radio, has been central to much of this work. Indonesia has also used distance education for teacher upgrading, with students numbered in the millions.

Surveys in 1991 and 1993 revealed a wide range of distance education programmes initiated by non-governmental organizations, private institutions and 11 out of 20 ministries (Indonesian Distance Learning Network (IDLN), 1999b, p. 5). Sixty-nine of these programmes catered for the pre-university level. To avoid duplication of effort and introduce a more co-ordinated, cross-sectoral approach to the implementation of distance education programmes, the UNDP and the Ministry of Education and Culture established the Indonesian Distance Learning Network in 1993 as a central co-ordinating body for distance education, providing information services and promoting research and the pooling of resources (UNESCO, 2001b).

Distance Learning at the Secondary Level

In the context of our proposal (see chapter 4) that governments should give open schooling a central and integrative role in the drive to achieve universal basic education, Indonesia is a particularly interesting case study. It is an example of an Asian model of open schooling, with parallels to India (NIOS) and South Korea, which is distinctive because it retains close connections with the regular secondary-school system. As Raza (2004, p. 213) noted: 'In Indonesia, the open schools were being integrated into the main framework for basic education provision...'

Both formal and non-formal routes have been adopted in pursuit of the goal of universal basic education. The Packet A and B programme and the Open Junior Secondary School (SLTP Terbuka) are large-scale non-formal programmes. They provide both alternative junior secondary systems and also educational opportunities to children who either have no access to primary and/or junior-secondary school or who have dropped out.

The Packet A programme provides education services to out-of-school children from ages 6 to 12 and works on the principle of harnessing available educational resources in the community. It combines print-based, self-instructional materials with face-to-face teaching in learning groups of about 30 pupils who meet about three times a week for two hours in community buildings or local schools. The materials are based on the primary level curriculum and include vocational and community development subjects, such as income generating skills. Eight million pupils were trained nation-wide through Packet A between 1978 and 1992, 60% of them female.

Packet B is a similar programme for junior-secondary level children from 12 to15 years old without adequate school provision, as well as for junior secondary drop-outs or adults who have not acquired a junior-secondary level education. The print-centred modules are designed to be used independently prior to discussion in learning groups of 30–40 people followed by tutorial groups. Tutors, who must be senior-secondary graduates, mark assignments and administer centrally produced tests. 1997 national exam results showed that of 104,826 candidates—40% of them female—95% graduated. Shortcomings identified in a 1998 evaluation included a low general perception of Packet B among parents and the desire for more vocationally oriented courses.

The Indonesian Open Junior Secondary School, SLTP Terbuka—also known as SMP Terbuka (Sadiman & Rahardjo, 1997)—represents a different approach to out-of-school education. In response to unmet demand for places at secondary level, the Indonesian government has created an alternative system for youngsters unable to get into mainstream school. They learn from self-instructional materials used in conjunction with different combinations of low-tech cassettes and broadcasts and various types of student support.

Learners are mainly from poor and rural families whose children have to work and can continue to do so alongside the SLTP Terbuka programme because they are not locked into a fixed timetable. SLTP Terbuka was first developed in 1984 in parallel with the expansion of regular secondary schooling and is considered an integral part of it because children follow the same curriculum and examinations. They attend open-school centres, often attached to regular schools or in a community building in their neighbourhood.

Centrally-produced self-instructional materials are designed to promote individual learning. These are backed up by twice-daily radio and television broadcasting and local student and teacher support groups. The students meet for three hours daily, four to five times a week. Untrained local teacher's aides attend meetings and mark assignments and the students attend a weekly three-hour session with subject specialists at the base school. This provides about 15–18 contact hours of supervised study per week, which contrasts with the 27 hours of contact in regular schools.

Expansion of the programme speeded up after Indonesia formally adopted a policy of universal basic education in 1994. In 1995 open schools were available in 59 provinces throughout the country with a total enrolment of about 50,000 students. By 1998–99 there were 3,773 open junior schools operating with 376,620 students. SLTP Terbuka aimed to have 13,000 centres and 2.25 million students by 2003–04 (IDLN, 1999a). For those who complete the course the examination results are good. di Gropello (2006) reported that 93% of participants who took the national exam passed, with no significant difference in academic performance between students from the programme and those from traditional schools.

Costs and Efficiency

Although the available data are some years old, they reveal that each of these approaches is highly cost-effective and competitive with the conventional schools. For Packet A the yearly cost for one 30-student group (including materials, tutors and examination) was calculated at 563,000 rupiahs or Rp 18,800 per student. As a comparison, the cost per regular primary school student is Rp 229,770 per year (IDLN, 1999b, pp. 12–13).

The unit cost per student of Packet B students was Rp 111,570. The programme evaluation noted above recommended the free distribution of uniforms, reference material and stationery to motivate these students, resulting in a cost per student Rp 169,988, which is still less than the regular student unit cost (IDLN, 1990b, pp. 27–29). The cost for an SLTP Terbuka student was Rp 293,936.

No detailed cost comparisons with regular secondary schools were available to the UNESCO study (UNESCO, 2001b), but expenditure on SLTP schooling was limited to 60% of the cost of mainstream schools (Perraton, 2000, p. 39). Earlier we reported a general estimate that in developing countries the unit cost of conventional secondary schooling is around 3.5 times the cost of primary. Assuming this is roughly true in Indonesia, then the unit costs of Packet B and SLTP Terbuka students range between 15% and 40% of those of regular secondary students.

SLTP Terbuka schools cut the teaching costs associated with regular schools by using more modest buildings and mobilising four different types of teachers from within the community: (a) a qualified subject specialist from the regular Junior Secondary School, (b) a primary school teacher or local person assigned to manage the learning centre and facilitate student learning, (c) a local person who has a specialised skill and can teach a practical subject, (d) a guidance and counselling teacher.

Botswana College of Distance and Open Learning (BOCODOL)

National Context

A small population of 1.8 million occupies a relatively large landlocked territory of 582,000 square kilometres, making Botswana one of the world's 10 least densely populated countries. The eastern part is more developed than the west, which is home to some nomadic peoples. Botswana's political and economic development is often held up as a model for the African continent, and it had one of the fastest growing economies in the world in the 1990s. However, a study at the end of that decade indicated that HIV/AIDS poses a great threat to continued economic growth in Botswana, mostly because of its impact on the labour force, savings and investment (BIDPA, 2000).

Most people speak Setswana as their indigenous language but English is widely used in government, business and post-primary education. Botswana has a young demographic profile with a median age between 19 and 21. Since 40% of the population is 14 years old or younger, education is especially important. Secondary school enrolment has increased by almost 30% in the past 15 years. Fifty-seven percent of girls and 50% of boys attend secondary school. Literacy rates for youths have increased from 83.3% in 1990 to 89.3% in 2003. Ninety-three percent of female youths in Botswana are literate, a figure that is 25% above the regional average.

Institutional History and Status

Although there is no national policy for open and distance learning, distance education in Botswana goes back half a century. It began with the correspondence courses to train primary school teachers from 1960–65 and an upgrading programme that enrolled 700 of these teachers between 1968 and 1973 (Tau, 2005). This showed the value of distance education and the Botswana Extension College was set up in 1973. This was phased out with the establishment of the Department of Non-Formal Education in 1979, which in turn gave way to BOCODOL.

The 1993 Presidential Commission on Education, which had a special focus on quality, made the recommendation to create BOCODOL. An Act of Parliament was passed in 1998 and BOCODOL became operational when its inaugural governing board was appointed at the end of 2000. BOCODOL was thus able to build on the earlier experience of trying to transform correspondence education into a country-wide system of distance education. It is the only public institution with the mission of delivering school equivalency programmes through ODL. In 2007 BOCODOL was also registered as a tertiary level provider and offered two diploma level courses. It is positioning itself to be an open university by 2016 (Maroba, 2009).

BOCODOL is a parastatal body (i.e. a semi-autonomous public institution run on business lines). To ensure its accountability to the public, the governing board makes an annual report to the Minister of Education, who in turn reports to the National Assembly. Members of its governing board, which includes stakeholders from the public and private sectors, are appointed by the Minister of Education for renewable terms of three years.

Although a self-perpetuating board with its own nominating process for members might be more independent, the current process works satisfactorily and has created a strong organizational model and culture (Tau & Gatsha, 2009). This culture reflects the national democratic ideals of democracy and consultation and since 2002 BOCODOL has gradually implemented an effective performance management system.

Curriculum and Results

BOCODOL offers 11 Junior Certificate level subjects, which account for 16% of enrolment; 11 Senior Secondary Subjects (72%) and adult vocational certificate programmes (12%). Annual enrolment in all programmes is nearly 6,000 and BOCODOL has attracted a cumulative enrolment of over 34,000 since its creation. Its annual enrolment makes up about 4% of the annual intake to the first year of the Junior Certificate programme. At the BGCSE level BOCODOL accounts for some 17% of pupils nationally. Open schooling is an attractive option at senior secondary level because universal secondary schooling goes up to Junior Certificate level (year 3) and there is only a 66% transition rate to year 4 (senior secondary) because of the limited number of senior secondary schools.

BOCODOL teaches to the national curricula, which are rich in national content but also prepare pupils to study internationally where they perform well (Tau & Gatsha, 2009, p. 69). In contrast to the conventional school system, where pupils must take nine Junior Certificate subjects in one sitting in order to be graded, BOCODOL pupils can sit examinations over more than one year. The pass rates of both groups are similar although, for the reason just given, a significant proportion of BOCODOL's results are ungraded. At the Senior Secondary level the results are also similar, and passing grades for BOCODOL completers are over 90%.

In addition to the usual challenges that often cause drop-out in distance learning, the separation of teaching from examinations (which are organized by the Botswana Examinations Council) creates special difficulties for BOCODOL pupils. At the Junior Certificate level the examination fee is roughly the same as the cost of tuition. However, because of the involvement of an overseas body (University of Cambridge, UK) in the examinations for the Botswana General Certificate of Secondary Education (BGCSE), the examination fee is ten times the cost of tuition. Many pupils begin study with BOCODOL in the hope that they will raise the examination fee as they study but fail to do so. Since BOCODOL's establishment, an average of just over one-third of pupils enrolling for the Junior Certificate have obtained it. The figure for the BGCSE is similar.

Clientele

Although BOCODOL expected that most of its pupils would be people who had never had a chance to study for the secondary certificates, today 60% of applicants have had some secondary schooling but want to obtain better grades or qualify for tertiary study. BOCODOL caters to the particular needs of these out-of-school youths and adults by offering vocational courses. Students can take these alongside their school equivalency programmes and a certificate level course in small business management is particularly popular.

BOCODOL admits students on the principle of first come, first served. Its entry requirements are a guide to help those who enrol to complete their programme and acquire the culture of lifelong learning. It gives pupils five years to complete the Junior Certificate programme and four years for the BGCSE—the figures for the conventional schools are three years and two years respectively. A policy for the recognition of prior learning is being developed.

Funding and Fees

BOCODOL is largely funded by the Ministry of Education but has its own policy of generating 15% of its budget through additional income. Funding is loosely based on enrolment projections but does not consider pupil throughput. Although, as a parastatal organization, BOCODOL can manage its own income and assets, fee levels are controlled by the Ministry of Education and set at between US$ 2–4 per subject, well below what the market rate might be.

Course Development

BOCODOL teaches to the curriculum set by the Ministry of Education. To convert this into self-learning materials, it puts together course teams, usually made up of external subject experts whom BOCODOL trains in the preparation of interactive self-learning materials. During this process the BOCODOL programme coordinator decides whether media other than print (e.g. audio-cassettes) should be included. Materials production is outsourced.

Course Delivery and Student Support

To ensure nationwide coverage BOCODOL has five regional centres that organize and administer all the courses offered in 92 learning centres that provide contact with the students. These are in three categories: community study centres in secondary schools with 50 or more BOCODOL learners; satellite learning centres in primary schools with a threshold of 10 learners; and study groups, also in primary schools, with fewer learners. These offer a range of services to provide administrative, academic and counselling support to the students. The community study centres arrange for the marking of assignments from students in the smaller centres.

Serving the remote western part of the country, with its difficult terrain and nomadic peoples, is the biggest challenge for the student support system. This part of the country also has poor ICT infrastructure compared to eastern Botswana. While ICT is used extensively in administration and course development, most course delivery uses print and student support is mostly done face to face. Even where connectivity exists, Internet access costs the equivalent of several US dollars for 30 minutes, so assignment submission and marking is not done electronically.

Quality Issues

BOCODOL takes quality very seriously. Its quality assurance policy is supported by an advisory committee backed by a department with technical expertise. The quality policy is linked to the performance management system, which has created a culture that ensures all staff consider quality assurance as their responsibility. This is supported by a proactive staff development policy that accounts for 2% of the institutional budget. The induction of new employees takes up to a year and all staff are encouraged to take internal and external courses in areas of ODL practice.

BOCODOL has an agreement with its neighbour, the Namibian College of Open Learning (NAMCOL) to do biennial quality audits of each other's operations. BOCODOL's most significant quality challenges are the cost of quality checks in remote areas and an unduly long revision cycle for course materials and, especially, assignments.

Efficiency, Synergy and Future Prospects

BOCODOL's costs per learner are about one-fifth of the cost in conventional schools. However, this does not include the use of conventional school facilities and services for its student support operation. One of BOCODOL's strengths is its synergies with the rest of the national education system that allows that shared use of classrooms, teachers, libraries and materials. Most of BOCODOL's tutors and markers are teachers from the conventional schools.

The major challenge preventing BOCODOL from serving the country better is the fees policy for school equivalency programmes. Because the government-controlled fees are set very low, BOCODOL cannot subsidise all applicants and has to turn many away. A policy that allowed higher fees and supported poorer or disadvantaged pupils with bursaries could be a more efficient use of public funds. By contrast, the vocational stream, which charges fees nearer to the market level, is able to handle the strong demand for the programme.

It also seems perverse that the senior secondary pupils, having paid low fees for their BOCODOL courses, are faced with a challenging fee for the BGCSE examination that deters some of them from getting the qualification they have studied for. A policy of charging higher course fees and using some of the revenue to offset the examination fee would seem more equitable.

A proposal to merge BOCODOL with the distance education activities of the University of Botswana did not attract support. BOCODOL now proposes to set up its own Open School Institute in 2010, to create structures for offering tertiary level distance education, and to introduce teacher education (Maroba, 2009).

General Implications

We suggest in this book that an open schooling system can play an important synergistic role in helping the whole of a national education system to achieve education for all cost effectively. Botswana seems well on the way to this situation in both principle and practice. BOCODOL is thoroughly embedded in the national education system. Its leadership would like to see open learning extended by encouraging private providers and helping conventional secondary schools to become dual-mode schools, using BOCODOL study materials for their open schooling operations (Tau & Gatsha, 2009, p. 81). If BOCODOL does introduce tertiary programmes, the long prior existence of the open schooling programme should ensure that it is not then seen as the poor relation of the tertiary level offerings.

Namibian College of Open Learning (NAMCOL) (Mega-School)

National Context

Namibia has a population of 2 million people in a large territory of 824,300 square kilometres. Two-thirds of the population lives in the rural areas, particularly the northern part of the country. Although it is classified as a middle-income country, Namibia's considerable inequalities in income distribution give it one world's highest Gini coefficients. By 2006 Namibia had achieved a net enrolment ratio of 92% in primary education. However, the school population at secondary level is less than 40% of the primary enrolments, making Namibia a good example of the challenge of scaling up secondary education.

Institutional History and Status

NAMCOL was established by an Act of Parliament in 1997 to offer secondary education to those wishing to study for the Junior Secondary Certificate (3rd year of the junior secondary phase) and the Senior Secondary Certificate (the exit level for secondary school). The Act also enjoins NAMCOL to offer training programmes to serve national needs. With 28,000 pupils annually it is Namibia's largest educational institution and accounts for 40% of the country's secondary pupils. NAMCOL has special political resonance because of its historic association with offering of distance education courses to Namibian refugees in Angola and Zambia in pre-independence days. The Act mandates NAMCOL to 'contribute towards the social and economic development of Namibia by upgrading the educational levels of adults and out-of-school youth through programmes of open learning' (Murangi, 2009, p. 87).

Unlike the rest of the Namibian public school system, which is run directly by the Ministry of Education, NAMCOL is a statutory entity with a governing board whose members represent difference sectors of society and are appointed by the Minister of Education. However, the Ministry provides most of the funds for NAMCOL and decides on appointments at the level of deputy director and above.

NAMCOL is better documented than most open schools. Murangi (2009) has given a recent account of its operations and Rumble and Koul (2007) performed a comparative evaluation of the cost-effectiveness of NAMCOL and India's National Institute for Open Schooling (NIOS).

Curriculum and Results

NAMCOL courses are mapped onto the national curriculum and prepare students for the Junior and Senior Secondary Certificate examinations of the National Examinations, Assessment and Certification Board. Although NAMCOL is represented on the various bodies and panels that develop and update the schools curriculum, the three-year revision cycle followed by the National Institute for Educational Development can cause NAMCOL to be left with quantities of out-of-date study materials that can no longer be issued to learners.

NAMCOL students write the same examinations as their counterparts in the conventional system at the same time. In general NAMCOL's part-time learners perform less well in these examinations than the full-time pupils from the other schools. Performance has, however, been improving significantly. In 2007 pass rates were 91% and 83% for grades 10 and 12 respectively, compared to figures of 76% and 67% in 1998. The 2007 figures for full-time candidates were 94% and 93% for grades 10 and 12 respectively. The comparisons look less rosy when examination grades are compared. At Grade 10, 22% of full-time candidates achieved grade C or above compared to 9% of part-time candidates. For Grade 12, the figures were 21% and 9% respectively.

Clearly, a major task for NAMCOL is to improve the grades of its students, since their performance in these examinations determines their access to employment or further study. Given that NAMCOL draws its student body from those who have achieved least success at school and therefore have low self-esteem this is a real challenge.

Clientele

NAMCOL's clientele is made up of out-of-school youth and adults. It is a mega-school with an enrolment of just over 28,000 in 2007. Many of its students have already studied in conventional schools without completing their courses. Whereas most pupils in the conventional secondary school system fall into the 15- to 18-year-old age bracket with almost a 50/50 split between males and females, 95% of NAMCOL's students are in the 18- to 34-year-old age bracket and 65% of them are female. Enrolments have climbed steadily over the last decade but are now flattening out. The overwhelming majority of students (99%) are enrolled in the secondary school programmes. In 2008 only 375 learners opted for its professional and vocational programmes that include post-secondary courses in community development, youth work and local government. Murangi (2009, p. 106) argues that the government should fund NAMCOL to expand its courses in technical and vocational education because at present these have to be cross-subsidised from the grant for the academic curriculum.

Perhaps surprisingly, given the age bracket in which they fall, only 1% of NAMCOL's learners is engaged in paid jobs or has other sources of income. Although a scholarship fund has recently been introduced, there are worries that the cost of study deters some potential students. Greater constraints on NAMCOL's openness are, however, the timing and entry requirements of the secondary examinations for which the students are being prepared (Murangi, 2009, p. 95).

Funding and Fees

When NAMCOL was established a provision of its state funding was that it should not be more expensive to provide secondary education through NAMCOL than through the conventional system. This has proved to be the case and today the government grant is set at 65% that of a conventional school learner. Funding is done on a per course basis and calculated on the enrolments in the previous year. There has been no attempt to make part of the funding conditional on successful completion of courses by students. The government also provides funds for capital expenditures, mainly for the construction of regional facilities since state-owned or rented facilities are used where available. Although NAMCOL is legally exempted from paying for school facilities made available outside normal school hours, it has an agreement with the schools that it uses to contribute to their operating costs.

NAMCOL charges its secondary level students compulsory learner fees of 20% of the course cost. This represents a higher fee than the voluntary contribution to the school development fund required in conventional schools, but a study showed that if the cost of books, uniforms and boarding is taken into consideration, full-time secondary education is more expensive than the NAMCOL fees (Du Vivier, 2007).

Course Development

Print remains NAMCOL's primary teaching medium although other media are being gradually introduced. The creation of NOLNET, the Namibian Open

Learning Network, as a consortium to assist with the development of ODL generally, is helping with capacity building for the introduction of ICT. NAMCOL has a systematic course development process, aimed most often at creating self-contained study guides that do not require accompanying textbooks. Teachers from the conventional schools are recruited on a part-time basis as members of the teams that develop these materials. Where possible the materials are co-published with commercial publishers.

Given the synergistic role for open schools that we promote in this book, an encouraging sign is the use of NAMCOL's materials by conventional schools. They have been approved for use by the National Institute for Educational Development and are used extensively by tutors in tuition centres. It is likely that when open educational resources (OER) are produced by NAMCOL in the context of the global project described in chapter 4, such use will increase further.

NAMCOL has been charged with managing a national educational radio project on behalf of the Ministry of Education and other publicly-funded ODL providers. This project is making good headway.

Course Delivery and Student Support

NAMCOL has a highly decentralized and locally rooted student support system. It uses a blended-learning approach that combines the self-instructional materials with face-to-face support. It offers students two study modes. Eighty percent opt for the Contact Open Mode, which gives access to weekly tutorials. The rest take the Non-Contact Open Mode which offers vacation workshops twice a year.

To ensure a national footprint NAMCOL divides the country into four regions, which together oversee more than 100 tutorial centres. Each of these has a centre management committee, similar to a school board in the conventional system, which includes representatives from learner, tutor and parent communities. This provides the main opportunity for students to play a role in the business of NAMCOL since travel costs, and the relatively short time that students study with NAMCOL (usually one year) make it difficult for the students to take up their place on NAMCOL's governing board.

Quality Issues

NAMCOL claims that quality is a process rather than a fixed set of criteria and that its quality management system is integrated into the strategic management process. Extensive consultation in the development of quality assurance policies has created a quality culture and a belief among staff that 'quality assurance measures will give the learner a fair and reasonable opportunity to achieve the required academic standards'. There are quality assurance teams in the various divisions and quality assurance is part of the performance management system, although NAMCOL finds, as do most organizations, that it is difficult to apply the system consistently (Murangi, 2009, p. 103).

NAMCOL also has an agreement with BOCODOL in neighbouring Botswana for the institutions to conduct quality audits on each other using common criteria. This has been done twice for each institution.

Efficiency, Synergy and Future Prospects

Rumble and Koul (2007) made a thorough comparative study of the costs of NAMCOL and the conventional school system. They concluded that NAMCOL had an efficiency rating per course enrolment of 0.994 at the Junior Certificate level and 0.356 at the Senior Certificate level respectively. This means that NAM-COL operates at about the same cost as conventional schooling at the Junior level but is substantially less expensive at the Senior level. The difference occurs primarily because NAMCOL learners do the two-year secondary curriculum (grades 11 and 12) in a single year.

These results mean that NAMCOL does meet the original condition for government funding that it not cost more than conventional provision. However, another study noted that as learner numbers have increased, more courses have been developed or revised and multi-media technology has been used to enhance course delivery, the costs of providing service to learners have almost doubled (Rumble, 2006, pp. 18–28).

A consultancy at the time of NAMCOL's establishment recommended that fees be set at a level that ensured the sustainability of the college (Du Vivier, 1998). NAMCOL has shown that it is scalable but there are still concerns that 'the current fee structure and grant have thus far only enabled the college to provide required services, which is a worrying factor for long-term sustainability for the college' (Murangi, 2009, p. 105). Were NAMCOL able to improve the examination grades of its students and introduce a range of technical and vocational courses that demonstrably helped students to improve their livelihoods, it would be able to charge higher fees.

General Implications

Although NAMCOL is a parastatal body with its own governing board, it remains very subservient to the Ministry of Education and therefore restricted in its ability to engage in its own strategic planning. The whole Namibian education system would benefit if NAMCOL were given more autonomy and encouraged, possibly through changes in legislation and funding arrangements, to extend its curriculum in livelihood-related areas and to increase its synergy with the whole education system. This could be particularly helpful in making high quality curriculum materials available as OER and in facilitating the further expansion of the use of ICT, an area where Namibia is already a leader through School Net Namibia (http://www.schoolnet.na/index.html).

Open College, Papua New Guinea (Mega-School)

National Context

Few countries are more apt candidates for an open school than Papua New Guinea. Its population of 6.25 million, growing at 2.7% annually and with a median age of 19 years, is scattered across a huge and inaccessible territory. Only 15% of the people live in urban areas—although the towns are magnets for internal migration. Moreover the country has 600 languages (800 dialects) and a strong tribal tradition. Literacy among those aged 15 years and over is around 45% overall and less than 40% in rural areas. Youth unemployment is 70% in urban areas with a high degree of disguised unemployment as well (Mannan, 2009, p. 154).

In the education system there is a very sharp drop-off in enrolment at successive levels: the elementary, primary, lower and upper secondary gross enrolment rates are 90%, 62%, 23% and 7% respectively. Another expression of the same reality is that for 3,300 primary schools there are only 170 secondary schools and 140 vocational schools. Furthermore a school-age population of two million in 2008 will grow to 2.3 million by 2015. The national education plan of 2004 proposed using ODL for graduates of grades 8 and 10 who will fail to secure a place in the conventional schools and the Certificate in Tertiary and Community Studies (CTCS) responds to that proposal.

Institutional History and Status

In view of one aim of this book, which is to explore optimal institutional arrangements for open schools, the open school programme of the Open College of the University of Papua New Guinea (UPNG) is a particularly interesting case. In principle it should suffer from a double whammy. First, the Open College is the distance learning arm of a conventional university. Such dual-mode institutions rarely provide fertile ground for distance learning and UPNG is no exception. Second, the Open College also offers tertiary level programmes. Often open school programmes are the poor relation in such circumstances. It is a tribute to the leadership and staff of the Open College that the open school programme, the CTCS, is successful in such an environment.

From 1978 to 2002 UPNG ran an adult matriculation programme to complement secondary schooling by increasing the intake to higher education and to give adults the opportunity to upgrade their education and qualifications. In its 2001 strategic plan UPNG proposed converting this into the CTCS but the University Senate, showing a typical academic attitude towards pre-tertiary programmes, decided to abolish it. Fortunately, it was persuaded to rescind that decision and the CTCS was made the sole responsibility of the Open College, which was created at the same time.

Curriculum and Results

Since UPNG has the power to approve programmes that are accepted nationally, the CTCS programme does not follow the national curriculum in the schools. It aims to:

- give students literacy and numeracy skills in readiness for lifelong learning;
- prepare them for study at the tertiary level; and
- help to upgrade skills for employment or self-employment.

The framework of the CTCS is based on the four pillars of the Delors Report: learning to know, to do, to live together, and to be (UNESCO, 1996). The curriculum includes a combination of vocational and academic courses. To gain the certificate students must complete courses in literacy (3); numeracy (3); life skills; civics and development; and three other courses chosen from a list of 15 academic and vocational courses. This curriculum evolves continuously, particularly in order to develop non-traditional skill-based courses to meet national and regional needs.

The minimum time for completion of these 11 courses is 18 months full-time equivalent. Learner assessment includes both formative and summative components. There are two or three assignments within each course which account for 40% of the final mark and a final examination that constitutes 60% of the overall assessment.

The CTCS programme has a low drop-out rate. In the examination sessions in 2007 and 2008 over 90% of students sat for the examination and pass rates were in the range 69%–73%. There was a normal distribution of passes between the four grades, half achieving A and B; the remainder C and D.

Clientele

The CTCS aims to provide opportunities to a large segment of the population who for some reason or other 'failed to pursue formal studies or have become social liabilities and would like to maximise their life potential' (Mannan, 2009, p. 158). This segment is clearly eager for learning opportunities because annual course enrolment grew from 3,700 in 2003 to nearly 20,000 in 2008. Over the same period the proportion of female students has grown from 40% to 45%. Seventy percent of the students are aged between 19 and 25 years old with only 15% over 31 years old.

Funding and Fees

The funding model for the CTCS and the Open College illustrates the undesirability of nesting an open school—or any distance learning programme—within a university whose main priority is classroom teaching. The Open College is a self-financing unit that meets its operational expenses through fees. UPNG denied the Open College any part of the University's government funding. Furthermore, UPNG takes 60% of the fees raised by the Open College's tertiary programmes and distributes them to the faculties (which do play a role in developing the programmes at that level). Because the Open College does not draw on the faculties for the CTCS programme it was supposed to receive all the fee income from this programme—but again funds are diverted to cover shortfalls elsewhere in UPNG. The Open College is not represented on the UPNG's planning and resource committee despite being a major source of the University's income.

Despite the UPNG's cynical treatment of the CTCS programme—and the Open College generally—as a milch cow, the UPNG Vice-Chancellor was, of course, delighted to travel to London and receive the award when the Open College was recognised for its excellence in ODL by the Commonwealth of Learning in 2008!

Course Development

The Open College follows a systematic instructional design process in developing courses for its unique curriculum. As well as using a multi-skilled team to produce the materials, there is special emphasis on consulting stakeholders to identify the needs and characteristics of the clientele. The aim is to create a well-integrated whole out of the study guide, the reading materials and learning activities that require students to interact with others in their community or workplace.

In commenting on the challenges of curriculum development, Mannan (2009, p. 163) notes that it is sometimes difficult to prepare learner-centred materials that suit both young and adult students. He also notes the challenge of finding part-time course writers and tutors in a country that has a low average level of education.

Course Delivery and Student Support

The course delivery system combines the packages of self-directed, printed learning materials with weekly face-to-face group tutorials at study centres. Some courses are enriched by cassettes and CD-ROM, while counselling is available at the study centres that are part of a network of open campuses and university centres. However, greater use of ICT is thwarted by the inadequacy of bandwidth and poor reliability of the networks in place. Access to computer facilities will remain a challenge for a long time. The Open College is exploring the use of community radio as a way of reaching students.

Being nested in UPNG handicaps the Open College not only in terms of funding and policy but also by obliging it to use a student record system that is not fit for purpose for ODL. Furthermore, because preference is given to on-campus students for data entry, the Open College has to maintain its own records on spreadsheets in order to give timely service to CTCS students.

Quality

Despite the considerable inefficiencies imposed by the host university, which does not have a quality assurance policy, the CTCS programme has evolved a systematic approach to quality assurance that is captured in an operational manual. The involvement of reference groups at various levels ensures a collective approach to good practice. Programmes are reviewed periodically and there are quality committees at both the Open College and UPNG level. A possible quality weakness—although it is shared with classroom instruction—is that the Open College relies on the rigour of its appointment process for tutors and markers, rather than monitoring their marking of admission tests and assignments directly.

Efficiency, Synergy and Future Prospects

The best estimate for the unit cost per CTCS student is around US$ 480. This compares to a unit cost for grades 8–12 in the conventional secondary system of some US$ 825—almost twice as much. There is scope for further efficiency gains from three sources: tightening up operations; greater economies of scale as enrolments increase; and more intensive use of ICT once the initial investment is made. The programme is being gradually scaled up by expanding both its network of study centres and its partnerships with NGOs. Given the enrolment growth and the gap between income and expenditure that makes it possible for UPNG to skim off resources for other uses, the programme is clearly sustainable.

However, for the CTCS programme to be able to contribute as much as it potentially could to the expansion of secondary schooling in Papua New Guinea, it would need to be freed from the current constraints of operating within UPNG. A consultancy commissioned by the government recommended that this option be examined (Abrioux, 2007). Implementing such a recommendation would require government action since UPNG is unlikely willingly to deprive itself of the chance to divert funds from the Open College to campus operations.

General Implications

The success of the CTCS programme owes much to the leadership and staff of the Open College, who manage to serve students effectively despite having to operate in an unfavourable organizational environment. To optimize benefits from open schooling governments should ensure that appropriate institutional arrangements are put in place. We examine this issue in chapter 4.

Contact North, Ontario, Canada

Context and History

From the perspective of the EFA GMRs Canada is considered to have achieved the goals of universal primary and secondary education even if, as in a number of richer countries, increasing drop-out from the secondary system, particularly by boys, is a cause for concern. Most of Canada's huge territory is, however, sparsely populated, posing serious challenges for educational provision. Northern Ontario is a good example. It covers a geographic area of more than 800,000 square kilometers, and its dispersed population, which includes 92 small, remote, Aboriginal and francophone communities, numbers only 900,000.

Contact North (http://www.contactnorth.ca/) was established in 1986 as part of the Ontario government's commitment to bring local access to secondary and post-secondary education to northern residents. Its mandate was: to improve access to formal education and training at the secondary and post-secondary levels; to extend informal education opportunities in Northern Ontario; to collaborate with Aboriginal peoples, francophones and local communities to facilitate response by educational providers (notably those in region) to identified needs; and to support innovation through testing and applied research on new modes of delivery.

With 92 Access Centres located in small, remote, Aboriginal and francophone communities across the region, it partners with 13 educational institutions, including all of Northern Ontario's colleges and universities, thus enabling residents to pursue the offerings of these institutions using three different learning technologies. This gives opportunities to people who live in remote communities to access secondary, college, and university-level programmes, as well as literacy and other training programmes, without having to leave home. It is headquartered in the northern cities of Sudbury and Thunder Bay.

Clientele

Over 23 years Contact North has facilitated 204,322 course registrations representing an estimated 68,000 learners, and it continues to grow rapidly. It targets disadvantaged groups including aboriginals, francophones, people with disabilities and those requiring literacy and basic skills. The 13,000 registrations in 600 synchronous credit and non-credit courses in 2009 represented a 27% increase over the previous year while enrolment in literacy courses, supported from 75 locations across Ontario, grew by over 400%.

Contact North is the only option for 30% of Northern Ontario's adult population (approximately 190,000 residents) to access education and training without having to leave their communities. Approximately 85% of course registrations come from students in communities with less than 100,000 residents. Students have to pay fees to the partner institutions but Contact North provides help with fees in cases of hardship.

It works with district school boards through joint secondary/college pro-grammes and offers orientation and training sessions to instructors at its col-lege, university, and secondary school partners on the effective use of audio conferencing, videoconferencing and eLearning platforms. Contact North also provides managers, distance education staff and faculty at educational partner institutions with access to expert resources on technology in learning, including workshops, seminars and discussion papers.

Teaching and Learning Methods

Unlike the other institutions profiled in this appendix, Contact North uses mainly synchronous technologies. Its real-time learning technology platforms include audio conferencing, videoconferencing and eLearning to 15 educational insti-tutions including Northern Ontario's colleges and universities such as Algoma University, Cambrian College, Canadore College, Collège Boréal, Confedera-tion College, Lakehead University, Laurentian University, Nipissing University, Northern College, Sault College and the University of Sudbury.

It tries to keep the region up to date on new technologies by showcasing new learning technology platforms during special briefings and by working with faculty and instructors at its educational partner institutions to do beta testing in its two FUTURE Labs through its Emerging Technologies programme. It also shares its expertise nationally and internationally with partners in China, Trinidad & Tobago, and South Africa. Most recently it expanded into the rest of Ontario through the establishment of *elearnnetwork.ca*, a distance education network serving learners in eastern and southern Ontario in small, rural and Aboriginal communities through 17 eLearning Centres and a partnership of 34 educational institutions including 19 colleges and 15 universities.

Organization

Contact North is both a technology and a human network. While the technology enables the delivery of the courses at a distance, local staff in the access centres in 92 communities provide personalised and individual support to learners in both of Canada's official languages by assisting them with: exploration of programme and course options; information on financial aid; the registration process at partner educational institutions; personal orientation on the use of the technology; exam invigilation services; and, perhaps most importantly, encouragement and moral support as students complete their programmes and courses on a full or part-time basis.

Staffed by local residents, each access centre is located in rent-free space provided by the community and includes audio conferencing, videoconferenc-ing and eLearning technologies that students use to access courses offered by the partner institutions.

Funding

Funded by the Government of Ontario, Contact North has an annual operating budget of approximately $5.7 million provided through the Ontario Ministry of Training, Colleges and Universities. This annual funding is supplemented by close to $0.5 million in annual sales of services and consultancies.

Future Prospects

After more than 23 years of operation, Contact North can claim to be one of the oldest synchronous distance learning networks. Its development plans include: achieving 20,000 course registrations by 2011; increasing support and expanding access in small, remote, Aboriginal and fly-in communities; expanding literacy and basic skills training throughout Ontario; providing much stronger backing for a range of asynchronous learning delivery platforms for its educational partners; and offering a dramatically expanded training programme for instructors to help them use technology more effectively in adapting curricula for distance delivery rapidly and cost-effectively (Jean-Louis, 2009, personal communication).

Programmes and Mechanisms for Expanding Teacher Supply

Introduction

Chapter 5 explores ways of increasing the supply of trained teachers in support of the EFA agenda. This appendix presents profiles of a variety of pre-service and in-service teacher education programmes in different parts of the world that are arranged in approximate chronological order of their establishment. The first profile, CNED, is a special case for two reasons. CNED is unusual in being both an open school and a teacher education institution. Furthermore, in 2008–09 it undertook a comprehensive strategy review which we report here for its relevance to other well-established programmes. We also describe the TESSA programme, through which a growing number of African institutions are working together as a consortium to develop materials for teacher education as open educational resources. Finally, because the global migration of teachers is a sensitive issue for countries that lose them in large numbers, we have also included a commentary on the Commonwealth Teacher Recruitment Protocol, which is an initiative intended to bring greater predictability to overseas recruitment and to protect the interests of migrating teachers.

Centre National d'Enseignement à Distance (CNED), France

History and Status

CNED operates both open schooling (see p. 110) and teacher education programmes alongside many other offerings. Founded at the outbreak of World War II in 1939, it operated as a correspondence school for primary and secondary pupils for its first decade. In 1949 it added programmes to prepare students for the national examinations giving entry to the teaching profession.

Programmes of Teacher Education

Entry to the teaching profession in France is through national competitive examinations for which CNED offers training courses. It does not administer the examinations. Compared to other countries educational qualifications in France have remarkable stability and longevity. Three of the qualifications for which CNED offered courses in 1949 are still available today: the CAPES, the CAPET and the Agrégation. A number of other qualifications have been added as school curricula have diversified and support functions (e.g. libraries, documentation, archives) have become more important. A new qualification for primary teaching is now CNED's most successful course.

Enrolments

CNED's enrolments in teacher education show a steady downward trend, having fallen increasingly rapidly from 73,000 in 2000 to 40,000 in 2007. This decline applies to all CNED's programmes that prepare people for the competitive examinations for entry to the education sector (CNED, 2008c, p. 60).

The Teaching-Learning System

Print, video, DVDs and CDs are the principal independent learning media. These are backed by various online services: virtual classes; electronic resources; tutorials (written or oral) and assignment marking; and language tests.

At 500 centres run by partner organizations across France students can buy a range of services, including coaching in study and examination skills, self-assessment and practical work.

Results

CNED does not make its own awards but prepares students for the national competitive examinations for teachers. This makes it impossible for CNED to know its success rates because it does not receive the examination results. Furthermore, most students are also enrolled at conventional universities, or are re-sitting examinations with them. However, CNED accounts for two thirds of those who gain the primary teaching qualifications and the teacher education courses are considered as very successful on a global basis.

Financial and Staffing

CNED's overall operating budget was €105m in 2006–2007. Student fees, which are set by the Ministry of Education for programmes teaching to national curricula, represented about half of its revenues. Staff, in full-time equivalents, numbered 2,641.

Opportunities and Challenges

In the area of teacher education, CNED faces opportunities and challenges consequent on reforms at the European level and within France (Cornu, 2006).

In 1999 Ministers of Education signed the Bologna Declaration in order to set up a European area of higher education that now includes 45 countries. This is based on a common system of three levels of certification and a European Credit Transfer System (ECTS): Bachelor (180 ECTS), Master (300 ECTS), and PhD. The aim is to facilitate the movement of graduates and professionals within Europe.

However, many countries, not only France, are hesitant about applying the ECTS system to teacher education. Finland is unusual in having a teacher education system that is fully compatible with the Bologna process. It requires a Master degree for all teachers, and teacher education programmes give access to ECTS in all universities. Perhaps Finland's impressive performance in the OECD's Programme of International Student Assessment (PISA) will make other countries less reticent about adopting the system.

France is, however, taking some steps in that direction. Since 1990 France has trained its teachers in IUFMs (Instituts Universitaires de Formation de Maîtres). Students do a three-year Bachelor degree and then spend two years in an IUFM. The first year, which students can take through CNED, prepares them for the national competitive examination and, if they pass and are recruited as teachers, they spend the second year with a salary in professional training and school practice.

France is now moving towards the award of a Master degree at the end of the IUFM process and the IUFMs are being integrated into universities. This presents opportunities for CNED. First, it will be able to adapt its courses for teaching qualifications to the new content and curricula of the national examinations so as to offer a distance learning option to students who cannot attend a course on campus or do not make it into the IUFMs' admissions quotas. Second, CNED will have the new challenge of developing new specialised Master degrees for teachers in collaboration with universities.

CNED's Strategic Review

CNED' development is of special interest to our study for three reasons. First, having been created in 1939, at the start of World War II, to serve children who were moved out of the cities and to replace male teachers who had to serve as soldiers, CNED is the oldest institution examined in this book. Second, with some 100,000 pupils in K–12 courses it is one of the largest mega-schools. Third, it also conducts teacher education at scale, helping nearly 40,000 students every year to prepare for the competitive national examinations for entry to the teaching profession.

Developing strategies for CNED's future is a special challenge since its combination of scale and tradition inevitably generates inertia and resistance to change. Conscious of this difficulty, CNED commissioned an external analysis of its requirements for modernisation from the VERTONE management consultancy in 2009 (VERTONE-CNED, 2009). Its findings and recommendations are relevant to all large distance teaching organizations—especially to those that operate across a range of levels and areas of education and training.

VERTONE's key strategic finding was that because CNED operates in so many markets its efforts have become too dispersed. This confuses potential students and reduces the profile of its key offerings. It makes it difficult to communicate CNED's mission clearly and generates wide variations in the economic viability of individual programmes. A corollary problem is poor market awareness and research, which prevents CNED from exploiting new markets with high potential. Finally, like all ODL institutions, CNED has the challenge of taking advantage of the burgeoning range of new teaching and learning technologies in a cost-effective manner.

In an analysis that could be useful for all institutions, VERTONE placed each of CNED's current programmes, along with potential new programme areas, on a plot with Market Potential on the x axis and Legitimacy on the y axis. This plot highlighted the fact that although CNED's schooling and teacher education programmes both have high legitimacy, their market in France is stable or declining. By contrast, CNED has less legitimacy in the stable market of university education and the growth market of professional development courses.

In summary, only 17% of CNED's enrolments come from the areas of its public service mission. For the remaining 83%, it operates in a competitive market. The report points out, however, that CNED could take advantage of its legitimacy in potentially important markets that it is not yet exploiting. Some of these are general home study courses, remedial schooling, online tutoring, and support for university students.

Modernisation is urgent because CNED's overall enrolments are declining. It had an operating deficit in 2008 and, on current trends, will exhaust its substantial financial reserves by 2012. It would be better to deploy some of these reserves now to prime the pumps of change rather than let its financial situation deteriorate further.

On the organizational side the consultancy concluded that CNED has become too decentralized. Devolving responsibility for the various programmes to its eight regional institutes has prevented the emergence of a common corporate strategy and vision that would translate into purposeful implementation of new options. However, the highly impressive centralized call-centre, which handles up to 12,000 new enquiries and student-support calls per day, shows that CNED can operate effectively as a unified organization.

The review recommended extending this type of corporate approach in order to transform both external relations and internal operations. To succeed in the 21st century environment it must become a student-facing organization with strong market awareness and a clear brand image. Internally it must seize opportunities for economies of scale by adopting similar course production and delivery processes where appropriate.

VERTONE concluded its analysis by outlining four possible future scenarios and assessing them first against CNED's current reality and future ambitions, and then in terms of the magnitude of organizational adaptation that implementing each scenario would require.

In scenario one (retrenchment) CNED would abandon the market sector and focus only on its public-sector offerings. This would require considerable downsizing in staff and physical plant.

Scenario two would involve rationalising and optimising current offerings for greater efficiency. It would require minimal reorganization and would restore financial equilibrium in the short term—but not necessarily beyond that.

The third scenario, which the consultants recommended, is a development scenario under which CNED would undergo significant re-organization and adopt a student-facing market-oriented approach. It would focus on CNED's current and potential legitimate markets.

Finally, there is a visionary scenario under which CNED would move aggressively into the competitive training sector. However, by requiring major changes in organization and institutional culture this scenario would present a high risk of being de-railed in its implementation.

At the time of writing CNED is in the process of making decisions about the implementation of the report under a new rector. In our earlier review of development strategies for mega-universities (Daniel, 1996, p. 137), we emphasised the importance of attending to both content and process when developing institutional strategies. In this respect CNED appears to be well placed since the VERTONE consultancy went to some lengths to involve and consult CNED's staff throughout the process of developing their recommendations. As a result people may feel a degree of ownership of the recommendations that will facilitate implementation.

While the consultancy was underway, France's Minister of Education made two potentially helpful decisions for CNED's future development. First, education legislation was changed to make it clear that courses taken from CNED are equivalent to courses taken in face-to-face institutions for official examinations and government purposes generally (JORF, 2009). Indeed, as the legislation now reads, CNED is the only distance-teaching organization to enjoy such blanket approval. The new legislation only applies, however, to courses for pupils who would normally attend a school (primary or secondary). This represents about 17% of CNED's student body. For the remaining 83% of its clients (higher education, adult education, etc.), CNED is simply part of the commercial market of distance education.

Second, and even more significantly, the Minister gave CNED the status of France's Online Academy for its primary and secondary teaching (*Le Figaro*, 2009, p. 2). Educational institutions in France are grouped into 30 regional academies, each with its own rector. CNED has now become the 31st academy, which also helps to put its offerings on an equal footing with those of other institutions. This decision presents CNED with new opportunities but will also require CNED to review its business model. As France's Online Academy, CNED must make its study materials available free on the Internet from June 2009, although it may charge fees for tutorial support and other services.

Putting all its course offerings online will likely stimulate considerable revisions to the material over time. Although the content of its courses is set by the national curriculum, putting this content online will present many opportunities to improve the instructional design and take advantage of evolving technologies. It is also likely to require much closer attention to copyright issues.

PERMAMA (Perfectionnement des Maîtres en Mathématiques), Québec, Canada

Introduction

The purpose of the PERMAMA programme was to train Quebec's secondary mathematics teachers in both pedagogy and content (Bélanger, 1976). It has a threefold interest for our study. First, PERMAMA offered its first course in 1972 so it is an early example of the use of distance education for in-service teacher education. Second, PERMAMA was modified substantially on the basis of feedback from teachers into a model that anticipates much of contemporary thinking. Third, the impressive performance in mathematics of Quebec's secondary pupils in both pan-Canadian assessments and the first OECD PISA (Programme for International Student Assessment) survey in 2000 was very likely linked to the retraining of the province's mathematics teachers through PERMAMA a generation earlier.

Purpose

In the 1960s and 1970s Quebec underwent a 'quiet revolution': a period of rapid modernisation that included a complete recasting of the education system. Catching the spirit of innovation in the wider world expressed by UNESCO's Faure Report (Faure, 1972), the province launched a series of initiatives that included the PERMAMA programme and creation of the Télé-université (Lamy & Henri, 1983), which operated the PERMAMA programme in its formative years. I should note a personal involvement in the programme since I joined the Télé-université as coordinator of educational technology in 1973. One of my first tasks was to set up a system for gathering student feedback on the PERMAMA courses.

At that time Quebec's secondary mathematics teachers fell into two groups, a younger group that had completed university degree courses with an extensive mathematical component, and an older group, starting with teachers as young as their late twenties, who had received teaching certificates prior to the extensive reforms of the late 1960s. Bélanger (1976, p. 20) noted: 'As new mathematics curriculum materials from Europe and the United States gradually entered Canada, it soon became obvious that many mathematics teachers had great difficulty in teaching, or even understanding, these materials due to their own insufficient mathematical background'.

To address this problem Quebec set up PERMAMA in 1971. The programme was designed to allow teachers to study for a degree while remaining in their jobs across the vast territory of the province. The basic purpose was to upgrade the teacher's knowledge of mathematics. Apart from one course on didactics the other 19 courses were in mathematics, although each tried to integrate material on the teaching of its content. In the initial model all 20 courses were obligatory. Courses were developed by writing teams from various parts of the multi-campus Université du Québec and 11 courses had been produced by 1975.

Implementation

The first course was offered in 1972 to some 1,700 students. It consisted of a package of materials with a series of TV tapes and evaluation materials. Seventy centres were created across the province where students met for three hours every week under the guidance of a facilitator. They spent a further six hours per week in informal sub-group meetings. The facilitators had similar backgrounds to the students and were not academic specialists. Their role was to promote the well-being of the group, lead discussions, supervise the students' work and their examinations, work the video equipment, and provide feedback to the course team (Daniel & Umbriaco, 1975).

Highlighting a temptation that faces all tutors in distance education, these authors comment: 'Despite warnings from the course team several facilitators tried to cast themselves in the role of instructors and to 'teach' the courses. These attempts failed and…nearly all the facilitators have become proficient at using the resources of the group to solve problems. Not surprisingly, we find that the better qualified ones are able to give more help with subject-matter problems, but those who are themselves taking the course are, in general, most successful at organizing group work and discussions' (p. 10).

However, three problems in particular became evident as the PERMAMA programme moved into its second year: (a) teachers had difficulty relating the content of the course to their classroom teaching; (b) the study work load was onerous for teachers in full-time employment and; (c) there were operational problems in the role of the facilitators. This led to a review of the programme that was 'remarkable for its searching self-analysis and for the candour in presenting its review of past years and future intentions' (Bélanger, 1976, p. 24).

Bélanger (1976, 24) quotes the report:

PERMAMA is not simply a machine to produce holders of a bachelor degree. PERMAMA has a social role to play: to offer to secondary school mathematics teachers an education that will enable them to transform their teaching. Reforming the teaching of mathematics is an essential social task when we note that the vast majority of the population leaves school with a distaste for mathematics, perhaps because all we teach is the art of conforming to the good methods, to correct definitions, and to good theorems infallibly proven in the correct order. We prepare for the society of tomorrow, and to prepare students to a point where they can develop autonomously; is it not therefore necessary that the teacher himself learn to be autonomous, to become open and confident in regard to mathematics and his own teaching? PERMAMA should help create competencies in terms of teaching, (preparing) teachers who have acquired the attitudes and the necessary resources to continue their own development and improve their own teaching.

The result was a radical overhaul of the programme to introduce a series of changes with the aims of:

- Making the programme less linear with fewer prerequisites.
- Mapping it more closely on the reality of classroom teaching.
- Changing teachers' attitudes to the teaching process rather than emphasising mathematical knowledge.
- Relating the courses more closely to the school curriculum.
- Putting more emphasis on problems of epistemology and the learning of mathematics.
- Orienting the mathematics content of the programme to relate it more closely to concrete problems.

Bélanger (1976, p. 28) notes with approval the risk taken by the PERMAMA team, not only in breaking away from traditional models of in-service training but in making that conceptual break explicit. The redesigned programme sees learning as a 'dynamic interactional process of exchanges between the learner and his environment where the learner is the central and active element... In this conception the chief agent is not the teacher as the transmitter of knowledge, but the learner as constructor of knowledge'. In this spirit students could continue to participate in the programme even after they received their diplomas if they felt their professional needs were being served.

In order to map the programme onto the teachers' professional tasks, rather than onto a fixed set of content, PERMAMA diversified its pedagogical methods and adopted a modular approach with three kinds of modules: management modules, intervention modules and content modules.

The introduction of the management module (one credit per year) was an ingenious way of addressing the considerable administrative challenge of handling 800 students taking a wide choice of courses in 70 centres. Students used the management module to plan their work over the year and report on its progress.

Intervention modules related directly to the students' professional tasks as teachers and might focus on topics such as a particular problem of learning mathematics, a new teaching method, or alternative ways of assessing pupils.

Content modules were of three types: modules dealing with a branch of mathematical knowledge; modules based on pupils' learning activities; and modules addressing the teaching of mathematics.

One organizational change that no doubt ensured the coherence of the revised programme and facilitated its implementation was establishment of a permanent course team to develop the new modules, instead of farming the work out to specialists around the province. The CalStateTEACH programme described later provides another example of the value of putting together a dedicated team to develop an innovative approach to teacher education. Bélanger (1976, p. 34) notes that some faculty on the conventional campuses of the Université du Québec thought that the new PERMAMA model was altogether too radical and ganged up against it. PERMAMA was closed in 1982, but one of its legacies was the creation of the *Groupe des responsables en mathématiques au secondaire* (GRMS), which continues to implement the philosophy developed by PERMAMA (Gagnon-Messier, 2005).

Impact

Finally, although it is impossible to establish cause and effect with certainty, we note that two decades after the introduction of the PERMAMA programme, when many of the thousands of teachers who went through it were still in post, Quebec's 15- and 16-year-olds demonstrated impressive mathematical achievements. In 1993 and 1997 when Canada's Council of Ministers of Education ran an assessment programme for 16-year-olds across the country, Québec students significantly outperformed the rest (Filion, 2000). Then in 2000 nearly 5,000 pupils from 165 Quebec schools participated in the first survey of the OECD's Programme for International Student Assessment (PISA) (Government of Quebec, 2000). They were part of a cohort of 265,000 pupils in 32 countries. PISA evaluated 'mathematical literacy' defined as the ability to pose and solve mathematical problems in a variety of situations. Quebec, with 550 points, ranked second among the participating jurisdictions after Japan (557 points) and just ahead of Korea (547). Quebec scored above the Canadian average (533) and well above the United States (493).

National Teachers' Institute (NTI), Kaduna, Nigeria

National Context

Nigeria is Africa's most populous country with a population of nearly 150 million (growing at 2.4% annually) spread over a territory of 923,000 sq. km. Life expectancy at birth is 47 years, partly because of high infant mortality (99 per 1,000 live births). The EFA goals pose a special challenge for Nigeria, which had 8 million children out of school in 2005—23% of the total for sub-Saharan Africa. Projections indicate that this figure will still be above 7 million by 2015

(UNESCO, 2008b, p. 66). By contrast similar projections show that India, which still had 7 million children out of school in 2005, will reduce this figure to fewer than 1 million by the same date.

The 2009 EFA GMR reports that the Government of Nigeria is forthright about the challenge and recognises that major renewal of all systems and institutions is needed. A major challenge is inequality. There are wide differences in primary school enrolment by region: the primary NER is 82% in the south west compared to only 42% in the poorer north-west. Girls' enrolment also varies greatly by region by family income. In Kaduna state, 48% of girls from the poorest 20% of households have never attended school, compared to 14% in the richest quintile (UNESCO 2008b, p. 62). The report also notes that 'a significant proportion of teachers lack the minimum requirement of three years of post-secondary education. Many have limited mastery of the subjects they teach'. Unfortunately the attempt to increase provision and keep costs low by recruiting volunteer teachers exacerbated this problem (UNESCO, 2006b).

History and Status

Nigeria's National Teachers' Institute, one of the world's largest institutions for teacher education at a distance, provides an excellent model for countries wishing to increase numbers of trained teachers rapidly within a national policy framework. The NTI was created in 1976 and began operations in 1978 to cope with a surge of enrolments in primary school following the launching of a campaign for Universal Primary Education by the Murtala/Obasanjo military administration (NTI, 2001, 2002a). This resulted in an explosion of primary enrolment from 5.5 million to 8 million. The government estimated that 250,000 teachers would be needed for the expanded system but only 180,000 were available and more than half of them were unqualified. Over 150,000 teachers were therefore candidates for immediate training and the numbers increased as more untrained teachers were hired to cope with the increased enrolment.

The NTI was mandated to establish a distance learning system for the purpose. The NTI decree mandated it to upgrade teachers at all levels, organize professional development events for teachers, conduct examinations, carry out research, formulate policy and foster international cooperation (Government of Nigeria, 1978). Although it has only recently begun to fulfil its mandates for research and policy, the NTI has carried out its upgrading tasks impressively in response to successive demands from government. Immediately after its establishment it trained thousands of teachers for the Teachers Grade Two Certificate (equivalent to five years of post-primary education) and was made the nationwide examining body for this qualification. By 2001, some 1.3 million teachers had taken this examination, which continued to be offered until phased out in 2006.

In 1989 the Nigerian Certificate in Education (NCE) was introduced. This qualification, which enabled its holders to teach at both primary and secondary level, required three years of training after secondary schooling (four years by distance education through NTI). All the holders of the Grade Two Certificate had incentives to upgrade to the NCE and 200,000 of them did so with NTI during the 1990s.

Although distance learning is NTI's main mode of instruction, it has also organized large-scale face-to-face upgrading schemes. In 2007, for example, it conducted a crash programme for the 50% of teachers who still did not have the NCE. This Special Teacher Upgrading Programme, which condensed the three-year NCE curriculum into two years, was done in a nationwide network of study centres in collaboration with Nigeria's colleges of education.

Having shown that it could operate at scale in both face-to-face and distance modes, NTI also undertook another face-to-face programme to retrain teachers in new methods of teaching for the four core primary subjects: Mathematics, Social Studies, Science and English from 2006–2008.

Renaissance and Renewal

By the late 1990s, however, NTI underwent a crisis of credibility due to poor management. Staff were unpaid, the examination system collapsed, and there were rumours of closure. Instead, however, NTI pulled itself together under a new management team, engaged in comprehensive capacity building for its staff with external help from agencies such as the Commonwealth of Learning, and developed a strategic plan (NTI, 2002b).

The purpose of the strategic planning exercise was to 'refocus, revitalise and restructure' NTI so that it can fulfil its mandate more effectively. The plan holds out the prospect of adding bachelors and postgraduate degree programmes but states the mission for the immediate future as: 'clearly focused on the production and regular updating and upgrading of teachers for Basic Level Education. This includes primary and junior secondary school education as well as non-formal and open education. The Institute will operate more clearly as a distance education centre with requisite capacity in the fast-changing world of technology assisted education' (NTI, 2002b, pp. 10–11). Such a focus is necessary because, even 25 years after NTI's creation, 'the reality of the Nigerian education scene today (is) massive shortfalls in teacher supply, particularly at primary level and the fact that a significant percentage of teachers in employment are untrained, under-qualified and professionally unqualified' (NTI, 2002a, p. 10)

NTI enjoyed a renaissance after this crisis and became, once again, the cornerstone of teacher education in Nigeria. Its base business is the upgrading of teachers to the NCE, with annual enrolments of approximately 150,000. It also undertakes a range of other tasks.

For example, one challenge which allowed the new administration to show its mettle was the Pivotal Teacher Training Programme that NTI introduced in 1999 to train 40,000 teachers annually by distance education to meet the needs of the Universal Basic Education (UBE) Programme in Nigeria's 37 states. Although this programme was jointly agreed by the federal and state governments, only

60% of the teachers trained were hired because some local governments did not follow through on their states' commitments. The programme was discontinued in 2003 but then restarted in 2005 on a smaller scale on the basis of specific agreements with some of the northern states.

NTI also carries out specific commissions at the request of states, for example in upgrading the pedagogical skills of primary teachers.

Pedagogy

NTI is concerned to ensure that its curricula for teacher education reflect best modern practice. In pursuit of this goal it has engaged with UNICEF's child-friendly schools programme since 2002 by developing some of the textbooks and training manuals for this programme. It is also one of the most active members of the TESSA (Teacher Training in sub-Saharan Africa) consortium (see p. 165). NTI prepared a special training manual for TESSA and disseminates TESSA materials, in the form of Open Educational Resources, into Nigeria's Colleges of Education.

Organizational Arrangements

NTI's large central campus, home to 400 staff, is located in central Nigeria at Kaduna, a city that is also a centre for military and police training. It also operates six zonal offices, each of which coordinates the work of a sub-group of the 37 state offices. To carry out its work the NTI engages some 17,000 part-time staff around the country, particularly as tutors and markers.

Media and Methods

The NTI operates a classic distance learning system based on printed self-instructional materials with an increasing use of audio and video cassettes and CD-ROMs. It is readying itself to make greater use of online technologies but these are not yet conveniently available to most of its students. NTI's study materials, which are developed and produced in house, are used extensively throughout Nigeria's education system and in other African and Commonwealth countries.

These self-study materials are supplemented by weekend contact sessions and intensive sessions during school vacations at some 900 study centres that take NTI into nearly all Nigeria's 700+ local government districts.

Since 2007 NTI has operated an FM radio station broadcasting interactive programmes for use by teachers and schools in a 70km radius of Kaduna. The time seems ripe for this successful venture to be expanding into a national AM radio channel to enrich teaching across Nigeria. NTI would also like to explore the possibility of hosting or participating in an educational TV channel.

Summary and Prospects

NTI is making a major contribution to the development of education in Nigeria, having trained nearly a million teachers since its inception. Given that of the world's high population countries Nigeria is one of the most challenged by the EFA goals, the NTI has important work to do for many years to come.

Allama Iqbal Open University, Pakistan

Context

With a population of 165 million spread over a partly mountainous territory of 800,000 sq. km., Pakistan has a particular need for distance learning but is a particularly challenging country in which to provide it. Communication within the country is difficult because of the rugged terrain and unrest in the regions bordering on Afghanistan. UNESCO includes Pakistan in its 'E9' group of high population countries singled out for special attention in the EFA campaign. In projections of the absolute numbers likely to still be out of school by 2015, Pakistan presents the biggest challenge after Nigeria, not least because the school age population will have grown by 10% between 2006 and 2015. Projections indicate that to achieve EFA and fill vacancies due to attrition Pakistan will need over half a million more teachers by 2015 (UNESCO, 2006b).

Pakistan was one of the first countries to follow the example of the UK in using distance learning at scale in higher education. Allama Iqbal Open University (AIOU) was established in 1974 and now enrols over 2 million students across all its programmes, meeting 87% of its budget requirements from its own resources. Its Institute of Education was created in 1976 and became the Faculty of Education in 1984. Now AIOU's largest faculty, it offers a variety of programme in education and training of teachers and educational professionals. These range from primary teacher education to M.Phil. and Ph.D. programmes and make a major contribution to teacher education in Pakistan (AIOU, 2009).

Through its B.Ed. programme AIOU has made a special effort to respond to the shortage of teachers: especially in Baluchistan, the North West Frontier Province and Azad Jammu and Kashmir. In these provinces there are special barriers for female teachers and financial obstacles for male teachers that prevent them undertaking conventional professional training. AIOU has become a beacon for such teachers.

Given its scale and national reach, AIOU works closely with the Government on various other priority initiatives. One such is the Students Access Centre for the promotion of English Language Teaching and Learning. This is creating online English Language teacher training courses, developing distance and online methods for language learning and testing, and providing training courses for teachers of English.

Through its Institute for Literacy and Mass Education, which is part of the

Faculty of Education, AIOU is also massively involved in providing basic education and training at grassroots level, especially to rural women.

Enrolments

In the period 2004–2008 AIOU enrolled over 1 million students in its teacher education programme. Taking a snapshot in 2008, the largest numbers were in the B.Ed. (General)—142,000; The Primary Teaching Certificate—43,000; the M.Ed. (Teacher Education)—26,000; the Certificate of Teaching—20,000; and the M.A. (Teacher Education)—13,000. There were also nearly 100 enrolments in Ph.D. programmes related to Education.

There is high enrolment of females in education programmes because in Pakistani culture they are socially and culturally restricted to their homes, so that distance education becomes their only opportunity (Masrur & Khan, 2007). The majority of female students of AIOU showed high satisfaction levels and positive attitudes towards their academic programmes.

Teaching-Learning System

AIOU faces the classic challenge of organizing technology-mediated learning in a developing country. It is extending its use of technologies (e.g. Wi-Fi Mesh) as they become available and, given the scale of its operations, is steadily modernising its use of data processing and databases in support of administrative operations.

The AIOU distance education system is a good example of the deployment of a variety of media in an integrated manner. Central to the system are sets of correspondence materials. These are augmented as appropriate by: national FM radio (The Voice of AIOU); satellite transmission (available in 45 countries); on-line teaching (when available in the region); non-broadcast audio-visual media; tutorial instruction (through contact sessions and academic guidance facilities at study centres); and face-to-face teaching in courses requiring lab work or skill development. Course assignments are also a component of instruction and there is continuous assessment as well as a final examination for each course.

In order to provide local support to students, despite Pakistan's difficult terrain, AIOU has 35 regional centres which manage nearly 700 study centres and over 30,000 tutors for the university as a whole.

Fees

To facilitate access AIOU sets the fees for its education programmes below those of the conventional universities. In this group the University of Education (UE) charges the lowest fees per credit hour but AIOU's fees are slightly above 60% of the UE fees for the B.Ed. programme and just below 60% for the M.Phil. In recent years AIOU has attracted larger numbers of teacher education candidates while minimizing committed costs and reducing flexible costs.

Comparisons with Conventional Provision

Research studies show that the B.Ed. curricula offered by AIOU and conventional universities are the same and school heads rated the performance of teachers trained by AIOU and conventional institutions as equivalent (Mumtaz 2002; Khan, 2006; Yasmeen, 2008). An evaluative study on the instructional design of AIOU material by Choudry (2003, p. 39) concluded that the 'scheme of studies are developed on principles of self learning, objectives of the courses are clear, contents are simple and easy to understand and useful to the student's needs, activities are placed properly in the text, sequence of the text is adequate, courses are at par with the courses of formal system, and length of each unit is suitable'. Furthermore, most of the teacher training institutions in the conventional system are using instructional material developed by AIOU and the AIOU course texts are stocked in the libraries of the most reputable universities.

The UK Open University (UKOU)

Context

As befits the world's leading distance-teaching university, the UK Open University has always been thoroughly engaged in teacher education. In 1971, when the University opened for business, teachers seeking to add subject-based degrees to their teaching diplomas made up a large part of the early clientele. Over the following decades tens of thousands of teachers obtained UKOU degrees. The formal training of teachers for certification came later, for it was not until the 1990s that the UK welcomed distance learning as an acceptable form of pre-service education. Having already given many non-graduate teachers the opportunity to obtain degrees, the UKOU has now developed programmes for older graduates who wish to be certified as teachers. Throughout its existence the UKOU has been engaged in various types of in-service teacher education.

This profile features the UKOU's teacher education work in the UK and Europe, but it also has a substantial influence in the wider world. The profiles of CalStateTEACH and TESSA later in this annex testify to the global impact of the UKOU's *Research Group on International Development in Teacher Education across Societies and Cultures* under the leadership of Professor Bob Moon. Here we shall first describe the UKOU's pre-service programmes for primary and secondary teachers and then report on one element of its provision: the use of electronic conference environments for the professional development of teachers at scale.

Origins of the Pre-Service Programmes

In their account of the UKOU programmes Leach and Moon (2000, p. 106) noted the 'global trend towards merging face-to-face instruction and open-and-distance modes of instruction brought about by new forms of communication technology'. The development of the UKOU's pre-service programmes, in line with this trend, took place in the 1990s during a turbulent period of reform of UK teacher education when the encouragement of innovation alternated with policies reflecting a traditionalist backlash (Moon, 1999). The PERMAMA programme described earlier had experienced a similar see-saw in attitudes 20 years earlier, although that had occurred within the Université du Québec network rather than at government level. The CalStateTEACH programme, described below, was also 'vigorously resisted by some parts of the teacher education and training community when first established' (Moon, 2007, p. 14).

In the early 1990s, following research carried out by the UKOU and the UK government, it became apparent that there were significant numbers of graduates currently pursuing other careers who would be interested in becoming teachers. Furthermore, the profile of these people was not only different from those entering teaching through conventional routes, but also corresponded to areas of teacher shortage in several ways. Graduates in science and mathematics were strongly represented among those interested in teaching at both primary and secondary levels. The numbers of women expressing interest in science and technology were unusually high and the proportion of potential entrants from ethnic communities was higher than in conventional programmes.

In order for these working people to become teachers, they had to be offered a part-time route through open and distance learning. The UKOU subsequently won the tender competition put out by the government for such a programme. The timing was good because the UKOU had reflected deeply on the shortcomings of previous ODL programmes of teacher education and was ready to address what it saw as their two major shortcomings: the lack of cost-effective means for interactive communication and the absence of school-based activity related to teaching competencies. It did so in a new model of a PGCE (Post-graduate Certificate of Education) programme that became Europe's largest ODL programme of pre-service teacher education, enrolling some 1,500 students each year in the mid-1990s.

Nature of the Programme

The new UKOU PGCE was a comprehensive programme, offering courses in seven secondary subject lines and a primary line where students could focus on either junior or senior primary. The programme was designed to meet the statutory time allocations for teaching experience laid down by government, so the 18-month course was sub-divided into three stages with a period of full-time teaching practice in each stage. Since the students were already graduates, the programme's focus was on teaching and subject/curriculum applications (Leach & Moon, 2000, p. 110).

The teaching-learning system was even richer than the UKOU provision in other subjects. In addition to comprehensive printed and audio-visual material, there was a detailed prescription of the curriculum activities to be conducted in schools and a student-assessment portfolio. Furthermore, to ensure regular interactive communication, all students were provided with a computer for the duration of the course—which was given to the school where they had done their teaching practice once the course was over. The computer enabled students to develop their ICT skills to communicate with their tutor and other students, and to access a range of electronic conferences.

The role of the tutor was also more intensive than in other UKOU courses. Responsible for a group of around 12 students, the tutor commented on and marked their assignments, contributed to day schools and provided tutorials at appropriate intervals. Each student also had another set of relationships in the school which was the base for their practical experience. Students were asked to nominate their own school, which was reviewed for its suitability as part of the application process. Once the school had been vetted by its regional staff, the University drew up a contract with it. Within the school the student had a designated mentor and was further supported by a senior member of the school staff—the school coordinator. Following special training these experienced teachers were primarily responsible for assessing the student's teaching practice.

Four aspects of the programme were particularly noteworthy: (a) its design, (b) the arrangements for quality assurance, (c) the integral role of the school, and (d) the use of interactive technologies. The design was done within an overall generic framework that was used by all subject specialists. This gave coherence and facilitated assessment and quality assurance. Quality assurance relied on a combination of student evaluation, the University's own QA processes, and government inspection.

Schools for Teaching Practice

Leach and Moon (2000, p. 113) comment in some detail on the issue of choosing schools, referring to Hargreaves (1995) writing on the social geography of teacher education. In selecting schools for teaching practice, an institution has essentially two choices. It can concentrate the work in a limited number of 'professional development' schools or it can disperse the students across the wider school system. The first choice risks giving the trainee teacher a false impression of the real world of schools, whereas the second makes administration more complex and gives fewer assurances of school quality.

The UKOU embraced the second option, both as part of its philosophy and because for many of the students, notably those from ethnic communities, their local city schools were the professional reality that they would encounter later, even if those schools did not have a tradition of hosting teaching practice for trainees. The University attempted to address potential problems through its quality assurance frameworks. Furthermore, an important principle of the programme was that all the ODL course texts and resources should be directly related to school practice. 'No activity, reading or observation could be set that did not relate directly to experience in schools' and 'the link had to be explicit' (Leach & Moon, 2000, p. 114).

Despite its best efforts, the University was not entirely successful in satisfying government inspectors about its provisions for teaching practice during the traditionalist backlash noted above. Here I should again note a personal involvement because I was the vice-chancellor of the UKOU during this period. We experienced the startling contradiction that the PGCE programme won a Queen's Anniversary Prize for Higher Education in 1997 and yet the next year we received a low quality rating from the Office for Standards in Education (OFSTED) for the Primary line of the programme following the introduction of a new national curriculum for teacher education and new inspection criteria. The Secondary line received a satisfactory rating.

The low rating of the Primary line was closely related to the fact that some of the schools chosen for teaching practice did not themselves receive high OFSTED ratings. Moon (1998) noted that 'political factors were clearly in play in relation to new requirements within a complex structure of government factions and competing national agencies'. Furthermore the OFSTED report on the Primary line for England and Wales was in sharp contrast to the favourable report by the inspectorate in Northern Ireland on the same programme!

Nevertheless, the poor OFSTED report on the Primary line created a serious dilemma for the UKOU, which then ranked among the top 10% of English universities for the quality of its teaching programmes—and was soon to rank in the top 5%. Should the University soldier on with a programme that had received a poor quality rating and revise it as it went along, or withdraw it and go back to the drawing board?

We decided to withdraw the Primary line, thereby earning the opprobrium of another branch of government because of the immediate loss of a large number of teacher education places. Today the UKOU PGCE for Secondary teachers has evolved into a much more individualised, flexible model that continues to make extensive use of interactive technologies. It now has the OFSTED top grade for quality but this has been achieved by reducing numbers significantly and increasing per capita costs.

Of all the decisions that I took during my time at the head of the UKOU this is the one I have revisited most frequently and I still think the choice of action was finely balanced. This incident is an example of a challenge facing large-scale ODL programmes in the politically sensitive and fast-evolving area of teacher education. Such programmes are highly visible because of their scale and also because all aspects of the programme are explicit and available for review. The UKOU mapped the PGCE onto the national teacher education curriculum at the time of its design, but it is impossible to change such a programme quickly when the winds of government policy shift direction. We noted a similar challenge on p. 71 for open schools, which also have difficulty reacting instantly to changes in the school curriculum. The lesson for governments that are serious about conducting either secondary schooling or teacher education at scale is that they must accept constraints on their ability to change curricula quickly—

or at least involve the large-scale providers in any curriculum revision process from the outset.

Interactive Technologies

The use of interactive technologies in the PGCE, and in the UKOU's teacher education programmes more widely, is of particular interest because of the scale of the operation and the care with which it has been researched (Leach, 2002). Given the lazy tendency to use the term *eLearning* to designate ODL generally, it is important to have a clear understanding of the strengths and weakness of interactive technologies.

In the PGCE programme every student and tutor has a computer, a printer and a modem for the duration of the course. Communication is carried out through the *FirstClass* software programme (now being replaced by a Moodle application), which enables the use of a personal mailbox, read-only bulletin boards, online conferencing and real-time chats, and document exchange. The aim is to create a virtual community among students and staff, who meet face to face only occasionally. Take up of the system is high: sampling revealed an average of four sessions per week by 1,117 students and 125 tutors (Leach & Moon, 2000, p. 116). As well as their tutor groups, there are electronic conferences, moderated by the course writers, for each of the subject lines.

More generally the computer conferencing system provides a secure setting and community of practice in which novices can gain experience through contact with experienced practitioners. The challenge is that 'learners do not automatically benefit from a communication and collaboration infrastructure' (Leach, 2002, p. 90). In this context an advantage of the PGCE programme is that it lasts much longer (18 months) than most online courses. This gives the opportunity to develop and sustain a genuine community of practice, which is not just a fancy term for a group, network or team, but 'participation in an activity about which participants share understandings concerning what they are doing and what it means for their lives and communities' (Lave & Wenger, 1991, p. 98). This means having a joint enterprise with an agreed goal, a shared repertoire of discourse and distinctive roles for participants in the joint work (Wenger, 1999, p. 74).

The challenge is that learning within a community of practice is always emergent and cannot be designed in from the start. As the UKOU gained experience of using electronic conferencing to sustain such communities of teachers, it came to appreciate and refine the new role of moderator of such conferences, about which Salmon (2000) has written extensively. Leach concludes that electronic conferencing is an ideal context for professional learning. In addition to helping teachers construct knowledge for themselves and be acculturated into their professional community, it also favours a process of social transformation whereby learning is jointly constructed and knowledge is distributed within and across communities. In this way electronic conferencing provides settings that enable development, transformation and creative change within professional communities.

Results

The UKOU's PGCE programme has successfully verified the initial hypothesis that graduates in other careers can transfer successfully to teaching. Eighty-two percent of the first cohort gained qualified teacher status and 80% of them went immediately into teaching posts, which is in line with figures for conventional provision. Later surveys showed that their retention in the profession was at least as high as that of teachers who had trained through conventional routes.

The cost of the first generation UKOU PCGE to the public purse was about 50% that of a conventional PGCE. Moreover, this figure fell to about 25% if the cost of the computer purchase and the payments to schools were taken out of the equation. With these elements removed the recurrent marginal costs per student were calculated as approximately US$663 (Leach & Moon, 2000, p. 121).

The Open University Malaysia (OUM)

Context

Malaysia has a population of 26 million in a territory of 330,000 sq. km. With nearly two-thirds of the population using the Internet in 2008, it is no longer a developing country. However, there are still disparities in wealth between the rural and urban areas, and Malaysia considers that its educational attainments do not yet match its national aspirations. While it has achieved universal primary education and high literacy rates among its young people, enrollment rates at the secondary level were just over 70% in 2004. Malaysia has a favourable pupil/teacher ratio of less than 20:1 at both primary and secondary levels. However, many teachers are non-graduates and completing their training is a key aim of the teacher education programme at the Open University Malaysia.

The Open University Malaysia (OUM) was established in 2000, since then student numbers have risen to 70,000. It has an unusual corporate structure because although it is formally a private university, the company that owns it, Multimedia Technology Enhancement Operations (METEOR) Sdn. Bhd., is a consortium of 11 public universities. This has proved to be an ingenious way of giving Malaysia's public universities a financial stake in the success of a potential competitor.

Upgrading Primary Teachers

Teacher education, both pre-service and in-service, is offered in distance learning mode by the Faculty of Education and Languages through a range of nine programmes extending from a Diploma in Early Childhood to the Ph.D. Between them these programmes enrol some 23,000 teachers. Following a successful programme to upgrade secondary school teachers that has already produced over 8,000 graduates, the Faculty is now focussing on improving the academic standards of the primary schools by upgrading the academic qualifications of those teachers.

Although some primary school teachers obtained degrees from local universities through distance education, most are non-graduates. The Faculty, in collaboration with the teacher education division of the ministry of education, was given task of providing in-service training to the non-graduates, who are taking bachelors degree programmes in either primary or pre-school education. The aim is that by 2010 at least half the primary school teaching force will have a bachelor degree. The programmes have been specially designed to give teachers the knowledge and skills that will ensure their effectiveness in the classroom.

The curricula are designed in an integrated manner to increase the teachers' skills and pedagogical verve in ways that enable them to stimulate their pupils' intellectual interest and foster their academic success. The 14 majors and 16 minors in the primary programme give teachers ample scope to explore their special interests. A first batch of 3,200 primary teachers graduated in 2009 and a further 5,000 are currently enrolled (Othman, personal communication, 2009).

The Teaching-Learning System

OUM adopts a blended approach to learning that employs multi-mode strategies; combining online learning, or more technologically advanced formats, with traditional methods such as face-to-face interaction. The aim is to provide the student-teachers with the best of both worlds, by giving them the high-level attention and guidance that can be achieved in an actual classroom, as well as the flexibility and openness of self-paced learning through online and virtual learning. They must attend the tutorial classes held every fortnight and be active in the online forum. In addition they have modules for self-managed learning.

A key feature of the system is *myLMS*, OUM's home-grown learning management system. This is a working and proven application package used by students, lecturers and tutors to assist them in their learning. Its comprehensive and flexible eLearning software platform delivers a course management system, institution-wide portals, online communities, and an advanced architecture that allows for web-based integration with multiple administrative systems.

Another example of OUM's advanced use of ICTs is the Tan Sri Dr Abdullah Sanusi Digital Library that has more than 25,000 volumes of printed books in the main campus and learning centres nationwide. The digital collection brings together online databases with more than 70,000 e-books and 23,000 e-journals. Other electronic collections include electronic theses, newspaper articles and legislative documents.

Advantages of University-Ministry Collaboration

The close collaboration between OUM and the Ministry on teachers' in-service education is helpful in a number of ways:

Teachers continue to work in schools, so the Ministry does not need to provide temporary replacements. Student-teachers are provided with a module for each course taken and the online *myLMS* forum to interact with their tutors as well as their peers. They attend the weekend face-to-face tutorials every second week, allowing them to be available for any extra school activities on other weekends.

OUM's flexible blended learning mode is scalable and available everywhere in the country through 56 learning centres, some of which are located in Malaysia's 27 Teacher Education Institutes. OUM rents these for the weekend tutorials—or upgrades the institutes' facilities with computers, etc. in lieu of rent. This arrangement also provides capacity building for their lecturers, who are recruited as tutors for the OUM programme. By operating in this way OUM is able to enrol some 400 teachers in remote areas such as the two states in Borneo: Sabah and Sarawak.

Challenges

In offering these in-service programmes OUM faces the following organizational challenges:

Conforming to the restrictions on the availability of teachers for tutorials and examinations is an administrative challenge. In the case of the tutorials the 'alternate weekend' requirement is not a major difficulty since the OUM has an ample number of classrooms in its learning centres. However, the restriction on examination days (Thursdays to Sundays only) is challenging given the number of courses offered each semester.

Developing and distributing the study modules throughout the country is a significant task that is handled by the OUM's Centre for Instructional Design and Technology.

Appointing and managing a large number of tutors is an ongoing operation. It is handled by the Centre for Tutor Management and Development, which recruits them from the Teacher Education Institutes and local public and private higher learning institutions. Providing appropriate classes for the courses that require practical work is both an administrative and pedagogical challenge.

Ensuring a good learning experience for student-teachers in remote areas requires special attention. These students do not have easy access to the Internet, phones and the postal service, so alternative communication channels between them and the Faculty and tutorial centres must be developed and maintained. In this context particular importance is attached to the formal tutorial and study review sessions organized at six tutorial centres during school vacations. Tutors work with the student-teachers on the study materials at these events and ensure that they leave with their modules and assignments for the following semester.

CalStateTEACH, California, USA

Background

Teacher shortage is far from being only a developing country issue. The United States has a dire problem of teacher wastage, with 50% of newly trained teachers leaving the profession within five years. In states like California, with high immigration, this is compounded by the challenge of a growing school population including many children from non-Anglophone backgrounds. In 1999 over 30,000 teachers in K1–3 were teaching on emergency credentials, that is, without any teacher education and training (Leach & Moon, 2000, p. 106).

Status and History

CalStateTEACH is one of the California State University's (CSU) responses to the critical teacher shortage in California. According to the National Education Association, California will need more than 300,000 teachers over the next decade. Although the CSU system would be educating roughly 60% of these new teachers, CSU Chancellor Dr. Charles Reed saw the need to do more in the late 1990s. He envisioned a programme that would combine the flexibility of online learning with the real-world experience that new teachers are already gaining in their classrooms. The result of this fusion is CalStateTEACH.

In August 1998 a group of CSU teacher education faculty met to design the programme and the first cohort entered CalStateTEACH in September 1999. With more than 700 participants now enrolled and over 7,500 alumni, CalStateTEACH is helping to fulfil the vision that 'every child deserves to be taught by fully prepared teachers' (CSU, 2009).

I declare an interest because the team developing CalStateTEACH had extensive discussions with the UK Open University, of which I was vice-chancellor at the time, during the design of the programme. The UKOU already had considerable experience of teacher education at a distance in pre-service, in-service and postgraduate programmes (see UKOU profile).

The UKOU team sometimes doubted whether the programme, even if approved, would be successful. American universities—not least their faculties of education—are rather conservative. However, CSU Chancellor Charlie Reed is a determined individual who made CalStateTEACH a personal campaign, and the faculty senate ultimately gave its blessing to the programme. Furthermore, the CSU faculty had insisted that the full-time faculty should support the students in the programme instead of operating more cost-effectively with part-time tutors. We feared that this would compromise the economic viability of the programme.

I am delighted, therefore, to observe its subsequent success, although it may be operating on a smaller scale than is desirable and possible. A strong validation of the programme is the favourable assessment of its graduates by their employers at the end of their first year of teaching. CalStateTEACH-prepared teachers as a group are rated as positively as those in any other CSU programme, and more highly than the graduates from most of them. Moon (2007, p. 14) notes that: 'External independent evaluation…is now giving the programme very high ratings'.

Clientele

The programme has two tracks. Students who have a teaching contract (employment) can be on the Internship track, which is a full-day, full-time experience. They must be teaching in a multiple subject public classroom in which the core curriculum is taught to all students. To be intern eligible they must have passed the California Subject Examination for Teachers (CSET) and met the Constitution requirement. Students who volunteer part time in a classroom are on the Student Teaching track/pathway, beginning as fieldwork participants, spending six hours per week in the classroom as volunteers. They are placed in schools by the programme.

The Programme

CalStateTEACH is a non-traditional programme for qualified candidates interested in earning their credential without attending traditional college classes. Instead, the curriculum is delivered online. In the academic jargon it is a 4 Term Multiple-Subject Teacher Education Programme for Interns and Student Teachers (http://www.calstateteach.net/) who wish to become elementary teachers. The curriculum is designed for self-directed learners comfortable with web-supported instruction. All courses are taken in blocks of 10 units and for those needing CSET support, there is an online tutoring course. Neither the intern (employed teacher) option, nor the traditional teacher preparation option (student teaching), has campus-based classes. The programme takes a minimum of 16 months to complete.

Participants use web, print, video, and CD-ROM materials. These include: a collection of print text books (one of which is a programme handbook with 28 essential learning outcomes); several electronic text books; the California Teacher Performance Expectations; the California Academic Content Standards; the California Frameworks; a spiral curriculum that guides the prospective teacher to develop in theory and practice; the California Standards for the Teaching Profession; a study guide; a classroom technology guide; a website with text and videos; CD-ROMs; and field-based learning. Students also come together at one of several regional sites across the state for six day-long seminars during the programme.

Students work through a series of 25 modules over the course of the programme, each taking approximately two weeks to complete and including both academic and field work. The intensity of the field work increases over the course of the programme, with one day required per week in the first term and a full-time experience scheduled in Term 4. They share ideas through web-based class discussions on the CalStateTEACH course website, and get professional feedback through on-site coaching. CalStateTEACH participants enjoy personal guidance from mentor teachers at their school site as well as CSU faculty.

Three design features appear to underpin the success of the programme; in all cases they reflect the integrated nature of the programme. Rather than discreet courses, CalStateTEACH features an integrated curriculum in which students encounter all aspects of a traditional teacher preparation programme on a need-to-know and spiralled basis. The premise of the original design is that the programme would give its students what they needed immediately to survive as teachers in a classroom and then gradually broaden, deepen, and refine that knowledge.

Related to this curricular integration is the interaction of academic work and field experience from the first week of the programme to the last. Students complete academic work and put it into practice simultaneously; this coincidental learning produces both a theoretical understanding and a maturity of practice that exceed the outcomes of many traditional programmes. Finally, all faculty members teach all aspects of the programme rather than specialise. The practice of assigning a faculty member to each new student insures that the student receives guidance from a professional who knows the entire scope of the teaching life. This structure also promotes the development of significant professional mentoring relationships which lead to a more intensive learning experience for the student.

The programme is integrated and completely school-based, with no separate course taken on campus. Each term is a 10-unit block of credit in a spiral curriculum without independent courses. CSET tutoring is provided to all enrolled students and first-time students taking the exam have a 96% pass rate. Support is also given for the Reading Instruction Competence Assessment exam with a 95% pass rate. There are four 15-week terms in the programme. Those on the fieldwork participant/student teaching track spend time in an assigned classroom each week with a gradual build up: term 1 = 6 hours per week; term 2 = 12 hours per week; term 3 = 15 hours per week; term 4 = solo teaching experience (full-time, full-day).

TESSA (Teacher Education in Sub-Saharan Africa)

Summary

When Nelson Mandela emerged from his decades in prison, he remarked how much smaller the planet had become because information and communication technologies had shrunk the world. He added that ICTs were a great weapon for eradicating ignorance and promoting democracy. The TESSA programme attempts to harness these technologies in order to widen access to teacher education programmes and increase their quality. It is not a training programme *per se* but rather it provides tools and content that will allow local developers to create school-based programmes. In its first two-year period (2005–2007) TESSA was a consortium spread across 9 African countries with the participation of 13 African universities and 5 international organizations (TESSA, 2008). In 2008 nearly half a million African teachers worked with materials and resources produced through the TESSA community. These materials, which are available in Arabic, English, French and Kiswahili, have a direct impact on millions of children through their use in the classroom. Thanks to its use of open educational resources (OER) the programme aims to take advantage of global cooperation in order to achieve high quality local provision.

The Programme

The key purpose of TESSA is to improve access to, and raise the quality of, all aspects of teacher education and training. For this purpose it has developed an extensive range of high quality multi-lingual OER and systems, which are designed to support all teachers, including those with little or no formal training. These OER are presented under the Creative Commons Attribution-Share Alike 3.0 License. Materials development draws on experts in each of the participating countries and by 2008 over 100 academics and more than 1,000 teachers had been involved in the design of the programme and the creation of OER.

TESSA materials cover the core areas of primary basic education teaching through text (print and online) and audio formats. Work on secondary teaching is planned. The materials are free for the TESSA community and others to adapt, share and use. There are 750 sections of study units that include 2,250 classroom-based activities for teachers to try out and implement.

Care is taken to ensure that the key focus of the materials is classroom-based activities for teachers. Key areas of teacher competence and skills have been defined as the foundation to the curriculum structure of the materials. From this work the consortium developed a structure of five module areas: Literacy, Numeracy, Science, Social Studies and the Arts, and Life Skills.

To facilitate their use, the materials have a similar format across the module areas. Each comprises three modules with five study units, and each section contains learning outcomes for the teacher, three classroom based activities, three case studies and a range of accompanying resources.

The programme is enriched and supported by a series of radio broadcasts, which reach millions of listeners across Africa. One series, broadcast during 'Teachers in Africa' week on the BBC World Service in June 2007, highlighted, in English and Kiswahili, the role of teachers in Africa. Another, *Story Story*, is a radio drama set in a busy market in West Africa. The series includes teaching and education story lines and, using actors from the drama, a series of audio clips have been made for the web portal where they enrich the teacher education materials.

The TESSA web portal, which is at the heart of the programme, is becoming an increasingly rich tool for teacher educators. The portal drew on the experience of the UK Open University's OpenLearn project and close co-operation continues. It provides access to a growing repository of relevant materials and is an important forum for communication and collaboration.

Particular attention has been paid to planning for implementation of the TESSA programmes. Plans for the use of the materials by all the participating teacher education and training providers were drawn up in 2005–07, with the TESSA Partner Advisory Council playing an important role. The use of TESSA materials by half a million teachers in 2008–09 is an indication of their overall success, but another strength of the programme is the way that these resources get embedded in local programmes because they fit the diverse needs of the participating countries and universities. For example:

- 65,000 Nigerian teachers were trained through in-service programmes.
- 53,000 students in the Open University of Sudan used the resources to guide their teaching practice on the B.Ed. programme. The University of Fort Hare, South Africa also uses the materials in this way.
- 500 students of the Open University of Tanzania have a new diploma course developed using TESSA materials, while Ghana's University of Education, Winneba is developing a new postgraduate diploma in mentoring using videos.
- In Kenya, the literacy materials are being used by teachers to create literacy rooms in schools to promote reading and writing.

As these examples imply, teacher educators are already making extensive use of the materials and the South African Institute for Distance Education (SAIDE) has developed four TESSA-based units to support the work of teacher educators with teachers across the consortium.

Research and Development

TESSA is carrying out its work in a spirit of reflective practice through a research and dissemination programme. One of its products is an important study on the experiences of female teachers working in rural areas of sub-Saharan Africa (TESSA, 2009). In a similar spirit TESSA plans to develop the OER materials continually in a dynamic fashion. This is facilitated by the adapt-and-share philosophy that underpins OERs—and the ability to draw in material from other OERs developed outside the TESSA framework.

Administration

The Partner Advisory Council is the main forum for driving forward the TESSA programme. There are also regional meetings and the consortium makes extensive use of electronic communication and video conferencing. An Administrative and Executive Committee, with sub-groups for specific issues (e.g. web and media), provides day-to-day support to the programme. The Council, the Committee and their sub-groups are supported by a small team at the UKOU.

Challenges

It is to the great credit of the TESSA consortium that it achieved its objectives for the 2005–07 launch period and is already having a major impact on teacher education in Africa. Many challenges have been overcome on the path to success. Three examples are the use of four languages, the development of a model to facilitate localisation of the materials and the identification of authors with the necessary skills and expertise. On the way the consortium has developed a publishing process to facilitate the transformation of original materials into a variety of OER formats.

However, the biggest long-term challenge is to establish policy frameworks to address, in a comprehensive way, the very difficult working conditions of many African teachers. The TESSA consortium aspires to make a major contribution to those working in the most disadvantaged circumstances, an ambition that drives its research agenda and its emphasis on dialogue within the community.

Protocol for the Recruitment of Commonwealth Teachers

Background

A significant factor contributing to the shortage of teachers in many developing countries is the recruitment of their trained teachers by richer countries. This is a special problem for the small states of the Anglophone Caribbean where there is considerable migration of teachers, both within the Caribbean region and to North America and the UK. Following a particular surge in the recruitment of teachers from Barbados, Guyana, Jamaica and Trinidad and Tobago in 2002, Jamaica's Minister of Education, Burchell Whiteman, asked for the assistance of the Commonwealth in addressing the problem of teacher recruitment. The result was the development of a protocol on teacher recruitment that Commonwealth Ministers of Education adopted in 2004.

The Protocol does not hold any legal authority, although member countries of the Commonwealth 'are encouraged to develop such regulations and legislation that are necessary to meet the commitments of the Protocol' (Commonwealth Secretariat, 2004, p. 8).

The aim of the Protocol is to 'balance the rights of teachers to migrate internationally, on a temporary or permanent basis, against the need to protect the integrity of national education systems, and to prevent the exploitation of the scarce human resources of poor countries. The Protocol also seeks to safeguard the rights of recruited teachers and the conditions relating to their service in the recruiting country' (2004, p. 7).

Highlights

The Protocol has five sections. We attempt a summary here but refer readers to the Protocol itself for the details and nuances of the carefully worded text.

Under Rights and Responsibilities of Recruiting Countries, it recalls that authorities in recruiting countries should manage domestic teacher supply and demand so as to limit the need for organized recruitment of teachers abroad. While recognising countries' right to recruit, it urges them to do so in dialogue with source countries in order to limit the damage to their education systems. In particular it discourages recruitment that leads to migration during the academic year. Recruiting countries are enjoined to provide the source countries with information about the status of the teachers recruited and should have a complaints mechanism for the recruitment process.

Recruiting countries are also asked to put in place a quality assurance mechanism for recruiting agencies that may be used in the process. Both these agencies and the recruiting countries should notify source countries in advance of recruitment activity with a view to agreeing the manner of its conduct and ensuring ethical practices.

A sub-section addresses the employment conditions for recruited teachers in an attempt to avoid exploitation of these migrants. Their employment conditions should be 'not less than those of nationals of similar status and occupying similar positions' and recruiting countries should provide them with opportunities for achieving fully-qualified status. The recruited teacher is subject to the laws and rules regarding employment in the recruiting country but should be given details of all teachers' unions and complaint mechanisms relative to employment contracts. Only schools and education authorities should obtain work permits for migrating teachers.

Under Rights and Responsibilities of Source Countries, the Protocol also gives source countries the responsibility of managing the supply and demand of teachers in ways that take organized external recruitment into account. They should also improve the attractiveness of teaching as a profession within the country and make clear any policies they establish to discourage recruitment of particular categories of teachers.

A source country has the right to be informed of recruiting drives and may refuse them, although it should do so within 30 days and try to reach agreement with the recruiting country if the latter requests dialogue. The terms and conditions of teachers in source countries should have provisions for the release of teachers for international exchange and recruitment and their re-integration into the source country's education system when they return.

Under Rights and Responsibilities of the Recruited Teacher, the Protocol gives the teacher the right to transparency and full information regarding the employment contract. Similarly the teacher is expected to behave transparently with current and prospective employers and give adequate notice of resignation or requests for leave.

Finally, the Protocol asks the Commonwealth Secretariat to monitor the phenomenon of teacher recruitment and to review the implementation and impact of the Protocol regularly. Calling for a comprehensive study of teacher flows, it also notes that Education Ministers requested the Secretariat to establish a working group on the assessment of equivalencies of teacher qualifications and professional registration across the Commonwealth.

Impact

The Commonwealth Secretariat has commissioned a study of the implementation of the Protocol and it has also been researched by Miller, Mulvaney, and Ochs (2007) who give figures for the scale of overseas recruitment. From 2001 to 2004 the UK recruited just over 20,000 teachers from abroad. Other Commonwealth countries bringing in significant numbers were South Africa (6,722), Australia (4,484), New Zealand (2,515), Jamaica (1,671), and Canada (1,591).

In response to the Protocol the UK introduced a Quality Mark which sets minimum standards for recruitment agencies and education authorities to reach in the way that they recruit, interview and manage supply teachers. In 2004 London introduced a preferred suppliers list which consists of bodies that hold the Quality Mark, and it also has a mechanism for verifying that they continue to meet the standards. Government agencies have also investigated cases where the guidelines have been breached and withdrawn the quality mark in some cases.

Miller et al. (2007, p. 159) are less sanguine about the response of developing countries to the Protocol noting that many do not have the capacity to implement it: 'Some of the more 'advanced' small states, for instance, do not possess a database of qualified teachers. How, then, are they supposed to make strategic decisions about quotas of teachers available for international recruitment? Systems for complaint mechanisms and clearance certificates are not yet pervasive throughout the Commonwealth. Monitoring failures and dealing with complaints and infractions is significant to the implementation of the Protocol'.

The review commissioned by the Commonwealth Secretariat (Commonwealth Secretariat, 2009, p. x) found that in addition to inter-Commonwealth recruitment, other countries (United States, Korea, Japan, Bahrain, Oman and Saudi Arabia) recruited at significant levels within the Commonwealth while Commonwealth countries were recruiting from countries such as Cuba and China. It also found a disjuncture between the information provided by recruited teachers and that from Ministries of Education in source countries. Rather disappointingly, more than four-fifths of teachers were unaware of the Protocol, which makes them unlikely to take advantage of its provisions. The review recommended that the Commonwealth Secretariat do more to publicise the Protocol and to work more closely with UNESCO on matters of teacher migration.

Bibliography

Abrami, P C, Bernard, R M, Borokhovski, E, Wade, A, Surkes, M, Tamim, R, & Zhang, D A (2008). Instructional interventions affecting critical thinking skills and dispositions: A stage one meta-analysis. *Review of Educational Research,* 78(4), 1102–1134.

Abrioux, D (2007). *Structural Framework for Higher Education Open and Distance Learning in Papua New Guinea.* Vancouver, Commonwealth of Learning. Retrieved from http://www.col.org/SiteCollectionDocuments/consultant_PNG_FinalReport_Abrioux_January08.pdf

Abrioux, D (2009). Special Issues and Practices in Open Schooling, in Abrioux, D & Ferreira, F (eds.) *Open Schooling in the 21st Century,* pp. 3–18. Vancouver: Commonwealth of Learning. Retrieved from http://www.col.org/PSOpenSchooling

Abrioux, D & Ferreira, F (eds.) (2009). *Open Schooling in the 21st Century,* Vancouver: Commonwealth of Learning. Retrieved from http://www.col.org/PSOpenSchooling

AIOU (Allama Iqbal Open University) (2009). *Vice-Chancellor's Annual Report 2007–2008.* Islamabad, Pakistan: AIOU.

Ashby, W R (1956). *An Introduction to Cybernetics.* London: Chapman Hall.

ASTD (2009). *The Top Five Trends in Learning Technology. American Society for Training and Development.* Retrieved August 8, 2009, from http://www.astd.org/LC/2008/1208_sumtotal.htm

Barber, M (1996). *The Learning Game: Arguments for an Educational Revolution.* London: Victor Gollancz.

Bates, A W (1995). *Technology, Open Learning and Distance Education.* Routledge: London.

Bates, A W (2004). Tony Bates on Trends in Flexible Learning. Retrieved June 9, 2009, from http://community.flexiblelearning.net.au/GlobalPerspectives/content/article_6525.htm

Bauman, K J (2001). *Home-Schooling in the United States: Trends and Characteristics,* U.S. Census Bureau. Retrieved from http://www.census.gov/population/www/documentation/twps0053/twps0053.html

Bélanger, M (1976). *Innovation in In-Service Education and Training of Teachers: Canada,* OECD-Centre for Educational Research and Innovation (CERI). Retrieved July 15, 2009, from http://www.eric.ed.gov/ERICDocs/data/ericdocs2sql/content_storage_01/0000019b/80/33/80/b1.pdf

Bennett, H (1972). *No More Public School.* New York: Random House.

Bentley, T (1999). *Learning Beyond the Classroom.* London: Routledge.

Bernard, R M, Abrami, P C, Lou, Y, & Borokhovski, E (2004). A methodological morass? How we can improve the quality of quantitative research in distance education. *Distance Education,* 25(2), 176–198.

Bernard, R M, Abrami, P C, Borokhovski, E, Wade, C A, Tamim, R, Surkes, M A & Bethel, E C (2009). A meta-analysis of three types of interaction treatments in distance education. *Review of Educational Research OnlineFirst,* published on July 6, 2009, as doi: 10.3102/0034654309333844.

Bhalla, S S (1995). Freedom and Economic Growth: A Virtuous Cycle? Background study for the 1991 World Bank Development Report. Retrieved from http://www.oxusresearch.com/downloads/Em150892.PDF

BIDPA (Botswana Institute of Development Policy Analysis) (2000). *Macro-Economic Impacts of HIV/AIDS in Botswana.* Gaborone: BIDPA.

Binder, M (2006). The Cost of Providing Universal Secondary Education in Developing Countries, in Cohen, J E, Bloom, D E & Malin, M B (eds.) *Educating All Children: A Global Agenda,* pp. 455–491. Cambridge, MA: American Academy of Arts & Sciences.

BOCODOL (2009). The Botswana College of Distance and Open Learning. Retrieved April 28, 2009, from http://www.bocodol.ac.bw/PGContent.php?UID=608

Brooks, V (2006). A quiet revolution? The impact of training schools on initial teacher training partnerships. *Journal of Education for Teaching: International research and pedagogy,* 32(4), 379–393. Retrieved from http://wrap.warwick.ac.uk/443/1/WRAP_Brooks_9270464_170209_AQuietRevolution_articleforJET.pdf

Chabbott, C (2003). *Constructing Education for Development: International Organisations and Education for All.* London: Routledge.

Charles, H (2008). *Advocacy and Change: Promoting Innovative Approaches to Education and Culture.* Roseau, Dominica: Pont Casse Press.

Choudry, M A (2003). An Appraisal of Instructional Design in Distance Education, *Journal of Elementary Education,* 13(2), 35–41.

Clemens, M A (2004). *The Long Walk to School: International Education Goals in Historical Perspective,* Working Paper #37. Washington, DC: Centre for Global Development, 74 pages. Retrieved from http://www.cgdev.org/content/publications/detail/2754/

CNED (2008a). *L'histoire du CNED Depuis 1939,* Chasseneuil-Futuroscope. France: Centre National d'Enseignement à Distance.

CNED (2008b). *Formations 2008: Catalogue détaillé,* Chasseneuil-Futuroscope. France: Centre National d'Enseignement à Distance. Retrieved from http://www.cned.fr/orientations

CNED (2008c). *Rapport d'activité 07,* Chasseneuil-Futuroscope. France: Centre National d'Enseignement à Distance.

Cohen, J E (1996). *How Many People Can the Earth Support?* New York: Norton.

Cohen, J (2007). Beyond Primary: Making the case for Universal Secondary Education – PowerPoint presentation. Retrieved July 27, 2009, from http://www.cfr.org/content/meetings/CUE%20Meetings/Cohen_CFR_Presentation.ppt

Cohen, J (2008). Make secondary education universal. *Nature,* 456, 572–573.

Cohen, J, Bloom, D E, Malin, M B, & Curry, H A (2007). Universal Basic and Secondary Education, in *Educating All Children: A Global Agenda.* Cambridge, MA: American Academy of Arts and Sciences. Retrieved from http://www.amacad.org/publications/cohen_intro.pdf

Colclough, C, Al-Samarrai, S, Rose, P, & Tembon, M. (2003). *Achieving Schooling for All in Africa: Costs, Commitment and Gender.* Aldershot, UK: Ashgate Press.

Commission for Africa (2005). *Our common interest.* Retrieved from http://www.commissionforafrica.org

Commonwealth of Learning (2009a). *The Open Schools Handbook: A Resource Guide for Managers.* Vancouver: Commonwealth of Learning. Retrieved from http://www.col.org/SiteCollectionDocuments/OpenSchoolsHandbook_web.pdf

Commonwealth of Learning (2009b). LIVES (Learning through Interactive Voice Educational System). Vancouver: Commonwealth of Learning.

Commonwealth Secretariat (2004). *Protocol for the Recruitment of Commonwealth Teachers.* London: Commonwealth Secretariat. Retrieved from http://www.africarecruit.com/downloads/Teacher%20Recruitment%20Protocol%20in%20PDF.pdf

Commonwealth Secretariat (2009). *Review of the Implementation of the Commonwealth Teacher Recruitment Protocol.* London: Commonwealth Secretariat.

Cornu, B (2006). Teacher Training: the context of the Knowledge Society and Lifelong Learning: the European dimension and the main trends in France, in Zgaga, P (ed.) *Modernization of Study Programmes in Teachers' Education in an international context,* pp. 26–36. Ljubljana, Slovenia: University of Ljubljana, Faculty of Education.

CSU (2009). CalStateTEACH: A California State University Multiple Subject Preparation Program for Elementary School Teachers. Retrieved from http://www.calstateteach.net/

Dangwal, R & Kapur, P (2008). Children's learning processes using unsupervised "hole in the wall" computers in shared public spaces. *Australasian Journal of Educational Technology,* 24(3), 339–354.

Daniel, J S (1996). *Mega-universities and Knowledge Media: Technology Strategies for Higher Education.* London: Kogan Page.

Daniel, J S & Umbriaco, M (1975). Distant Study in French Canada: The Télé-université. *Teaching at a Distance,* 4, 8–13.

Daniel, J S & Marquis, C (1979). Independence and Interaction: Getting the Mixture Right. *Teaching at a Distance,* 14, 29–44.

Devereux, J & Amos, S (2005). The University of Fort Hare's learner-centred Distance Education Programme. *Open Learning* 20(3) 277–284.

DFID (1999). *The Effectiveness of Teacher Resource Centre Strategy,* Knamiller, G (ed.) London: Department for International Development. Retrieved from http://www.greenstone.org/greenstone3/nzdl?a=d&c=dfid&d=HASH7b26d8e95ed5d575e3978d.6&sib=1&p.a=b&p.sa=&p.s=ClassifierBrowse&p.c=dfid

DFID (2001). *The Challenge of Universal Primary Education.* London: Department for International Development. Retrieved from http://www.eric.ed.gov/ERICDocs/data/ericdocs2sql/content_storage_01/0000019b/80/19/76/69.pdf

di Gropello, E, Ed. (2006). *Meeting the Challenges of Secondary Education in Latin America and East Asia: Improving Efficiency and Resource Mobilization,* Directions in Development: Human Development. Washington, DC: World Bank.

Du Vivier, E (1998). *Market Options for NAMCOL.* Windhoek, Namibia, NAMCOL.

Du Vivier, E (2007). *Financing NAMCOL into the Future. A study of the College's Efficiency, Cost Effectiveness, Fee Structure and Funding Formula.* Namibia, NAMCOL.

Du Vivier, E & Ellis, J (2009). Enabling Policy for Open Schooling, in Abrioux, D & Ferreira, F (eds) *Open Schooling in the 21st Century.* Vancouver, Commonwealth of Learning, pp. 21–34. Retrieved from http://www.col.org/PSOpenSchooling

Easterly, W (2001). *The Elusive Quest for Growth: Economists' Adventures and Misadventures in the Tropics.* Cambridge, MA: MIT Press.

Easterly, W (2006).*The White Man's Burden.* New York: Penguin Press.

The Economist (2009a, March 14). Global heroes: a special report on entrepreneurship.

The Economist (2009b, August 19). The quality of teachers: Those who can.

Education in Labour Relations Council (2005). *The health of our educators; A focus on HIV/AIDS in South African public schools.* Cape Town.

Eee PC-Blog (2009). India buys 250,000 OLPC laptops for schoolchildren. Retrieved May 8, 2009, from http://eeepc.net/india-buys-250000-olpc-laptops-for-school-children/

Estrada, R Q (2003). Telesecundaria: Students and the meanings they attribute to elements of the pedagogical model. *Mexican Journal of Educational Research* 8(17), 221–243. Retrieved from http://www.comminit.com/en/node/70742/36

Farrell, G & Isaacs, S (2007). *Survey of ICT and Education in Africa: A Summary Report Based on 53 Country Surveys, info*Dev/World Bank. Retrieved from http://www.infodev.org/en/Publication.353.html

Farrell, G Isaacs, S, & Trucano, M (2007). *The NEPAD eSchools Demonstration Project: A Work in Progress. A Public Report.* Commonwealth of Learning & *info*Dev/World Bank. Retrieved from http://www.infodev.org/en/Publication.355.html

Faure, E (1972). *Learning to Be: Report of the International Commission on the Development of Education.* Paris: UNESCO.

Ferreira, F (2009). The Bright but Challenging Future of Open Schooling, in Abrioux, D & Ferreira, F (eds.) *Open Schooling in the 21st Century,* pp. 193–204. Vancouver: Commonwealth of Learning. Retrieved from http://www.col.org/PSOpenSchooling

Le Figaro (2009, January 22). Darcos: 'L'absentéisme, un fléau pour l'école' [Truancy, the scourge of the school system], p. 2.

Figueredo, V & Anzalone, S (2003). *Alternative Models for Secondary Education in Developing Countries: Rationale and Realities.* Washington, DC: American Institutes for Research.

Filion, P (2000). Performances des élèves québécois en mathématiques [Performance of Quebec pupils in mathematics], *Retrouvailles CRPM et PERMAMA.* McMasterville, Quebec, Canada: Maison Primevère.

Flores, R C & Albarrán, A M R (2007). La Telesecundaria, ante la sociedad del conocimiento [Telesecundaria and the knowledge society]. *Revista Iberoamericana de Educación,* 44(7). Retrieved from http://www.rieoei.org/expe/2197Flores.pdf

FTI (2009). *Mid-term evaluation of the Education for All Fast Track Initiative.* Retrieved from http://www.camb-ed.com/fasttrackinitiative/

Gagnon-Messier, D (2005). *Historique du GRMS.* Retrieved from http://www.grms.qc.ca/info2.htm

Gakio, K (2006). African Tertiary Institutions Connectivity Survey (ATICS), IDRC Canada. Retrieved from http://www.aau.org/renu/docs/ATICS2006.pdf

Gates, W with Hemingway, C (1999). *Business @ the Speed of Thought: Using a Digital Nervous System.* New York: Warner Books.

Gauthier, C (2009). Case Study – Vancouver Learning Network (Secondary) British Columbia, Canada, in Abrioux, D & Ferreira, F (eds.) *Open Schooling in the 21st Century,* pp. 173–189. Vancouver: Commonwealth of Learning. Retrieved from http://www.col.org/PSOpenSchooling

Glennie, J (1999). Distance Education: A way of providing cost-effective access to quality education? *Education in Africa Forum,* Education in Africa, First Edition. Johannesburg: Education Africa.

Glewwe, P, Ilias, N, & Kremer, M (2003). Teacher Incentives, National Bureau of Economic Research, Working Paper Series. Cambridge, MA. Retrieved from http://www.jourdan.ens.fr/piketty/fichiers/enseig/ecoineg/articl/Glewweetal2003.pdf

Government of Alberta (2009). *Roles and Mandates Policy Framework.* Retrieved June 9, 2009, from http://www.advancededucation.gov.ab.ca/post-secondary/policy/roles.aspx

Government of India (2009). *Sarva Shiksha Abhiyan.* Retrieved May 11, 2009, from http://india.gov.in/sectors/education/sarva_shiksha.php

Government of Nigeria (1978). Supplement to Official Gazette No 20, Vol 65, 27th April – Part A, Government of Nigeria.

Government of Quebec (2000). 4: Results – Evaluation of Learning: 4.5: Mathematical Literacy in 15-year-olds. Retrieved from http://www.mels.gouv.qc.ca/STAT/indic02/indic02A/ia02405.pdf

Griswold, S (1838). *Fireside Education,* Retrieved from http://www.archive.org/stream/firesideeducatio00gooduoft

Hanushek, E A & Wössmann, L (2007). *Education Quality and Economic Growth.* Washington, DC: World Bank.

Hargreaves, A (1995). Towards a social geography of teacher education, in N K Shimahara,N K & Holowinsky, I Z (eds.) *Teacher Education in Industrialised Nations: issues in changing social contexts.* New York: Garland.

Hatakka, M (2009). Build it and they will come? Inhibiting factors for reuse of open content in developing countries. *The Electronic Journal on Information Systems in Developing Countries,* 37(5), 1–16. Retrieved from http://www.ejisdc.org

Hole-in-the-Wall (2009). Research Findings. Retrieved August 8, 2009, from http://www.hole-in-the-wall.com/findings.html

Holt, J C (1983). *How Children Learn.* New York: Delacorte Press.

Hutchings, M, Maylor, U, Mendick, H, Menter, I, & Smart, S (2006). An evaluation of innovative approaches to teacher education on the Teach First programme: Final report to the Training and Development Agency for Schools. London: London Metropolitan University, Institute for Policy Studies in Education. Retrieved from http://www.tda.gov.uk/upload/resources/teach%20first%20evaluation%20report%2005-06.doc

Illich, I (1971). *Deschooling Society.* Harmondsworth, UK: Penguin.

Inamdar, P & Kulkarni, A (2007). 'Hole-in-the-Wall' Computer Kiosks Foster Mathematics Achievement – a comparative study. *Educational Technology & Society,* 10(2), 170–179.

Indonesian Distance Learning Network (IDLN) (1999a, 1999b). Jakarta: Pustekkom.

IRFOL (2004). *Improving the Quality of Primary School through Distance Education.* Report prepared by the International Research Foundation for Open Learning for the EFA Monitoring Report Team. Paris: UNESCO. Retrieved from http://portal.unesco.org/education/en/files/36185/11005342603IRFOL.doc/IRFOL.doc

Jones, P W (1988). *International Policies for Third World Education: UNESCO, Literacy and Development.* London: Routledge.

JORF (Journal Officiel de la République Française) (2009). Décret n° 2009-238 du 27 février 2009 relatif au service public de l'enseignement à distance [Decree…concerning the public provision of distance education].

Khan, M (2006). *Comparative study of the Effectiveness of formally Trained and non-formally trained Secondary School Teachers.*Unpublished Thesis, Secondary Teacher Education Department. Islamabad, Pakistan: Allama Iqbal Open University.

Kigotho, W (2006). Facing Financial Difficulties, African Virtual U. Revamps Itself. *Chronicle of Higher Education,* 53(7), A44.

Krstić, I (2008). Sic Transit Gloria Laptopi. Retrieved August 8, 2009, from http://radian.org/notebook/sic-transit-gloria-laptopi

Kubler, J (2008). Is technology dazzling everyone? *Bulletin of the Association of Commonwealth Universities,* 166, 4–5. Retrieved from http://www.acu.ac.uk/Bulletin_Dec08.pdf

Lamy, T & Henri, F (1983). The Télé-université: Ten Years of Distance Education in Quebec. *Innovations in Education and Teaching International,* 20(3), 197–201.

Laurel Springs School (2009). College Preparatory Distance Learning. Retrieved August 9, 2009, from http://www.laurelsprings.com/home

Lave, J & Wenger, E (1991). *Situated Learning.* Cambridge, UK: Cambridge University Press.

Leach, J (2002). The curriculum knowledge of teachers: a review of the potential of large-scale electronic conference environments for professional development. *The Curriculum Journal,* 13(1), 87–120.

Leach, J, Ahmed, A, Makalima, S, & Power, T (2006). *DEEP IMPACT: an investigation of the use of information and communication technologies in teacher education in the global south,* Researching the Issues, Report #58. London: Department for International Development. Retrieved from http://www.research4development.info/PDF/Outputs/DeepReportFeb2006.pdf

Leach, J & Moon, R (2000). Changing Paradigms in Teacher Education: A Case Study of Innovation and Change, in Scott, A & Freeman-Moir, J (eds.) *Tomorrow's Teachers: International and Critical Perspectives on Teacher Education,* pp. 106–122. Canterbury, New Zealand: Canterbury University Press.

Leach, J & Moon, R (2008). *The Power of Pedagogy.* Newbury Park, CA: Sage.

Lewin, K M (2002). The costs of supply and demand for teacher education: Dilemmas for development. *International Journal of Educational Development,* 22(3–4), 221–242.

Lewin, K M (2008). *Strategies for Sustainable Financing of Secondary Education in Sub-Saharan Africa*, World Bank Working Paper No. 136. Washington, DC: World Bank.

Mandela, N (2007). A Message from Mr. Mandela… Retrieved from http://www.mandelainstitute. org.za/messages.aspx

Mankiw, N G (1995). The Growth of Nations, *Brookings Papers on Economic Activity*, 1, 275–326. Washington, DC: Brookings Institution.

Mannan, A (2009). Certificate in Tertiary and Community Studies: An Alternative Learning Pathway, Open College, Papua New Guinea, in Abrioux, D & Ferreira, F (eds.) *Open Schooling in the 21st Century*, pp. 149–167. Vancouver: Commonwealth of Learning. Retrieved from http:// www.col.org/PSOpenSchooling

Maroba, M (2009). Botswana Country Report. Paper presented at the *Commonwealth of Learning Forum on a Decade of Open and Distance Learning in the Commonwealth: Achievements and Challenges*. Abuja: National Open University of Nigeria.

Mason, R (1994). *Using Communications Media in Open and Flexible Learning*. London: Kogan Page.

Masrur, R & Khan M A (2007). Academic Satisfaction and Involvement of Distance Education Learner. *The International Journal of Humanities*, 5(6), 157–162.

Massingue, V (2006). Mozambique Towards Connectivity and Access for All: Slide presentation. Retrieved August 8, 2009, from http://74.125.155.132/search?q=cache:YTO6tRluumYJ:unpa n1.un.org/intradoc/groups/public/documents/apcity/unpan025038.pdf+mozambique+mass ingue+cprd+shanghia&cd=1&hl=en&ct=clnk

Mayer, A P (2008). Expanding Opportunities for High Academic Achievement: An International Baccalaureate Diploma Program in an Urban High School. *Journal of Advanced Academics*, 19(2), 202–235.

Mill, J S (2004). *The Principles of Political Economy – Preliminary Remarks*. London: Prometheus Books (Original work published 1848)

Miller, P W, Mulvaney, G, & Ochs, K (2007) The Commonwealth Teacher Recruitment Protocol: Its impacts and implications for the global teaching profession. *Research in Comparative and International Education*, 2(2), 154–161. Retrieved from http://www.wwwords.co.uk/pdf/vali-date.asp?j=rcie&vol=2&issue=2&year=2007&article=6_Miller_RCIE_2_2_web

MIT (2009). MITOpenCourseware. Retrieved from http://ocw.mit.edu/OcwWeb/web/home/home/ index.htm

Mitra, S (2008). What can children teach themselves? Lessons from a hole in the wall. *Bulletin of the Association of Commonwealth Universities*, 164, 4–5. Retrieved from http://www.acu.ac.uk/ Bulletin_June08v7.pdf

Mitra, S, Dangwal, R, Chatterjee, S, Jha, S, Bishtm Ravinder S, & Kapur, P (2005). Acquisition of computing literacy on shared public computers: Children and the "hole in the wall". *Australasian Journal of Educational Technology* 21(3), 407–426. Retrieved from http://www.ascilite. org.au/ajet/ajet21/mitra.html

Mitra, S, Dangwal, R, & Thadani, L (2008). Effects of remoteness on the quality of education: A case study from North Indian schools. *Australasian Journal of Educational Technology*, 24(2), 168–180. Retrieved from http://www.ascilite.org.au/ajet/ajet24/mitra.html

Moon, R (1998). *Towards a New Generation of Open Learning Programmes in Teacher Education*. Paper presented to the American Educational Research Association Conference, San Diego, California, 12–17 April.

Moon, R (1999). *The English Exception? International perspectives on the initial education and training of teachers* (Occasional Paper No 11). London: Universities Council for the Education of Teachers.

Moon, R (2007). Research analysis: Attracting, developing and retaining effective teachers: A global overview of current policies and practices, Working Paper ED/HED/TED/2007/ME/20. Paris: UNESCO. Retrieved from http://unesdoc.unesco.org/images/0015/001516/151685e.pdf

Moon, R (2008). The role of new communication technologies and distance education in responding to the global crisis in teacher supply and training: an analysis of the research and development experience. *Educação & Sociedade*, 29(104). Retrieved August 5, 2009, from http://www.scielo. br/scielo.php?pid=S0101-73302008000300008&script=sci_arttext&tlng=en

Moore, R S, Moore, D R, & Moore, D N (1975). *Better Late Than Early: A New Approach to Your Child's Education*. New York: Reader's Digest Press.

Morawczynski, O & Ngwenyama, O (2007). Unravelling the Impact of Investments in ICT, Education and Health on Development: An Analysis of Archival Data of Five West African Countries Using Regression Splines. *Electronic Journal on Information Systems in Developing Countries*, 29(5), 1–15. Retrieved from http://www.ejisdc.org/ojs2/index.php/ejisdc/article/viewFile/352/198

Mumtaz, R (2002). *A study of Practical Component of Allama Iqbal Open University B.Ed. Programme Comprising Workshop and Teaching Practice.* Unpublished M.Phil. thesis, Allama Iqbal Open University, Islamabad, Pakistan.

Muralidharan, K & Kremer, M (2007). Public and Private Schools in Rural India. Boston: Harvard University. Retrieved from http://www.econ.ucsd.edu/~kamurali/public%20and%20private%20schools%20in%20rural%20india.pdf

Murangi, H V (2009). Open Schooling in Educational Transformation: The Case of the Namibian College of Open Learning, in Abrioux, D & Ferreira, F (eds.) *Open Schooling in the 21st Century*, pp. 85–109. Vancouver: Commonwealth of Learning. Retrieved from http://www.col.org/PSOpenSchooling

NAAC (2007). *Quality Assurance Toolkit for Teacher Education Institutions.* Bangalore, India: National Assessment and Accreditation Council.

National Institute for Open Schooling (2005). International Conference on "Promotion of Open Schooling": Open Schooling Models, Goa, India. Retrieved from http://www.nos.org/goa-iii.htm

NCES (National Centre for Educational Statistics) (2003). Homeschooling in the United States: 2003. Retrieved from http://nces.ed.gov/pubs2006/homeschool/index.asp

Negroponte, N (2006). *TED Talks: Nicolas Negroponte.* Retrieved August 9, 2009, from http://www.ted.com/talks/nicholas_negroponte_on_one_laptop_per_child.html

Nelson Mandela Foundation (2004). *Emerging Voices.* Cape Town, South Africa: HRSC Press.

Nock, S (2006). *Teachers for All: What governments and donors should do.* Global Campaign for Education. Retrieved July 24, 2009, from http://www.eldis.org/go/topics/resource-guides/education/key-issues/human-resources-in-education/human-resources-for-education-service-delivery&id=22481&type=Document

NTI (2001). *25th Anniversary Brochure.* Kaduna, Nigeria: National Teachers' Institute.

NTI (2002a). *Information Booklet.* Kaduna, Nigeria: National Teachers' Institute.

NTI (2002b). *The Strategic Plan of the National Teachers' Institute: 2002–2006.* Kaduna, Nigeria: National Teachers' Institute.

Nugroho, D & Lonsdale, M (2009). Evaluation of OLPC programmes globally: a literature review, Australian Council for Educational Research. Retrieved from http://www.scribd.com/doc/12729094/Evaluation-of-OLPC-Programs-Globally-a-Literature-Review

OECD (2009).OECD Programme for International Student Assessment (PISA). http://www.oecd.org/pisa

OER Africa (2009). OER Africa: Building African higher education capacity through openness. Retrieved August 8, 2009, from http://www.oerafrica.org/

OFTP (Ontario Federation of Teaching Parents) (2009). Homeschooling Frequently asked Questions. Retrieved August 9, 2009, from http://www.ontariohomeschool.org/FAQ.shtml

OLPCNews (2009a). One Laptop Per Child Overview, March. Retrieved from http://www.olpcnews.com/files/One_Laptop_Per_Child_Overview_2009.pdf

OLPCNews (2009b). What Do We Know About OLPC Pilots Worldwide? (3). Retrieved from http://www.olpcnews.com/implementation/evaluations/what_do_we_know_about_olpc_pil.html

OLPCNews (2009c). Ivan Krstić: XO Crippled by Crack-Smoking Hobos, Not Sugar, (23). Retrieved from http://www.olpcnews.com/software/operating_system/ivan_krstic_xo_crippled_by_cra.html

Open University (1978). *T102 Foundation Course in Technology.* Milton Keynes, UK: Open University.

Open University (2009). OpenLearn http://www.open.ac.uk/openlearn/home.php

Orivel, F (2000). Finance, Costs and Economics, in Yates, C & Bradley, J (eds.) *Basic Education at a Distance*, pp. 138–154. London: RoutledgeFalmer.

Packer, S (2008). *International EFA Architecture Lessons and Prospects: A Preliminary Assessment, Background Paper prepared for the 2008 EFA Global Monitoring Report: Education for All, will we make it?* Paris: UNESCO.

Palfrey, J & Gasser, U (2008). *Born Digital: Understanding the first generation of digital natives.* London: Basic Books.

Pant, M C, (2009). National Institute of Open Schooling, India: A Case Study, in Abrioux, D & Ferreira, F (eds.) *Open Schooling in the 21st Century*, pp. 111–128. Vancouver: Commonwealth of Learning. Retrieved from http://www.col.org/PSOpenSchooling

Papert, S (1980). *Mindstorms: Children, Computers and Powerful Ideas.* London: Basic Books.

Paul, R (1990). *Open Learning and Open Management: Leadership and Integrity in Distance Education.* London: Kogan Page.

Perraton, H (2000). *Open and Distance Learning in the Developing World.* London: Routledge.

Perry, W (1976).*The Open University: A personal account by the first vice-chancellor.* Open University Press.

Peter, L J (1977). *Peter's Quotations: Ideas for our time.* New York: Morrow.

Phillips, M (1996). *All Must Have Prizes.* London: Warner Books.

Phillips, S (2006). Exploring the Potential of Open Schooling, *Connections* 11(1), 8–10. Vancouver: Commonwealth of Learning. Retrieved from http://www.col.org/SiteCollectionDocuments/Connections_vol11_no1.pdf

Phillipson, R (ed.) (2008). *Low-cost Private Education: Impacts on Achieving Universal Primary Education.* London: Commonwealth Secretariat.

Piaget, J (1952). *The origins of intelligence in children.* New York: International Unilever Press.

Pollard, H M (1956). *Pioneers of Popular Education.* London: John Murray.

Pope, A (1734). *Essay on Man.* Retrieved from http://theotherpages.org/poems/pope-e3.html

Pscharapoulos, G (2008). *Economics of Education: A 50-year recap* [slide presentation]. Retrieved August 8, 2009, from http://elearn.elke.uoa.gr/2ndICEE/psach.pdf

Pyle, K B (1969). *The New Generation in Meiji Japan.* Palo Alto, CA: Stanford University Press.

Raymond, M, Fletcher, S, & Luque, J (2001) *Teach for America: An Evaluation of Teacher Differences and Student Outcomes in Houston, Texas.* CREDO. Retrieved July 25, 2009, from http://credo.stanford.edu/downloads/tfa.pdf

Raza, R (2004). Benefits for students, labour force, employers and society, in Perraton H & Lentell, H (eds.) *Policy for Open and Distance Learning,* Perraton, pp. 209–223. London: RoutledgeFalmer & Commonwealth of Learning.

Robinson, B & Latchem, C (2003). *Teacher Education through Open and Distance Learning.* London: RoutledgeFalmer & Commonwealth of Learning.

Rumble, G (2006). *Costs and Funding of NAMCOL,* A Report of a Short-term Advisory Mission to Conduct a Study on the Costs and Funding of the Namibian College of Open Learning. Namibia: NAMCOL.

Rumble, G (2009). Costs of Open Schooling, in Abrioux, D & Ferreira, F (eds.) *Open Schooling in the 21st Century,* pp. 55–64. Vancouver: Commonwealth of LearningRetrieved from http://www.col.org/PSOpenSchooling

Rumble, G & Koul, B N (2007). Open Schooling for Secondary and Higher Secondary Education: Costs and Effectiveness in India and Namibia. Vancouver: Commonwealth of Learning. Retrieved from http://www.col.org/resources/publications/consultancies/Pages/2007-07-openSchl.aspx

Sadiman, A S & Rahardjo, R (1997). Contribution of SMP Terbuka toward Lifelong Learning in Indonesia, in, Hatton, M J (ed.) *Lifelong Learning: Policies, Practices and Programs.* Toronto: Humber College. Abstract retrieved from ERIC database http://www.eric.ed.gov/ERICDocs/data/ericdocs2sql/content_storage_01/0000019b/80/14/fa/98.pdf

Salmon, G (2000). *E-Moderating.* London: Kogan Page.

Schocroft, J (2009). Case Study: Open Access College, South Australia, Australia, in Abrioux, D & Ferreira, F (eds.) *Open Schooling in the 21st Century,* pp. 21–34. Vancouver: Commonwealth of Learning. Retrieved from http://www.col.org/PSOpenSchooling

SchoolNet Namibia (2009). SchoolNet NA http://www.schoolnet.na/index.html

Schrock, J R (2009). US: Problems Teaching Science Online, University World News, June, Issue 0079. Retrieved August 9, 2009, from http://www.universityworldnews.com/article.php?story=20090604191432435

Sen, A (1999) *Development as Freedom.* Oxford: Oxford University Press.

Shaw, G B (1903). *Man and Superman – Maxims for Revolutionists.* New York: Penguin Classics.

Smith, A (1776a). *The Wealth of Nations, Book V Chapter 1 para. V.1.189.* Retrieved from http://www.econlib.org/library/Smith/smWN.html

Smith, A (1776b). *The Wealth of Nations, Book V Chapter 1 para. V.1.185.* Retrieved from http://www.econlib.org/library/Smith/smWN.html

Smith, A (1776c). *The Wealth of Nations, Book 1 Chapter 1 para. I 1.3.* Retrieved from http://www.econlib.org/library/Smith/smWN.html

Solano, L P (2008, January 13). La telesecundaria cumple 40 años; vive una "crisis profunda". *La Jornada.* Retrieved from http://www.jornada.unam.mx/2008/01/13/index.php?section=sociedad&article=038n1soc

SouthAfrica.info (2009). *Opening SA's Digital Doorway.* Retrieved from http://www.southafrica.info/about/education/digitaldoorway.htm

Stephens, C (2005). *Responding To The Need for Resource Materials Through Distance Education: In Pursuit of a Collaborative Model.* Retrieved from http://pcf4.dec.uwi.edu/viewpaper.php?id=190&print=1

Stiglitz, J E (1998). An Agenda for Development in the 21st Century, in *Annual World Bank Conference on Development Economics 1997,* Pleskovi, B and Stiglitz J E (eds.). Washington, DC: World Bank.

Swarup, V (2005). *Q&A: A Novel* New York: Scribner.

Tapscott, D (2009). *Grown up digital: how the net generation is changing your world.* New York: McGraw Hill.

Tau, D R (2005). BOCODOL: Its background and educational context, in Hope, A & Guiton, P (eds.) *Strategies for Sustainable Open and Distance Learning,* pp. 30–32. London: Routledge.

Tau, D R & Gatsha, G (2009) Open Schooling in Botswana: The Case of Botswana College of Open and Distance Learning, in Abrioux, D & Ferreira, F (eds.) *Open Schooling in the 21st Century,* pp. 67–83. Vancouver: Commonwealth of Learning. Retrieved from www.col.org/ PSOpenSchooling

TESSA (2008). *The Teacher Education in Sub-Saharan Africa (TESSA) programme progress report 2005–2007.* Retrieved from http://www.tessaprogramme.org

TESSA (2009). *Pride and Light: Female teachers' experiences of living and working in rural sub-Saharan Africa.* Retrieved from http://www.tessafrica.net/images/stories/pdf/tessateacherslives.pdf

Thakrar, J, Zinn, D, & Wolfenden, F (2009). Harnessing Open Educational Resources to the Challenges of Teacher Education in Sub-Saharan Africa, *International Review of Research in Open and Distance Learning,* to be published. (www.irrodl.org)

TimesOnline (2009). *Schools hiring bouncers to ensure pupils behave, teachers say.* Retrieved August 8, 2009, from http://www.timesonline.co.uk/tol/life_and_style/education/article6083162.ece

Tooley, J (2000). *Reclaiming Education.* London: Cassell.

Tooley, J (2005). Private Schools for the Poor: Education where no one expects it. *Education Next,* 5(4), 22–32.

Tooley, J (2009). *The Beautiful Tree.* Washington, DC: Cato Institute/Penguin.

Trucano, M (2009). *Computers in secondary schools: Whither India?* EduTech. A World Bank Blog on ICT use in Education. Message posted at http://blogs.worldbank.org/edutech/ computers-in-secondary-schools-whither-india

UIS (UNESCO Institute of Statistics) (2009). Table 20C Regional Sum of Teaching Staff by ISCED Level. Retrieved August 10, 2009, from http://stats.uis.unesco.org/unesco/TableViewer/ tableView.aspx?ReportId=193

Umar, A (2008). Nigeria, in Phillipson, R (ed.) *Low-cost Private Education: Impacts on Achieving Universal Primary Education,* pp. 91–129. London: Commonwealth Secretariat.

UNESCO (1991). *World Education Report.* Paris: UNESCO.

UNESCO (1994). *Donors to African Education: A Statistical Profile of Education in sub-Saharan Africa in the 1980s.* Paris: UNESCO.

UNESCO (1996). *Report of the Task Force on Education for the Twenty-first Century* (The Delors Report). Paris: UNESCO.

UNESCO (2000). *Statistical document: Education for All 2000 assessment.* Paris: UNESCO.

UNESCO (2001a). *Monitoring Report on Education for All.* Paris: UNESCO.

UNESCO (2001b). *Distance Education in the E9 Countries: The Development and Future of Distance Education Programmes in the Nine High-Population Countries.* Paris: UNESCO. Retrieved from http://unesdoc.unesco.org/images/0012/001231/123157e.pdf

UNESCO (2001c). Applying new technologies and cost-effective delivery systems in basic education, Thematic study for the World Education Forum, *EFA 2000 Assessment.* Paris: UNESCO.

UNESCO (2001d). Background document, UNESCO International Expert Meeting on General Secondary School Education in the 21st Century: Trends, Challenges and Priorities. Beijing, May 21–25.

UNESCO (2002a). *Education for All: Is the World on Track? EFA Global Monitoring Report Summary.* Paris: UNESCO.

UNESCO (2002b). *Education for All: Is the World on Track? EFA Global Monitoring Report.* Paris: UNESCO.

UNESCO (2003a). *Gender and Education for All: The Leap to Equality. EFA Global Monitoring Report Summary.* Paris: UNESCO.

UNESCO (2003b). *Gender and Education for All: The Leap to Equality. EFA Global Monitoring Report.* Paris: UNESCO.

UNESCO (2004a). *Education for All: The Quality Imperative. EFA Global Monitoring Report Summary.* Paris: UNESCO.

UNESCO (2004b). *Education for All: The Quality Imperative. EFA Global Monitoring Report.* Paris: UNESCO.

UNESCO (2005a). *Literacy for Life. EFA Global Monitoring Report Summary.* Paris: UNESCO.

UNESCO (2005b). *Literacy for Life. EFA Global Monitoring Report.* Paris: UNESCO.

UNESCO (2005c). Telesecundaria, Mexico. Retrieved from http://www.unesco.org/education/ educprog/lwf/doc/portfolio/abstract8.htm

UNESCO (2006a). *Strong Foundations: Early Childhood Care and Education. EFA Global Monitoring Report Summary.* Paris: UNESCO.

UNESCO (2006b). *Strong Foundations: Early Childhood Care and Education. EFA Global Monitoring Report.* Paris: UNESCO.

UNESCO (2006c). *Teachers and educational quality: Monitoring global needs for 2015.* Montreal: UNESCO Institute of Statistics.

UNESCO (2007a). *Education for All by 2015: Will we make it? EFA Global Monitoring Report Summary.* Paris: UNESCO.

UNESCO (2007b). *Education for All by 2015: Will we make it? EFA Global Monitoring Report.* Paris: UNESCO and Oxford University Press.

UNESCO (2008a). *Overcoming inequality: why governance matters. EFA Global Monitoring Report Summary.* Paris: UNESCO.

UNESCO (2008b). *Overcoming inequality: why governance matters. EFA Global Monitoring Report.* Paris: UNESCO and Oxford University Press.

UNESCO (2009a). *Communiqué: 2009 World Conference on Higher Education: The New Dynamics of Higher Education and Research for Societal Change and Development.* Paris: UNESCO. Retrieved from http://www.unesco.org/en/wche2009

UNESCO (2009b). Multipurpose Community Telecentres. Retrieved from http://www.unesco.org/webworld/public_domain/mct.html

United Nations (2003). *World Youth Report.* New York: United Nations. Retrieved from http://www.un.org/esa/socdev/unyin/documents/ch01.pdf

United Nations General Assembly (1948) *The Universal Declaration of Human Rights, Article 26.* New York: United Nations.

University of Alberta (2009). Legislation will reshape post-secondary education. *Express News,* May 5, Retrieved August 9, 2009, from http://www.expressnews.ualberta.ca/article.cfm?id=4456

VERTONE-CNED (2009). *Etude de Modernisation: Présentation au Conseil d'Orientation* [Modernisation Study: Presentation to the Steering Committee]. Paris: Centre National d'Enseignement à Distance.

VSO (2006). *Making Education for All a Reality.* Retrieved from http://www.beso.org/Images/Making_Education_for_all_a_reality_tcm76-22712.pdf

VUSSC (2009). *The Virtual University for Small States of the Commonwealth.* Retrieved from http://www.col.org/vussc

Walden, G (1996). *We Should Know Better: Solving the Education Crisis.* London: Fourth Estate.

Watkins, K (2000). *The Oxfam Education Report.* Bath, UK: Redwood Books.

Wedemeyer, C A (1974). Characteristics of open learning systems, in *Open Learning Systems.* Washington, DC: National Association of Educational Broadcasters.

The Week (2009, July 25). Have you ever thought about working for your country?

Wenger, E (1999). *Communities of Practice.* Cambridge, UK: Cambridge University Press.

West, E G (1994). *Education and the State* (3rd ed.). Indianapolis, IN: Liberty Fund.

Wikipedia.com (2009). PLATO (Computer System). Retrieved from http://en.wikipedia.org/wiki/PLATO

Witte, D E, & Mero, P T (2008). Removing Classrooms from the Battlefield: Liberty, Paternalism, and the Redemptive Promise of Educational Choice. *Brigham Young University Law Review,* 30, 377–414. Retrieved from http://www.sutherlandinstitute.org/uploads/lawreview2008witte.pdf

World Bank (2000). *Education for All: From Jomtien to Dakar and Beyond.* Paper prepared for the World Education Forum in Dakar, Senegal, April 26–28.

World Bank (2004). *World Development Report 2004: Making Services Work for Poor People.* Washington, DC: World Bank Retrieved from http://econ.worldbank.org/WBSITE/EXTERNAL/EXTDEC/EXTRESEARCH/EXTWDRS/EXTWDR2004/0,,ImgPagePK:64202988~entityID:000090341_20031007150121~pagePK:64217930~piPK:64217936~theSitePK:477688,00.html

World Bank (2007). *Investing in Indonesia's Education: Allocation, Equity and Efficiency of Public Expenditures.*Washington, DC: World Bank.

World Bank (2009). Education in India. Retrieved from http://www.worldbank.org.in/WBSITE/EXTERNAL/COUNTRIES/SOUTHASIAEXT/INDIAEXTN/0,,contentMDK:21493265~pagePK:141137~piPK:141127~theSitePK:295584,00.html

Yasmeen, B (2008). *A Comparison of Cost Effectiveness of Formal and Non-formal systems of Education at B.Ed. level in Faisalabad Region.* Unpublished M.Phil. thesis, Allama Iqbal Open University, Islamabad, Pakistan.

Zittrain, J (2008). *The Future of the Internet and How to Stop It.* New Haven, CT: Yale University Press.

Subject Index

Name Index